.

OXFORD PHILOSOPHICAL MONOGRAPHS

Editorial Committee
J. J. Campbell, R. S. Crisp, Michael Frede, Michael Rosen,
Ralph C. S. Walker

The Grounds of Ethical Judgement

OTHER TITLES IN THE SERIES

Against Equality of Opportunity
Matt Cavanagh

Causality, Interpretation, and the Mind
William Child

The Kantian Sublime
From Morality to Art
Paul Crowther

Semantic Powers
Meaning and the Means of Knowing in Classical Indian Philosophy
Jonardon Ganeri

Kant's Theory of Imagination
Bridging Gaps in Judgement and Experience
Sarah L. Gibbons

Determinism, Blameworthiness, and Deprivation
Martha Klein

Projective Probability
James Logue

Understanding Pictures
Dominic Lopes

Wittgenstein, Finitism, and the Foundations of Mathematics
Mathieu Marion

False Consciousness
Denise Meyerson

Truth and the End of Inquiry
A Peircean Account of Truth
C. J. Misak

The Good and the True
Michael Morris

Hegel's Idea of Freedom
Alan Patten

Nietzsche and Metaphysics
Peter Poellner

The Ontology of Mind
Events, Processes, and States
Helen Steward

Things that Happen Because They Should
A Teleological Approach to Action
Rowland Stout

Metaphor and Moral Experience
A. E. Denham

The Grounds of Ethical Judgement

NEW TRANSCENDENTAL ARGUMENTS IN MORAL PHILOSOPHY

Christian F. R. Illies

CLARENDON PRESS · OXFORD

OXFORD
UNIVERSITY PRESS

Great Clarendon Street, Oxford OX2 6DP

Oxford University Press is a department of the University of Oxford.
It furthers the University's objective of excellence in research, scholarship,
and education by publishing worldwide in

Oxford New York

Auckland Bangkok Buenos Aires Cape Town Chennai
Dar es Salaam Delhi Hong Kong Istanbul Karachi Kolkata
Kuala Lumpur Madrid Melbourne Mexico City Mumbai Nairobi
São Paulo Shanghai Taipei Tokyo Toronto

Oxford is a registered trade mark of Oxford University Press
in the UK and in certain other countries

Published in the United States
by Oxford University Press Inc., New York

© Christian Illies 2003

The moral rights of the author have been asserted
Database right Oxford University Press (maker)

First published 2003

All rights reserved. No part of this publication may be reproduced,
stored in a retrieval system, or transmitted, in any form or by any means,
without the prior permission in writing of Oxford University Press,
or as expressly permitted by law, or under terms agreed with the appropriate
reprographics rights organization. Enquiries concerning reproduction
outside the scope of the above should be sent to the Rights Department,
Oxford University Press, at the address above

You must not circulate this book in any other binding or cover
and you must impose this same condition on any acquirer

British Library Cataloguing in Publication Data

Data available

Library of Congress Cataloging in Publication Data

Data available

ISBN 0–19–823832–0

1 3 5 7 9 10 8 6 4 2

Typeset by Cambrian Typesetters, Frimley, Surrey
Printed in Great Britain
on acid-free paper by
T. J. International Ltd.,
Padstow, Cornwall

Preface

This book concerns the (literally) fundamental question of moral philosophy: how do we ground our judgements concerning good and bad or right and wrong? To be frank about the spirit of this book from the very start, it should be added that I will raise this question in a Kantian way: I am looking for a *rational* basis for our notions of good and bad. It has often, and I think quite convincingly, been argued that if practical philosophy remains less ambitious than this, then it is in danger of sinking into the quagmire of historical and sociological relativity.

Ever since Descartes, however, any such project has become very difficult; the standards required for a successful justification have risen dramatically. That is why a major part of this book is dedicated to epistemological investigations about the appropriate method practical reason should adopt. For reasons given in Chapter 2, I think that transcendental arguments—more specifically one type—are the most promising and probably the only path which practical reason should explore in order to fulfil this ambition. In brief, such a transcendental argument is designed to show that we cannot rationally deny some things because they are essential for reasoning itself. Any rational attempt to reject them would be at odds with itself and thus irrational. If, however, something cannot be rejected rationally, then we are entitled to accept it as justified and true—there is simply no consistent, and hence rational, alternative to doing so.

This type of indirect argument is admittedly very simple. And, as with many very simple arguments, its real power has therefore often been overlooked. Many philosophers 'sigh with ennui' when any such argument is presented to them; they will 'want to ignore the whole thing and to turn their attention to more important matters' (Nielsen 1984: 59). Others regard the idea as too simple to provide any interesting knowledge for moral philosophy. I hope to show that, on the one hand, annoyance itself is no argument, and that, on the other hand, we have good reasons to be more optimistic about the achievements of transcendental arguments. In brief, my book is but one extended argument for a transcendental grounding of our notions of right and wrong.

In the first chapter the project is located in the debate about 'moral realism' which can be found in current analytic philosophy. The position of moral realism and anti-realism and the main arguments which proponents of both sides raise will be outlined. It seems that we cannot easily hope for a rational solution of the conflict between these very different perspectives, since realists and anti-realists not only disagree heavily about whether moral facts are 'real' in any meaningful sense, but also about the *criteria* for deciding upon this question. As I see it, moral realism has the burden of proof in this debate—and it can only make a proper claim to be right if it is able to provide a rational justification of moral judgements. In a very brief survey at the end of Chapter 1, possible methodologies for such a justification of normative notions, like deduction, induction, intuition, etc., are analysed and discarded as inappropriate to the task. This rejection of traditional routes only serves the purpose of sketching the methodological landscape within which I wish to place my own argument. It is therefore neither an exhaustive investigation of all alternative approaches nor does it include a discussion of anti-foundationalist positions.

In Chapter 2 transcendental arguments are introduced as the most promising prospects. I will distinguish two types of transcendental argument, of which I consider only one—the retorsive type—to be fully promising.

Two highly developed transcendental arguments exist in the current ethical and meta-ethical debates: Karl-Otto Apel has developed what I will call an 'argument from discourse', while Alan Gewirth has suggested an 'argument from agency'—again, these are my words. Although it seems to me that neither argument works as it stands, nonetheless they deserve a careful investigation.

In Chapter 3 the focus is upon Apel's account and on a similar account by Wolfgang Kuhlmann. Both understand truth as a consensus and, consequently, reason as a form of discourse. Their central argument is that to reason at all everyone (including the sceptic) must accept the rules and principles which are required for any discourse to be rational. Therefore, to deny the constitutive rules of this discourse is irrational; hence these rules have found an ultimate grounding. The main flaw of this argument from discourse seems to me the consensus theory of truth on which it rests. Apel and Kuhlmann cannot show that every reasoner necessarily anticipates a *universal* discourse community in his reasoning. But if the reasoner does not, why should he follow these rules towards *everyone*?

The shortcoming of Gewirth's argument from agency, which I discuss in Chapter 4, is similar. Gewirth has proposed that a reflection on the nature of agency in general reveals that it contains certain implicit value judgements which no one can deny without falling into a pragmatic inconsistency. What he argues is implied in all agency is a placing of positive value in our own freedom to act. From the necessity of this value judgement for every agent he concludes that we are entitled to consider our individual freedom to act as a right. There is a crucial error in this step of his argument. Although he can convincingly show the absolute necessity of our placing positive value in our freedom to act, he cannot show how *my* placing value in *my* freedom to act can claim to affect anyone else unless they are already committed to respecting both me and my evaluations in the first place. Gewirth, like Apel and Kuhlmann, jumps too quickly from the personal to the universal, or so I will argue.

In Chapter 5 I suggest a new transcendental argument of the retorsive type. I hope to show how it can overcome the criticized insufficiencies of the former transcendental approaches. It seems that there are indeed two moral judgements to which *everyone* (including the sceptic) is committed; namely, a judgement concerning the *universal* freedom to act and another concerned with the *universal* making of true judgements. The universal 'must' used in making these judgements, however, is generated not by a threat of performative inconsistency, but by the threat of what will be termed a 'normative inconsistency'. To deny the truth of these moral judgements would be a performative contradiction to certain *demands* which every rational free agent must necessarily impose upon himself implicitly by acting or arguing. Although the justification provided by this argument is transcendental, it is of a special kind and is different from the justifications attempted by Apel and Gewirth. It will be argued that it is nonetheless a good justification and indeed the *only* sort of justification we could ever expect to find for moral reasoning.

In the concluding chapter the epistemological level of discourse—the main battlefield of this book—is put aside, and the reach of the suggested 'argument from normative consistency' is sketched. In particular, I hope to show that it can provide an apt and useful basis for the main tenets of moral realism.

A book, like a life, is a product of its debts. The thoughts and ideas which have culminated in this book originate in the context of some earlier studies on Kant's moral philosophy. Ralph Walker and Gabriele Taylor, the supervisors of my doctoral dissertation on Kant's ethics, were the first with whom I was able to discuss some ideas in this area; their critical yet consistently friendly comments were of great value. I am also very thankful for constructive discussions with Michael Inwood and Raymond Geuss, and the very helpful comments and enlightening criticisms made by Dieter Wandschneider and Wolfgang Kuhlmann about a penultimate draft of this book.

For some years I was highly privileged to work with Vittorio Hösle at the University of Essen in Germany. Those years have been of inestimable value and I am more than grateful to him both as a teacher and as a friend. This book, though not always in accordance with his views, is the best testimony of Hösle's significance in shaping my philosophical thinking.

There is a long list of philosophical friends who have undertaken the chore of reading and commenting on earlier versions (or parts) of this book: Melissa Lane, my constant philosophical companion; Thomas Kesselring, who scrutinized my argument sharply; Georg Kamp, Miriam Ossa, and Thorsten Sander, whose annotations have helped me in several ways. I should also mention Michel Bourdeau, Geno Fernandez, Bernd Göbel, Bernd Gräfrath, Dietrich Koch, Tracy Lounsbury, Jong Seok Na, Michel Sherwin OP, Andreas and Christian Spahn, and the students who participated in my seminar on transcendental arguments at Essen University. They were always willing disputants, critics, and supporters of my work.

I wrote this book in a language which I considered to be English. Not all of my friends thought that that was true, and some of them were so kind as to spend many hours transforming it into a language which can more justifiably be described in that way. Besides Melissa, Tracy, and Geno, I should also mention Amir Sadighi Akha, Emily Filler, Brian Herlocker, Christiania Whitehead, and, particularly, Graeme Napier, who provided me with indispensable help. Last but not least, Jane Wheave, the remarkable copy-editor at OUP, performed miracles.

I should also like to thank Peter Momtchiloff at Oxford University Press, who encouraged me to write this book and whose friendly and patient way of dealing with delayed typescripts has been remarkable. I also want to mention the anonymous reader for OUP whose careful comments on this book proved to be extremely valuable.

My main gratitude, however, is reserved for three people: my wife, Friederike, to whom I owe too much for words, and my parents, whose love made me believe in the possibility of moral realism becoming practical. It is to them that this book is dedicated.

Contents

1. Claims and Counter-claims: A General Introduction to Moral Realism ... 1
2. The Promise of Transcendental Arguments ... 30
3. The Argument from Discourse ... 64
4. The Argument from Agency ... 93
5. The Argument from Normative Consistency and the Goodness of Truth and Freedom ... 129
6. Truth and Beyond ... 168

References ... 199

Index ... 211

CHAPTER I

Claims and Counter-claims: A General Introduction to Moral Realism

I.I. THE STEEP CLIFFS OF MORAL REALISM AND ANTI-REALISM

The grandest canyon in ethics separates two views about whether normative judgements can be true. It is not a difference of easily determinable matters of fact; rather the steep cliff walls mark a fundamental divergence of moral attitudes.

On the one side spires 'moral realism'; that is, the view—in the way the term is commonly used (and will be in this book)—that there are moral facts. According to this position, judgements on matters of norms and values are literally true, if they get the moral facts right. Thus, moral realists see moral judgements as expressions of our beliefs about some factual matter, not simply as assertions of subjective preferences and feelings of approval, or as judgements about the practices of groups of people. Though not always put in these terms, moral realism has been the view of most, though not all, philosophers up to the advent of modernity.

This view has been severely and powerfully challenged by the proponents of anti-realism, who occupy the opposing ridge. They hold that no facts exist of the kind required by the realists. Moral judgements are either considered to be expressions of people's thoughts or feelings, so that there is no 'truth' to be found at all, or they are seen as true only to the extent that they are appropriate accounts of subjective interests, social conventions, or such like. If, as some anti-realists argue, people do indeed make normative judgements about alleged moral facts, then they are mistaken and their judgements are simply *wrong* or meaningless because they are in fact contentless. Moral anti-realism has been the dominant philosophical outlook for the last century. It is mainly an expression of a deeply felt suspicion against the possibilities of reason discovering anything more than means–end relations.[1] For many, to search for any timeless truth in moral judgements has appeared to be nothing but the atavistic relics of a theological, pre-scientific age. Others, however, have stated and continue to state that anti-realism has failed entirely to understand morality.

It is one of the central tasks of contemporary 'meta-ethics'—the endeavour to advance (or discover) a systematic understanding of what morality is or pretends to be—to adjudicate between the two positions of realism and anti-realism. The current meta-ethical debate ranges over three not always sharply distinguished nor distinguishable levels of analysis: at a semantic level about the meaning of normative terms; at an ontological level about the existence of moral facts; and at the epistemological level about possible truth-conditions for moral judgements.[2] It is with the meta-ethical debate that this book is engaged. Its

---

[1] This critique of practical reason was put in place by empiricists like Hume, and since the second half of the nineteenth century it has been ubiquitous in philosophical discussion. There are many motives for this radical break with the traditional conception of reason, but I want to name but a few. The triumph of natural sciences and technology, and hence of a specific use of reason, is surely one of the most important motives, since it gave support to the impression that reason is incapable of achieving anything comparable in ethics—and therefore that ethics is not a rational matter at all. The theory of evolution, which explains man and reasoning as a product of a natural process of adaptation, and as being selected in a struggle for existence, endorses this conviction. After all, human 'reason'—that evolution selected positively—seems of an instrumental type rather than value-oriented. The rejection of reason as a faculty to come to true judgements was further nurtured by the historicist school and sociology, especially by the new insights that values have varied substantially in different times and cultures.

[2] Up to the late 1970s analytic meta-ethics was primarily occupied with the semantic question, mainly spurred on by G. E. Moore's *Principia Ethica* (1903). Since then the weight of discussion has shifted for several reasons to the ontological and epistemological level. One of the reasons might be serious objections to the project of basing any authority on linguistic analysis (cf. P. Foot 1961, A. Montefiore 1961, and A. Gewirth 1981: 9–12). After all, it is hard to see how the linguistic approach could escape the danger of committing the naturalistic fallacy.

The late 1960s brought political events, outside the domain of philosophical arguments, which made people aware of the importance of more material issues in moral philosophy—the Vietnam War being the most striking example. There was an obvious need for substantial answers to the ethical problems of the time, answers which the exercise of linguistic analysis could not accommodate. John Rawls's *A Theory of Justice* (1972) responded most

aim is to propose fulfillable truth-conditions for moral judgements and thus to support a realist understanding of morality.

1.2. THE THREE CLAIMS OF COGNITIVIST MORAL REALISM

Let us look more carefully at what moral realism states. There are three fundamental claims mostly made by moral realists (though not all of its representatives would necessarily hold all three of them). The first and most crucial one is an *epistemological* claim. I will call it the truth thesis of moral realism:

> We can make moral judgements with truth-value that we are able to determine.

This statement expresses a commitment to cognitivism in moral philosophy. Moral utterances are not simply viewed as expressions of emotions but are structured as judgements that have a truth value, and the criteria for their truth can actually be fulfilled. Kant, for example, makes the same point when he talks about practical reason's capacity to arrive at 'a priori synthetic judgements'—hence he grants moral judgements the highest status his epistemology offers with regard to truth. Although the different forms of moral realism will vary widely in their view of what the relevant truth-conditions are, i.e. what criteria justify calling a moral judgement true (whether they are based on intuition, a kind of observation of moral facts, or something else), they agree that to call them true is not merely a *façon de parler* but to be taken in a literal sense. That's why

---

powerfully to this challenge and 'changed the subject', as Thomas Nagel wrote in the dedication of his book *Equality and Partiality* to John Rawls (1991: p. v.; see also S. Darwall et al. (1992: 122 ff.) and J. Habermas (1996: 65)). Disputes about the appropriate status of moral judgements, their underlying epistemology, and the possibility of rational justifications dominated major parts of the debate.

There have always been philosophers in the analytic tradition raising the question of the ontological status of value (e.g. A. J. Ayer 1936 in *Language, Truth and Logic*), but intense disagreements did not start before J. L. Mackie's *Ethics* (1977) and Gilbert Harman's *The Nature of Morality* (1977). Both triggered a far-reaching debate about the status of moral facts and their function in morality. To use the traditional terminology, the new area of meta-ethical discourse was largely about the metaphysics or ontology to which a moral philosophy is committed. (For the development of meta-ethics see M. Warnock 1978, S. Darwall et al. 1992, and H. Spector 1992.)

this first claim can also be expressed as follows: 'Moral judgements can be literally true.'

There is also a tradition of a restricted understanding of the truth thesis and thus of what 'moral realism' amounts to. Probably because of Moore's rather paradigmatic position in the analytical world, several authors see intuitionism like that of Moore, Prichard, or Ross as constitutive for moral realism. According to these authors ethics must embrace supernatural, indefinable properties and thus a unique power of (intuitive) recognition. It follows that not much informative can be said about the truth-conditions of moral judgements. There are, however, no good reasons to see this as the only way of being a moral realist; at least, that is the position I will argue for at some length in this book.[3]

Let us now look at the ontological claim of moral realism—I will call it the 'moral-fact thesis':

There are moral facts, which exist independently of our evidence for them.

There are many varying conceptions of this ontological claim; which one a moral realist defends will depend on the theory of truth to which he is committed in the moral realm.

Some moral realists talk about 'facts' in the sense of an independent class of ideal entities which serve as a standard for our judgements about the ordinary entities we deal with in our life and actions. Plato's concept of forms is a rich ontology of this type. For him, forms constitute not only a realm over and above everyday reality, but are much more 'real'— they are the ultimate source of all empirical realities of the world around us.

Others have a very minimal conception of moral 'facts'. For several

---

[3] There is a further variation of moral realism worth pointing out. Someone might be more objectivist about moral truth than about moral knowledge. In this case, one would hold that moral judgements can be literally true but would deny our capacity to identify them. This position, however, would raise many profound questions about the architecture of the world—at least if it were connected with the claim that moral truth, though inaccessible for us, is about the way *we should act*. The extreme case would be poor Joseph K. in Kafka's *Trial*, who is quite sure that there is an absolutely demanding law, and that he is accused of having acted against it, but will never find out what its content is. It might be that his case strikes us as so bizarre exactly because his ignorance is *not* complete: he is aware at least that he has acted against this law. Raskolnikov in Dostoevsky's *Crime and Punishment* comes also to see an absolute moral law, which is 'hidden from all minds' and thus provides the paradox of human experience. The contrasting figure in the same novel is Razumieken, who not only accepts the universal moral law and the truths contained therein, but insists that we, *all men of goodwill*, have access to these truths. I hope that my book shows that Razumieken is right.

A General Introduction to Moral Realism · 5

authors the fact *that* it is, for example, wrong to lie is seen as the only relevant moral fact. In this case, the moral-fact thesis seems itself to be interpreted in terms of the truth-value of a moral judgement and the epistemological and the ontological claims cannot easily be distinguished. This is probably the reason why many proponents of moral realism either avoid reflecting about the appropriate ontology accompanying their epistemology or argue vividly that moral realism does not have any further ontological implications. Thomas Nagel, for example, defends explicitly the truth thesis of moral realism but is very reluctant to adduce any ontological claims: 'There is no moral analogue of the external world' (1997: 101). To characterize this position, Christine Korsgaard has suggested a helpful distinction between a 'procedural moral realism' and a 'substantial moral realism' like Plato's (1996: 34 ff.): The proceduralist argues that there are right or wrong answers to moral questions, but sees their rightness as constituted by their being the result of a correct procedure. Hence procedural moral realism seems to give up the ontological thesis; the 'moral facts' are not considered independent from our evidence for them.[4]

Although the moral-fact thesis is controversial even amongst moral realists, it is necessary to account for some forms of moral realism. There are philosophers whose conception of morality is based upon the moral-fact thesis; for example, Kierkegaard with his non-cognitivist moral realism, but also in some sense Moore and several other intuitionists. They are committed to a rich notion of normative entities, which they see as prior to and the basis for any true moral judgement (if Kierkegaard with his weird notion of 'subjective' truth can be said to hold the truth thesis at all).

The characterization of moral realism must be completed by the addition of a third claim. Most moral realists would hold the following:

---

[4] This raises the question whether the label 'realism' makes any sense for a strict proceduralist. Habermas thinks it does not. He would agree that right moral judgements are the result of having employed the right procedure for reaching them. For him the special conditions of moral discourse are but a subset of the general conditions of rational argumentation. But he is opposed to any subsequent ontological claim about what is good because of his strict consensus theory of truth. And this is probably the reason why he rejects being labelled a moral realist 'like a poisoned pawn' (F. J. Davis 1994: 136).

But if he sees the result of these normative discourses as rationally justified norms (i.e. moral judgements), and if he affirms that the consensus is ultimately what 'truth' amounts to, he does seem committed to a version of the truth thesis. Using Korsgaard's expression, he could therefore, *contre coeur*, be called a procedural moral realist.

6 · *The Grounds of Ethical Judgement*

> There is a correspondence between a person's moral judgements and his motives. If he judges sincerely y to be morally better than non-y, then he has a motive to do or support y.

This third claim will be termed the 'motivational thesis' of moral realism.[5] The correspondence is not taken to be an empirical thesis about the influence of judgements on preferences or motives but rather an *analytic* truth about making moral judgements. While even the anti-realist will probably agree that it is an analytic truth that a moral judgement *ought* to have motivational force, many realists argue that a moral judgement *has* by itself motivational force.

Two clarifications must be made. First, moral realists do not normally imply that the motive which is connected to a judgement will override all other (and possibly conflicting) motives that an agent harbours. All they say is that the judgement plays *some* role in the preferences of the person making the judgement. Secondly, it must be noted that the motivational thesis does not allow any conclusion from the presence of a motive to a previous moral judgement. It is obvious that there can be entirely different (for example, selfish) motives for doing some y. Motives can have all sorts of origins and one of them is making a moral judgement.

1.3. MORAL ANTI-REALISM

1.3.1. *Anti-realism as Scepticism*

Anti-realism in its different forms can be characterized as a scepticism about the three claims of moral realism. It states that there are no normative facts *sui generis* and consequently that there are no (or no fulfillable; this is the point made by Mackie 1977 and 1985) truth-conditions for these alleged judgements about moral facts. It is further questioned whether we can ever be motivated by moral judgements or whether we need external reasons (Williams 1979).

It is important to note that not just any kind of scepticism is relevant for the meta-ethical debate. The sceptic must be someone who accepts the possibility of reasoning in general. As already pointed out, an anti-rational sceptic who is so radical as to deny even the laws of logic, and

---

[5] Following F. v. Kutschera (1994: 54 ff.) we might also call it the 'correspondence thesis'. However, in order to avoid any association with the correspondence theory of truth the label above seems more suitable.

who is consequently willing to see his own 'utterance' as no argument whatsoever, is outside reasoning altogether. Already Aristotle reminds us of the impossibility of dealing with him (Met. 1008ᵃ).[6] While this radical form of scepticism is meaningless, it is also, in a certain sense, irrefutable. What argument could possibly convince someone who, let us say, does not accept *modus ponens*? Someone who ignores the authority of all reasons whatsoever will not be moved by rational argument to the effect that his position is irrational. But this is also the *reason* why no one can or need take the radical sceptic as the interlocutor or addressee of any argument seriously. Moral realism does not have to be concerned about his contributions (at least not philosophically).

It should be added that it is simply irrelevant whether or not the anti-realist sceptic actually believes her objections, or whether she is merely constructing a sceptical straw man in order to investigate the strength of the claims made by moral realism. 'It is entirely irrelevant whether anyone has really these doubts or not,' as M. Schlick rightly says (1925: 141). The anti-realist's arguments are not disproved if she does not really believe that everyone is free to murder her husband.[7]

Rational sceptical objections can be found at different levels of generality: they may be of a very general kind, querying the ability of reason to attain any secure knowledge: 'No one is ever justified or at all reasonable in anything' (P. Unger 1975: 197). But whatever epistemological position one assumes with regard to other realms of knowledge, the only relevant objections here are the ones to the three claims of moral realism. That is why anti-realist scepticism can also allow descriptive judgements in the area of moral sociology or moral psychology to be true;

---

[6] Aristotle affirms that it is impossible to hold that all assertions are true and false at the same time. Everyone who argues or acts must stick with this minimal demand for rationality. Otherwise, it seems, whatever he says could simply mean the opposite. Such a sceptic does not really argue at all; Aristotle asks therefore: 'what difference will there be between him and the vegetables?' (Met. 1008ᵇ39). This has also been acknowledged by Descartes. We have no 'reason' to consider as meaningful any scepticism of this fundamental type, which argues that we might be radically deceived by a *malin génie*, even about the laws of logic (1985: 145). See also Wittgenstein (1963: 114) and Stegmüller (1969: 381 ff.); for the possibility of a meaningless scepticism see R. C. S. Walker (1989a).

[7] Annas and Barnes (1985: 7–8, and 166 ff.) and M. F. Burnyeat (1980) argue that modern scepticism since Descartes retains beliefs and merely sees no justification for them, while the ancients tended to abandon unjustified beliefs. It is interesting that this difference between ancient and modern scepticism reflects the close connection between an insight and a motive to act which was held by many philosophers in antiquity (cf. Aristotle, *NE* vii—knowing what the good life means *is just living* the good life).

that is, judgements that are *about* evaluations, beliefs, or desires of individuals or groups of people. The sceptic can accept them without losing the force of his objections, because these judgements must be distinguished sharply from *evaluative* judgements, which are, according to anti-realism, either all meaningless or all false.

1.3.2. The Main Arguments of Anti-realism

Part of the anti-realist case is straightforwardly (but not all-out) sceptical; it questions the validity of the arguments of moral realism. In addition, there are three direct criticisms of any realist interpretation of moral matters. Let us look at them briefly and also at the most common replies given by moral realism.

(1) The first argument is to offer some explanatory, reductive thesis about moral phenomena. According to this, the alleged 'moral facts' are not crucial to the explanation of moral observations. There is, so the anti-realist says, no difficulty in replacing them with psychological observations about human attitudes or beliefs. These are sufficient to explain why we make certain judgements. A classic example is Friedrich Nietzsche's moral psychology, which exposes all moral judgements as power-acquisitive activities of the will and thus not as rational judgements at all. (For more recent versions see, for example, Blackburn 1984, Gibbard 1990, Hare 1952, and Mackie 1977). Therefore, judgements about moral facts are either meaningless in the strictly moral sense or they have some other, non-moral point of reference.

Several moral realists who argue that moral facts have exactly this necessary explanatory function (like Boyd 1988, Brink 1989, Railton 1986, and Sturgeon 1985) have questioned this analysis. They accuse anti-realists of a circular argument, which does not accept that moral facts can provide a satisfying explanation, because they doubt that there are such facts in the first place. Only if, realists argue, they are regarded as doubtful entities does their explanatory role seem so questionable.[8]

(2) The second, and probably more important, argument against moral realism comes from recognizing the diversity of moral opinions in different cultures and the intractability of moral disagreements. This argument from relativity is the most prominent and the oldest objection

---

[8] The other means of refuting this first objection is to question the entire picture of moral realism on which it is based, and of the explanatory role moral facts are supposed to play (Korsgaard 1996: 45–6).

to the existence of universal norms or values; it is already to be found as the basis of Herodotus' relativism and has not changed much in the subsequent two and a half thousand years. An anti-realist position is seen as the more plausible explanation of this diversity. Though it is generally acknowledged that this does not show positively that anti-realism is right, it is seen as strong enough for 'a reasonable inference' to this end (Harman 1996: 9; see also D. B. Wong 1984).

Countering this objection, some moral realists reply that the differences between cultures are not so strong; they point to a core of moral judgements which are culturally invariant. Examples for commonly shared convictions are the rejection of 'murder, deception, betrayal and gross cruelty' (M. Walzer 1987: 24).[9] Besides this, it has been objected that the differences are more apparent than real, since the same fundamental norms or values, when applied to different circumstances, may lead to different results. Further, to apply moral principles always requires some beliefs about matters of fact (in particular, difficult assessments of the future), but in many cases people make different judgements about these facts and therefore might hold different moral beliefs although they share the same fundamental normative principles. Furthermore, moral judgements have an important impact on our interests and on the way we should behave. Thus, there is a tendency to be influenced by egoistic desires—and so to mellow down the sometimes strict demands of morality in order to serve our own interests. In addition, people tend to be reluctant to change beliefs on which they have based their lives or in which they have invested a lot—Judith Thomson calls this the phenomenon of 'walling off' (1996: 205). All this might explain why moral judgements could vary so widely even if there were moral facts (cf. v. Kutschera 1994: 245–7 and 1999: 246–9).

(3) The third objection to moral realism is Mackie's 'Argument from Queerness' (1977: 38–42). For Mackie it is unacceptable to postulate a moral fact which is objective and has prescriptive authority because such a fact would be a metaphysically inconsistent, 'queer' entity. And, in fact,

---

[9] The counter response of the anti-realist would be that appealing to these so-called shared convictions is really making a linguistic point about what various cultures perceive as their individual moral goods or evils: a wide range of descriptive activities is labelled in such a way that the scope of 'cruelty' is ultimately variant and the term merely indexical. It can be specified in very different and partly mutually exclusive ways by socially conditioned variant customs. Thus, the relativistic thesis is not denied but merely moved one step back into the relativistic content of equivocal descriptive terms.

realists who hold some version of the moral-fact thesis are probably committed to the existence of an entity with these features, which seem to 'pull against each other' (Smith 1994: 5). It would seem that there are several problems to be distinguished in Mackie's criticism of queerness—the ontological, the motivational, and the epistemological. The first, the ontological point concerning what sort of 'entity' values with these properties might be, arises because they do not seem to fit into a suitably scientific picture of the world. The motivational question concerns how the connection—and distinction—between beliefs and desires are to be understood. Based upon the controversial positions of Hume and Kant, an ongoing debate in philosophy has queried whether this double demand of moral realism, to give an objective account of moral facts which at the same time are practical in that they have demanding force, could ever succeed. The third, epistemological, problem is the closely related one of how we can ever come to make true judgements of a kind which also involves an influence on our motives—what would the truth-conditions of these (queer) judgements be? Mackie's objection is so powerful because it can be directed against all three theses of moral realism.

In response, moral realists have tried to give accounts of moral facts which can explain both their objectivity and their practicality. They do so either by proposing a suitable ontology of moral facts, or by questioning Hume's underlying psychological picture of motivation in general (for example, Galvin 1991, Nagel 1978), or by separating the underlying epistemology from any ontological claim—and placing the weight of queerness at the ontological level alone, which they hope to be able to dismiss. Another common defence is to argue that Mackie's objection is overdetermined and can be directed against any fact whatsoever, hence against realism in general. Whatever the defence strategy is, there is no doubt that for moral realists the objection against an apparently motivating yet objective fact is the most difficult challenge; M. Smith has argued convincingly that this is *the* 'moral problem' at the centre of the contemporary debate which explains most of the argumentative manoeuvres made by philosophers on both sides of the canyon of meta-ethics:

> The objectivity of moral judgement suggests that there are moral facts, wholly determined by circumstances, and that our moral judgements express our beliefs about what these facts are. This enables us to make good sense of moral argument, and the like, but it leaves it entirely mysterious how or why having a moral view is supposed to have special links with what we are motivated to do.

And the practicality of moral judgements suggests just the opposite, that our moral judgements express our desires. While this enables us to make good sense of the link between having a moral view and being motivated, it leaves it entirely mysterious what a moral argument is supposed to be an argument about; the sense in which morality is supposed to be objective. (1994: 11)

1.4. INSUFFICIENT RESPONSES TO MORAL ANTI-REALISM

Let us now look at the chief objections to moral anti-realism. Roughly speaking, all realists claim in one way or another that anti-realism gives an *inadequate* account of what morality is.

(1) First, it is argued that the anti-realist's account of the phenomenology of moral experience is not compelling, because it denies that we talk about 'objective' rightness or truth in the moral arena. Thus, the common-sense understanding of our normal normative discourses cannot be captured by the anti-realists' interpretation.

(2) It is argued that anti-realism (which presents itself most commonly as a version of subjectivism or intersubjectivism) gives highly implausible accounts of the truth-conditions for moral claims. It construes morality as a reflection of our attitudes, rather than a standard for them, and is therefore incapable of making sense of the idea of moral progress or of the possibility that we might make fundamental moral mistakes, namely wrong moral judgements.

(3) Lacking an appropriate notion of moral truth, the anti-realist would deprive morality of its claims to importance, and it could no longer fulfil its necessary function. But, then, morality seems to become reduced to practical rules, as Kant famously reminds us (*KGS* IV. 389). This is particularly crucial in areas where moral obligations demand a great deal or even everything (as in the case of self-sacrifice) from people: all those demands which go beyond any self-interest of the agent could not be made plausible if there were no normative standard transcending the subject and his interests.

Against these objections the anti-realists defend their scepticism in two main ways: either they try to give a plausible account of our normal manner of speaking which still challenges the common (but according to anti-realism *wrong*) realist interpretation (for example, Harman 1996 and

Blackburn 1993), or they challenge our normal manner of speaking and give therapeutic advice as to how to make moral claims properly; Nietzsche's rather drastic suggestions are an extreme example.

Consequently, the first realist's objection is not allowed to be a genuine objection as such, but rather a restatement of the point of dispute between realism and anti-realism. Similarly with the second realist objection: according to anti-realism there are no *wrong* judgements, as the realists assume; if this is indeed the ordinary interpretation of the way we speak about moral issues, then this interpretation should be replaced by a more adequate one. Anti-realists will answer the third objection in the same spirit: why *should* we think that there *are* strong moral obligations of the characterized kind? Realism might simply err, and anti-realism helps to get rid of an unnecessary moral burden, which results from a fanciful metaphysics.

We should briefly look at a kind of 'immunization strategy' against scepticism that is based on Rudolf Carnap's distinction between internal and external questions. According to Carnap, internal questions refer to entities *within* an accepted framework while external questions are about the existence of this framework itself (1972: 259; a similar position is held by Wittgenstein 1970: § 84). Carnap argues that only internal questions are capable of being answered, while external questions are decided in a practical manner on the basis of their utility. So scepticism about the framework itself would miss the point—external questions about a particular framework are not a matter of reasoning (and thus a scepticism about reasons) at all; it is only a matter of choice, or of a 'jump' as we might say with Kierkegaard. Yet not only is it highly counter-intuitive to claim that it is meaningless to question the legitimacy of the framework itself, as Descartes reminds us with his *malin génie*, but any rejection of external questions themselves is highly dogmatic. Even worse, it is self-refuting. To reject all external questions as meaningless is taking the alleged meaningless viewpoint of those external questions. Apart from these problems, the immunization strategy is in fact surrendering to the sceptic. It would undermine at least the first and second claims of the realist by making their validity depend on a framework accepted merely for pragmatic reasons. There could be nothing literally true about moral judgements, since the foundation of the framework and thus (indirectly) of the subordinate judgements would be decision-based. Moral demands would turn out to be, in Kant's terminology, mere *hypothetical* imperatives, whose authority would be conditionally linked to prior wishes, decisions, or other contingent states of affairs—and that is exactly what the realist denies.

Similarly, the debate does not seem to allow for an easy and pragmatic escape in simply leaving the question open. Why? When we disagree about what we should do, and when we want to praise or criticize the behaviour of people, someone might argue in a Rortyian spirit that this can be done without deciding whether moral judgements are true in any literal sense. In a world of famine, violence, and ecological catastrophes, one might say, it seems to be more relevant to look for the best solution possible to our pressing moral challenges, whatever the exact status of moral judgements is. Philosophers should engage with practical ethical problems, the pragmatists argue, and they should not bother too much about the status of right answers. However, this rejection of the entire realism/anti-realism debate will not succeed. Without coming to a decision about the meta-ethical controversy, we will have no clear and useful standard for rational decisions in applied ethics, especially in cases that are controversial. And the individual decision making that the pragmatist urges upon the philosophical community will have no procedural validation. It is only when we have come to terms with what moral judgements *are* that we can hope to know to our satisfaction how to deal with them. If moral realism is right, then we must aim at moral knowledge and use the truth-conditions given by the realist's theory in order to overcome the patent fact of ethical disagreement. It will provide us with the standard against which we have to check substantial moral claims. If, on the other hand, anti-realism wins the debate, then this would have a great effect on our practical approach. The answers we should aim at in moral debates would not necessarily be rational. Agreements about what to do might then have to be found on the basis of balancing the power of people and their interests in a Hobbesian fashion. In brief, normative debates should look quite different depending on whether moral realism or anti-realism gets things right. This explains why we cannot simply investigate which of the two positions gives the better result in practice; that is, which is most successful in dealing with ordinary moral problems. For the above-mentioned reasons this will fail—both sides have very different criteria for the definition of a 'moral problem' and even more for what a 'successful' solution of such a problem would amount to. A merely pragmatic solution of the meta-ethical problem is futile since there is not one common praxis of evaluation between moral realists and anti-realists.

14 · *The Grounds of Ethical Judgement*

The problem is profound. Where is the common ground between the disputants on which the meta-ethical question could be decided? What makes it so difficult to think of a solution is that the positions express a fundamental divergence of moral attitudes: realists and anti-realists have very different standards by which to measure what counts as a reasonable, satisfying account of morality. How can the problem be solved?

1.5. THE DEMAND FOR A RATIONAL JUSTIFICATION OF MORAL JUDGEMENTS

Let us summarize the last discussion. Both sides of the debate seem convinced that their opponents' case is not built on banks of reason but on a shoal of errors. The situation is, however, not symmetrical. The burden of argumentation lies on the side of moral realism because it makes a strong claim. And this burden is a heavy one: it would not suffice to reject the three positive arguments of anti-realism; the rightness of the claims of moral realism must be demonstrated in a way which cannot be rebuffed by the anti-realist. Without such a positive demonstration, i.e. a justification of the truth of some moral judgements, there will always be a strong *motive* (though not a further argument) to use Ockham's razor in an ontological and epistemological fashion: entities as much as claims to truth must not be multiplied without necessity.

What does the required justification amount to? It will have to explain not why we make a certain kind of judgement, but why some moral judgements ought be made. We can also say that in order to be rationally justified a judgement must turn out to be the only coherent way in which we can think about things. If a judgement fulfils this demand, then the main requirement for an epistemological justification is met and we are entitled to call it 'true' or 'right' (at least according to a plausible and common interpretation of these notions). It is, as Kant put it in the *Critique of Pure Reason*, the question *quid juris*, investigating the validity of judgements—and not the question *quid facti*, asking for the genesis of a judgement (A 84).

This is our understanding of justifications in general and also in the realm of morality. The moral realist must show that a certain normative principle (like the categorical imperative) or a fundamental value is rightly understood to be or imply a basic demand upon our action. Then, this principle or value can be regarded as rationally justified. This enterprise takes place at the most fundamental level of morality and must be sharply distinguished from judgements at subordinate levels (or 'internal questions', as Carnap would put it). Given some general norm or normative framework, there will always be a deductive justification of particular judgements, based on an understanding of the situation in which the agent acts. If we *presuppose* that 'torture is wrong', then even the anti-realist will see it, *ceteris paribus*, as justified to deduce that it is wrong for some specific person to torture someone else in a particular situation. But this is not the level of investigation under discussion.

In order to be successful realism needs, as it were, a 'meta-ethical' argument; that is, a justification for the *ultimate* normative framework itself. To put it rather metaphorically: an 'Archimedean point' of leverage for practical philosophy is needed (B. Williams 1985: 28). This Archimedean point must serve to establish a framework which is both *justified* and *normative*—more exactly, justified *as* normative. By 'normative' it is intended that such a framework will describe an ideal state of affairs (or actions); that is, how things should be (which leaves it open whether the actual states of affairs are already like this or not). That is why we must see justifications of normativity as having an imperative dimension, at least so long as reality does not match the justified norms.

To justify a value or moral principle means to give a reason why people should act in this or that way. And anything which is a reason in one case must be a reason in every comparable one. This is what is meant by proposing reasons or arguments in general, and is also true for practical philosophy. It follows that the rationally grounded normative framework must be universal, at least to the degree that it is universally relevant and tells everyone what he ought to do—although it does not necessarily universally determine what he ought to do in every particular case (cf. Philipps-Griffiths 1967: 177). Thus, even a sceptic must allow that a normative judgement, if it cannot be refuted, would have this authority and that he should support the ideal state set out in the judgement. Further, the justification sought must show that even the most radical rejecters of reason and arguments will fall under those demands which the normative framework establishes, even if they are unwilling to acknowledge the justification and will surely never be motivated by it. If the justification is valid, then it spells out norms for everyone. Yet the justification cannot be burdened with absurd demands. No reasoning could ever motivate someone to acknowledge its validity or to obey an imperative if he were unmoved by the force of arguments in general. R. Nozick has rightly remarked on this point: 'The motivational force of the argument . . . can be no stronger than the motivation to avoid the particular inconsistency specified by the argument' (1981: 407).

It is important not to confuse the task of justification with other investigations, like the search for explanations. To explain *why people think* that they should do something is not a justification, so long as it does not say why they actually *should* do so. A good test for discriminating between a 'justification' and an 'explanation' can be run by applying the motivational thesis. We must ask whether someone who has fully understood what has been argued remains under the obligation to act in the way set up by the normative framework under discussion—or whether it sets him free to challenge its authority. Let us assume, for example, that a socio-biological explanation of morality could establish why certain modes of behaviour have evolved in human evolution as the most successful strategies (Gibbard 1990). If this were *all* we could say about moral norms, then it would deprive morality of its unconditionally obligatory character. Even if it were difficult or impossible to act against this genetic programme, this would only set up a compulsion, not a moral obligation. Someone who has understood the explanation might simply say: 'Now I see why we hold certain things as valuable: it is all connected with evolutionary success. But to the extent to which I can act freely, I won't play the gene game any more. I don't care about the survival of the fittest, about proliferation or evolutionarily stable strategies!'. No evolutionary explanation alone could tell him why he should not reject the norms that evolution brought about.

A justification must retain the normative force of moral principles even if we know everything about them—they must, as this point has been put, have a 'psychological stability' (Rawls 1972: 177) or 'survive reflection' (Korsgaard 1996: 49). A mere explanation can fall short of this because its whole force is the 'translation' of the normative framework into a descriptive one. The point can also be expressed in terms of Moore's 'open-question test'. To ask whether something is 'really good or right' amounts to questioning whether the given account is sufficient to survive reflection and still tell us why we are *obliged* to act in a certain way. This is exactly where a mere explanation differs from a justification: the former fails, the latter (if successful) passes Moore's test question.

A notable point should be added. Expressions such as 'normative framework', 'ultimate normative principles', and so on have been generally used here. This is not to imply that they all amount to the same thing, but rather in order not to limit the meta-ethical task by presupposing any specific sort of 'moral fact'. Moral realism has expressed itself in very different forms. Mostly—but not always helpfully—it is characterized as either value-based (for example, 'freedom' or 'justice') or centred on fundamental principles (like the categorical imperative). The former are generally labelled as 'teleological theories', the latter as 'deontological theories'.[10] For the present purpose, the question about the best form of moral realism can be left undecided until a successful justification has been found. This might tell us more about moral facts—what they are and what their ontological status is. Therefore, the rather neutral expression 'source of normativity' (following Korsgaard 1996) might be the most appropriate term at this stage of the discussion.

Of course, so far it has not been shown that any such justification can be provided; that will be the project of this book. And it will have to start by looking at the appropriate methodology for moral philosophy. Both questions are intimately linked; scepticism about the validity of some meta-ethical argument will mostly be a scepticism about the methodology behind it. Thus, the moral realist's task of providing a rational justification for an ultimate normative framework will have to begin by providing a justification for an appropriate *method* of reasoning in the moral realm. As Nagel rightly remarks (1997: 102): 'It is mainly because we have no comparably uncontroversial and well-developed methods for thinking about morality that a subjectivist position here is more credible than it is with regard to science.'

1.6. INADEQUATE METHODS OF ETHICS

What method or sort of argument might do practical reason's job in providing rational justification? It is necessary to look briefly at the different methods of rational justification in general so that we can find out which one serves this purpose best—if indeed there is any satisfactory method at all.

1.6.1. *Induction*

In most areas wherein we aim to acquire knowledge, induction plays a

---

[10] The *locus classicus* for this distinction in the analytic tradition is to be found in Rawls (1972: 24 ff., 30, 40).

crucial role. However, there are two main reasons for the inadequacy of induction as a rational justification of ethics.

First, induction cannot achieve anything stronger than a hypothetical knowledge, and never full necessity. Already Sextus Empiricus (*Outlines of Pyrrhonism* II. 15) pointed out that the problem with induction is that we cannot possibly know all particular propositions (including future-tensed propositions) by which the mind is led to the general proposition; and only this general proposition would safeguard against a counter example (see also Aristotle *Prior Analytics* 69^{a} [11]). Thus, Karl Popper has rightly called it a mere conjectural knowledge (*Vermutungswissen*; see 1983: 11–158 and 1984: 1–31). While hypothetical knowledge might be sufficient for science, where the investigator can move from a weaker, falsified hypothesis to a stronger, as yet unfalsified one—because science is not normative in the moral sense—it is not enough for the strong claims of moral realism outlined above. Hypothetical knowledge is insufficient since it cannot verify value judgements in the sense of showing them to be literally true. What moral realism needs is a *grounding* for our moral claims. Kant never tires of dismissing induction for this reason as a basis for truth; he emphasizes over and over again that it can only provide general, but never universal, judgements with absolute necessity.

Secondly, induction alone cannot explain why it should be regarded as a reliable method of justification. This is crucial: if we want to escape from a kind of epistemological fideism we need a reason why we should accept some methodology. But there is no reason for taking the results of inductive processes as true, and induction itself cannot provide one by its own means. If we try to explore induction inductively we will only find that many people—possibly everyone we look at—use induction. But this would not demonstrate that it could make a claim to truth. Induction's self-grounding attempts will always be circular, as Hume points out on many occasions in his *Treatise of Human Nature*.

Thirdly, and pivotally for our purpose, induction fails as a suitable method because it cannot simply start from 'normative elements' without already applying a standard that allows the selection of some elements as good, some as bad, and others as neutral and hence irrele-

---

[11] Interestingly enough, Aristotle regards the general proposition obtained by induction as more certain than the particulars that lead up to it. Also, he is not entirely against some form of induction as the basis of ethics—but makes it very clear that we will not have strict, absolute knowledge in moral matters.

vant for the inductive process. It does not suffice to begin in a Humean fashion by looking at the things we actually desire or dislike, or from our passions, since even if there were general agreement concerning the nature of human needs and passions (unlikely as that is), an argument would still be required for the 'good' of satisfying our desires.[12]

It has been suggested that one should start an inductive process from commonly agreed particular normative judgements about 'goods', which are then connected to general judgements.[13] But this will hardly circumvent the problem, since there is still a difference between stating that some or even all people make certain value judgements (which is a descriptive fact and a result of sociological research) and the claim that these judgements (whether or not they are universally shared) are valid. At most, induction can show that people always regard something as good—but 'it cannot tell us that any one ought to seek it', as Sidgwick reminds us (1901: 98).

It should be mentioned that a similarly dogmatic starting-point is taken by ethical theories which proceed from the analysis of the concepts of moral language. They hold that the task of justifying a first principle is achieved simply through the meaning of the relevant terms, most importantly the term 'moral' itself. Here, the alleged givenness of language breaks down all rational enquiry in the same way. This seems already flawed on empirical grounds—to find one commonly agreed-upon analysis of language is difficult and many tend to project their preferred ethical system into the alleged meaning of words.[14] But even if there were only one meaning to moral terms (and in order to reflect on ethical issues we must indeed presuppose that a shared language for all rational people is possible), the central problem is not solved: why should

---

[12] See e.g. J. Harrison's reasoning against 'objective naturalism'; i.e. an ethical theory based on natural facts which are considered 'good' (1967). Any such theory seems to covertly presuppose some moral principle as a criterion of goodness, or some values as an underlying moral framework.

[13] See for a contemporary version Chisholm (1957: 32, 96–7), Goodman (1965: 63 ff.), and Rawls (1972: 20–1, 48–51, 120, 579).

[14] There are emotivists (like Ayer, Carnap, and C. L. Stevenson), and those who see moral language as descriptive—the latter camp including both a naturalistic fraction considering moral language to be about natural facts like subjective preferences (e.g. Foot and Harman) and an intuitionist fraction which assume language to be about moral facts *sui generis* (namely, Moore, Prichard, and Ross). Some claim that language reveals that morality is inherently egalitarian and universalist (e.g. Baier 1958: 200–1, Benn and Peters 1959: 56, Hare 1952, and Toulmin 1970: 145). Others detect inbuilt notions of desired well-being and the avoidance of ill-being (Foot 1958: 502–13; 1958–9: 83–104).

we consider what is given by language as some kind of Archimedean point beyond need of proof? The sceptic can easily argue that the actual normative notions which are built into our language are simply wrong and a mirror of our prejudices.[15] Of course, even this questioning will happen within some language and it is surely not possible to be sceptical about the meanings of all words. We need some basis to stand on when we argue. But this does not prove anything as long as we can detach ourselves from the evaluations our language might happen to imply. If we can establish a modified language without the evaluations in question and if we can question the normative meaning of words within this (new) language consistently, then we will be on firm ground from which to volley the Moorean missile.

All the particular types of starting-point for inductive reasoning are therefore question-begging for a sceptic. Moral inductivism tries to justify values by reference to apparent normative elements without being able to give a rational justification of them (cf. Gewirth 1981: 17–21). Nonetheless, people might be willing to accept its results since, in many cases, they were gained on the basis of what people already accepted in practice. But it is not difficult to see that this manoeuvre will not impress the sceptic, who by definition questions the beliefs of ordinary folk.

1.6.2. Intuitionism

There is a common antithesis between 'inductive' and 'intuitive' approaches (Sidgwick 1901: 98) according to which intuitionism is the only way to secure the givenness, or objectivity, of morals. Intuitionists claim 'that we have the power of seeing clearly that certain kinds of actions are right and reasonable in themselves, apart from their consequences' (ibid. 200). Different accounts are given of the faculty that discerns the moral properties of actions and states of affairs. Philosophical empiricists like A. Shaftesbury and F. Hutcheson argue that intuition must be a sense like eyesight, since this is the most reliable guide to the nature of objective reality. The early rationalists, unwilling to grant the senses this authority, based intuitionism on Cartesian epis-

---

[15] Cf. e.g. Foot (1961), Gewirth (1981: 9–12), and Montefiore (1961) on the problems of basing any authority on linguistic analysis. It is hard to see how this linguistic approach could escape the danger of committing the naturalistic fallacy: no mere analysis of usage can either grant or reject the possibility of unquestionable moral demands. At least without further argument, usage tells us only about already shared practices and conventions. The result is likely to be a very static notion of morality, which hardly accounts for ethical progress.

temology, according to which the ultimate logical constituents of reasoning are clear and distinct ideas grasped by some unique faculty. As the vaguest form of intuitionism we might count the appeal to common sense—most people would say that it is 'obvious' that murder or torture is wrong, without being able to give any further justification for these judgements, or even without thinking that this is necessary.

What makes intuitionism so attractive for moral realism is that it can serve as a basis for all three of its central claims. According to its picture of morality, moral judgements are about moral facts and are true if they give an adequate account of these facts. Thus, their truth is, as the second claim demands, independent of our evidence for them—quite to the contrary, the evidence follows from some moral facts being truly there. In addition, it seems plausible to link an intuitive understanding of good and bad with some impulse to act; human conscience as a magisterial voice within has often been seen as such a mediating intuitive faculty which pushes the agent to do the right thing. Hence the motivational thesis would be satisfied. Another attractive feature of intuitionism is that it avoids, as Moore argues most eminently, the naturalistic fallacy. Intuitionism does not undermine the strict distinction between descriptive and normative judgements as long as the intuition of the goodness of something is not mixed up with any other perception but is regarded as an epistemological access to normative truth, which is *sui generis*.

Yet it seems that moral realism is well advised not to base its authority on intuitionism, since this shows profound methodological deficiencies. Its two central problems are: like induction, it is simply not a justification proper, and therefore vulnerable to several criticisms from the anti-realist; and it cannot satisfyingly account for people having different intuitions.

Let us look at the first deficiency. 'Intuitions' are not strictly speaking a *justification* of any judgement at all. Moore saw that quite clearly when he wrote: 'I would wish it observed that, when I call such propositions "intuitions", I mean merely to assert that they are incapable of proof' (1903: p. x). At the most, intuitions are a window that opens on to some fascinating insights, but they cannot grant the truth of the picture they show. All might be but dreams. This corresponds to the problem that intuitionism as a methodology cannot find any rational support. Any attempt to argue for the capacity of intuitions to grasp the truth will make intuitionism itself either superfluous or circular. This is so because any argument which attempts to show that moral facts can only be known intuitively must have some access to those moral facts independently from intuition, in order to come to this conclusion. But, *ex hypothesi*, this is claimed to be impossible. If, however, we did have this alternative avenue to the moral facts, then we would no longer need intuitions to ground ethics—intuitionism would become superfluous. The threat of a vicious circle would come up if we wanted to justify intuitionism by intuitions: A further meta-intuition is supposed to tell us that the only access we have to moral facts is intuition itself. Obviously, this does not work either, since it would be a circular approach—already Wittgenstein reminded us that we cannot prove the truth of information in a newspaper by looking at a second copy of the very same newspaper.

The second weakness of intuitionism is that it cannot account for the varieties or lack of the relevant intuitions. What can the intuitionist answer to the rather wicked Antonio who remarks in the *Tempest* about the conscience: 'where lies that? If 'twere a kibe, | 'Twould put me to my slipper: but I feel not | This deity in my bosom' (II. i. 267–9). This possibility weakens any pragmatic appeal to intuition substantially. But even if intuitionism claims that some people simply do not have this capacity (in the same way as, say, some do not have an ear for music), the problem of disagreement amongst those who claim to have the faculty remains. And even if we grant that most people seem to have some intuition at least *that there is* good and bad, they certainly do not always have the same concrete 'intuitions' about *what exactly is* good and bad.[16] Intuitionism will have to offer a satisfying explanation for these varieties, and for what enables some people to truly 'see' goodness and why others fail to do so. But the method is not designed to explain this—Moore continues, after having stated that intuitionism is not a 'proof', with: 'I imply nothing whatever as to the manner or origin of our cognition of them' [propositions that assert what kinds of things ought to exist for their own sake] (1903: p. x). To exclude unpleasant convictions from being intuitions proper the intuitionist would have to offer a rational procedure by which this can be done, an 'independent, agreed test' for moral blindness (Hudson 1967: 58). This, obviously, requires a *separate* standard of good and bad (not intuitions again) against which the results of people's intu-

---

[16] It is not sufficient to make only the limited claim that though the contents of people's intuitions differ all have some intuition about good and bad. Even if this were true, which is highly dubitable, and if nothing else could be said to make intelligible fundamental moral mistakes, then the method would simply be useless for the purposes of moral realism: it would not be a way to come to substantial true moral judgements.

ition could be tested—the problem leads back to the impossibility for intuitionism to ground its methodology.

The second problem is particularly bad because we have more powerful explanations at hand to tell us why people have certain views about the good and the bad rather than postulating some direct access to an alleged normative realm. Karl Marx, Friedrich Nietzsche, and especially Sigmund Freud have given alternative and non-moral descriptions in terms of the hidden motives for the views we hold. They have rightly taught us to be suspicious of taking moral judgements at face value—P. Ricoeur calls them the three 'maîtres du soupçon' (1965). If the strength of a theory reflects the variety of phenomena which can be explained by it, then their theories are surely very strong, since there are few, if any, phenomena which they cannot explain by their means (but NB: an explanation is not a justification nor itself an argument against the possibility of justifications). Freud's theory can even tell us why intuitionist views were in vogue at certain times. When, for eighteenth-century philosophers, the truth of certain moral judgements appeared to be clear-cut and indisputable, Freud could put this down to the consequences of an imperious superego which developed in times when the authority of parents, teachers, or priests was austere and received unquestioned respect (Hudson 1967: 61). I am not saying that Marx, Nietzsche, and Freud always give us satisfying answers, but their account of what constitutes intuitions is very powerful and cannot be facilely rejected by intuitionists when they themselves do not have a convincing story to tell about our access to the moral realm. That is why intuitionism has often been blamed as simply 'obscurantist' (J. O. Urmson 1958: 207).

All of this does not prove positively that intuitionism is wrong or inconsistent, but it questions whether it is a promising path to explore. As it stands it does not provide a sufficient basis for moral realism, at least while it cannot give a justification for its central thesis. It can only emphatically affirm the normativity of a principle or value and must remain silent when its own rationality is questioned (cf. Korsgaard 1996: 40, 65 n.).

1.6.3. Contractual Theories

Contractual theories are not an option for moral realism since they are not aimed at the *truth* of judgements. Yet they are considered as providing a rational justification for normative principles and deserve therefore a very brief investigation.

According to most contractual theorists, self-interest and prudential considerations are an apt basis for an agreement on moral norms. Hobbes, for example, defends the extreme version of the contract as a means to protect one's life from one's neighbours. Obviously, this can only ground what Kant called hypothetical imperatives; that is, the advice to behave in a certain way if one wants to achieve a certain end. The theories differ in complexity and the exact account they give of this agreement—whether it is real, imagined, or a regulative idea. There are also very sophisticated contractual theories (esp. by Rawls, Tugendhat, and possibly Habermas) which consider something as rationally justified if it has been, or could be, accepted in a fair discourse. The obvious strength of these approaches is that they presuppose very little. Some of them, like Hobbes' version, only assume everyone's self-interest. But it is obvious that this kind of theory does not lead immediately to true moral judgements—it might be 'true' that it is in the self-interest of all people to set up a society in order to preserve their interests, but there is no compelling step towards the 'goodness' of the resulting state in the sense of a moral fact.

A further difficulty is that contractual theories cannot provide any argument for the validity of the central underlying claim that all of them presuppose in some form or another. They face a methodological problem, which is structurally similar to the one faced by intuitionism and also by induction. If a contractual theory wants to demonstrate the claim that something should be regarded as justified when agreed upon, then this claim *itself* cannot be validated by mere agreement or contract. Otherwise we would face circular reasoning and mere self-affirmation. To base the claim itself on an imagined or real contract cannot show why rules of behaviour—or procedures to come to them—are rightly or wrongly judged as moral in any objective sense (cf. Wimmer 1980: 164–5 and Gewirth 1981: 20–1). Further, a strict contractualism (which does not allow any non-contractualist justification of practical principles) would be powerless against general agreements or contracts amongst all philosophers that might come up saying, for example, that no contractual agreement ever provides any justification—apart from this very one which condemns all other contracts. Contractualism is not immune to the possibility of self-destruction.

This problem might be avoided if the contractualist added some procedural requirements to his theory in order to exclude the self-destructive contract. He would have to show through different means than by mere agreement that a consensus constitutes truth in the required sense if it is achieved by the right procedure—and that this procedure makes the self-destructive contract impossible. (If, for example, the requirements are that the contract must always be open to further revision, then a contract which makes all possible past, present, and future contracts (besides itself) invalid would be impossible.) But, then, these additional rules will be the first moral principles which might be of interest for moral realism; contractualism will turn into a secondary, dependent, not a grounding, methodology. Let us assume that someone could justify that a consensus resulting from a procedure which includes universal respect towards everyone's contribution would provide true judgements. Then this would spell out some obligations or demands for agents—and to act upon these procedures itself turns into a moral demand *prior* to any contract. Thus, if the contractualist wanted to justify the consensus theory by independent means, his contractualism would ultimately cease to be the ultimate basis for moral realism. At least, it would turn out to be underdetermined, because contractualism itself gives us no justification of the procedural mechanism for acting out the moral obligation derived from the theory. Instead, the alternative means (or methodology) which it employed to do this prior job would provide the most essential moral judgements. (It would be inconsistent to assume that the procedural obligations would not be *moral* demands. If there is some ideal state of affairs to be established through the contract that we are obliged to care about, then it seems that we are also obliged to find out what this state of affairs is—hence to follow the procedure that leads us to this insight.)

Thus, for the purpose of moral realism contractualist methodologies are either useless (because they do not lead to moral facts at all) or they are secondary to some other rational procedure. But what could this be?

1.7. A FUNDAMENTAL PROBLEM OF GROUNDING OUR ETHICAL JUDGEMENTS

In 'Baron Münchhausen's Narrative of his Marvellous Travels and Campaigns' (2001) we find the story of an accident. In the darkness, Baron Münchhausen leaves the path across a marsh and is in danger of being submerged with his horse in the black, smelly liquid. No one is around to help him. However, as a man of practical intelligence and great strength, he bravely grasps his own hair—luckily he is not bald—and pulls himself and his horse up, so that he does not sink. Thus, so the story tells us, they are saved.

I agree with the general opinion—and the laws of physics—that the baron's impressive and grand effort cannot succeed.

For more than two thousand years it has been argued that philosophers' attempts to use deduction in order to make ultimate claims for truth fall into a similar marsh—a hopeless situation.[17] As we know from Sextus Empiricus and Diogenes Laertius, Agrippa already argued in the second, fourth, and fifth 'tropoi' that deduction, otherwise a safe road for reason to true judgements, must necessarily fail when it comes to first principles. (For a brief history of this trilemma see Hösle 1990: 152.) The core of this objection lies in the fact that deduction will never lead to absolute knowledge, but only to hypothetical truth, because the conclusions of deduction always depend on some prior axiom whose knowledge it has to hypothetically presuppose. If deduction wants to justify its own starting-point, it faces a three-horned lemma.[18] Either:

1. The deductive method is used to justify principles by mutual, circular reference from one principle to the other. In this case the deduction would be based upon a *petitio principii*.

Or:

2. The deduction is interrupted at some point which is either arbitrary or at least requires a further justification which cannot be given by deduction. This possibility can be seen as dogmatic.

Or:

3. In order to avoid a dogmatic solution, one might face an endless regress. This would mean that every judgement is seen as being deduced from a further, more fundamental, one without there ever being discovered a truly first ground.

The difficulty becomes even greater in the area of practical reason, which is my concern. Is deduction a suitable method for a non-

---

[17] For this, see Popper (1979: 120–8) and Albert (1980: 11–15), who have introduced the term 'Münchhausentrilemma' into the recent debate.

[18] In Anglo-American literature the difficulty is mostly presented as a dilemma (e.g. J. Harrison 1967, Phillips-Griffiths 1967), leaving out the first horn above. In particular, because of the transcendental argument I wish to suggest below, I think it is important to be aware of the first horn as well.

subjectivist, cognitivist ethics? The double demand on first normative principles, to be normative and to have logical priority, seems only to sharpen the horns of the trilemma of deduction. Here the entire deductive enterprise appears, from the start, to fall into the naturalistic fallacy. If the first principle itself must be deduced from a further normative principle, then it must cease to be rightly regarded as the 'first'; if it is deduced from a non-normative principle, then it will have to find a further justification for its normativity. Deduction can only ever mediate normativity—it can never provide a justification for first normative principles. (It is of course obvious that some deduction plays a role in more or less all moral theories, in that it is necessary to deduce rules and right ways of behaviour from the fundamental moral values or principles in particular situations. But this is not the deduction at issue here.)

Let us look at some examples. While the fallacy of the third horn is rare amongst philosophers,[19] there are many examples at hand of the first and second ones, probably because they are in many cases much less obvious.

When it comes to the notorious problem of providing a criterion for the good, Aristotle's *Nicomachean Ethics* can be interpreted as committing the fallacy of circularity. Roughly, his reasoning seems to go as follows. A virtue is a disposition to choose the mean between two extremes. How do we decide where the mean lies? Aristotle derives this knowledge from common opinion, yet not from the opinion of the many, but of the few. Only those people who already accept virtues as first principles of their behaviour and habits—the ones Aristotle calls the 'beautiful and the good' (*NE* 1099^{a}6, 1124^{a}4, 1179^{b}10)—have the *phronesis* (understanding) to determine the mean. Only they have the right sort of 'eye' (*NE* 1109^{b}20–3, 1126^{b}2–4, 1142^{a}23–30). This does not mean that they propose arguments or criteria for what the mean (and thus a virtue) is; excellence in understanding is rather itself a virtue which alone allows them to grasp the good. In brief: the good can only be determined by good people. And how do we determine who the good people are? Well, by asking good people. Here the argument faces circularity.[20]

---

[19] Adorno sees an endless regress in Kant's ethics when he writes that this ethics is based upon 'a bad infinity of deductions' (1966: 281). This is, however, not a very convincing interpretation, since Kant seems to take the 'fact of reason' as a definite starting-point for ethics (though not a well-justified one).

[20] A more sympathetic reading would be that although Aristotle says that good people are the kinds of people that we should go to for practical wisdom regarding the moral life, these

Neo-Aristotelian virtue ethics tries to avoid this problem and often does so only by falling short of avoiding the second fallacy. For many theories of virtue ethics the fundamental notion is the good person; that is, someone who possesses moral virtues. At the same time, this goodness is identified with human flourishing. And, hence, one ought to be virtuous in order to flourish. But either we have nothing more than a piece of advice about what to do in order to live a certain life (a hypothetical imperative according to Kant) or the representatives of virtue ethics must rely on some prior principle which they presuppose; namely, the identification of goodness and human flourishing. Appealing as this might be, it is still a substantial thesis in need of further justification. The situation is similar to that of utilitarianism, according to which happiness of some form is to be seen as the highest good. On the whole, the neo-Aristotelian's project stops here and does not attempt to give a further justification which would allow it to escape from the second horn of the trilemma.

It is hard to see how moral realism could be based on deductions without being staked by one of the three horns. This should not be surprising, since it is exactly the *point* of deduction that it starts from prior axioms, and the question will always remain as to where these are to come from. Induction and intuition cannot offer these starting-points, as has been argued above. But if no other candidate for justification can be found, then Hume would be right in claiming that reason must be the slave of passion, or at least of something else—the only practical answers reason could give would be of the means–end type. It can compare the advantages of different means, or investigate their unwanted implications or possible inconsistencies with other means, and might help to co-ordinate them. Yet the actual ends would spring from different sources; for example, from desires, the will to power, from the determining force of the economic situation, or from ultimately arbitrary conventions. The categorical difference between the ethical theories of Kant, Nietzsche, and de Sade would melt away (T. W. Adorno and M. Horkheimer 1998: 105 ff.) and we might be left with, as Kant says in the second *Critique*, a moral philosophy for the 'rogues' (*KGS* v. 100).

good people do not need to be identified by people who have full goodness themselves but by all non-bestial men, hence by those who are even trying to grow in the moral life. Does this help? This interpretation would only avoid circularity if it could offer an independent criterion which everyone—including the wicked—could apply in order to know whether he or she is non-bestial even in this minimal sense.

This challenge, however, transcends the foundational problems of moral realism—it marks the current crisis of epistemological foundationalism in general. If this crisis cannot be solved, then the classic tasks of philosophy will have to be given up. Ultimately, philosophy will sink in the marsh of uncertainty (at the most held by some pragmatic safety belt—but where should this be fixed?) or will be 'buried to history', as Ross Harrison has put it (1989). The only possibility of avoiding the aporia of reason is to look for a method of rational justification other than those explored above. After all, their failure alone cannot exclude the possibility of a different and more successful alternative. A claim to this end, namely that there cannot be a method besides deduction, induction, or intuition, and that therefore no method could ever do, would be a fundamental claim (or first principle of epistemology) which itself requires a justification. But how could this ever be provided, if the very claim is that there is no possibility of justifying first principles? *Categorically* to reject the possibility of any alternative method to achieve secure knowledge is therefore inconsistent. Hence we have no reason to assume that the search for a different method must be in vain—and with transcendental arguments we have further candidates for the task. It is worth examining whether they might salvage moral realism.

CHAPTER 2
The Promise of Transcendental Arguments

2.1. TRANSCENDENTAL ARGUMENTS: GENERAL CHARACTERISTICS

Transcendental arguments were originally designed by Kant to lead to synthetic judgements a priori. A huge number of these arguments have been developed since then. Authors as different as Fichte, Hegel, Peirce, Husserl, Wittgenstein, Malcolm, Strawson, Davidson, Shoemaker, and Bennett, to name just a few, became engaged in the project. The last forty years especially have brought something of a revival, and transcendental arguments have been explored in numerous ways. Although the high hopes attached to them in the beginning have declined over the last years, they are still seen by many as the most promising path to epistemological advance in the face of sceptical objections. If any kind of reasoning might, then transcendental arguments might securely establish some non-empirical knowledge for use in theoretical or practical matters.

Transcendental arguments are supposed to achieve their ambitious aim by a special form of conditional, their *differentia specifica*. It is argued that we can know in a non-empirical way that something must be the case for something else to be possible, because the latter is the necessary condition for the possibility of the former. This condition is supposed to be non-contingent, but, rather, a constraint for every possible world; transcendental arguments are therefore meant to lead to a priori knowledge.

Transcendental arguments can vary widely with regard to their starting-points as much as with regard to the exact kind of conditions they employ. To avoid limiting the investigation to any particular interpretation of this condition, I will call the second premiss the 'transcendental conditional', whatever its exact nature might be.

An important reservation must be expressed. There are many rivals for what is the most adequate account of the structure of transcendental arguments. Further, it is unclear whether all arguments which call themselves 'transcendental' have sufficient structural similarity to be categorized as one species (or at least one family) of arguments by any account. In addition, transcendental arguments are often closely linked with other types of reasoning or reflections. Kant, for example, seems to have seen his transcendental deduction as inseparably bound to transcendental idealism (a conjecture that has famously been criticized by Hegel and Strawson). It is particularly confusing when philosophers label the resulting *combination* of structurally different forms of reasoning 'transcendental argument'. As Moltke S. Gram notes quite rightly: 'The history of transcendental arguments is the chronicle of a series of disputed claims to a title' (1978: 23). However, this chronicle does not have to concern us too much. Our purpose is not to develop an exhaustive analysis of transcendental arguments, but to investigate whether they might suffice for a justification of a source of normativity, and hence for the project of moral realism. For this aim it will be enough to distinguish two groups or types of transcendental arguments on the basis of two tasks for which they are employed.

On the one hand, transcendental arguments are engaged in furthering the explanation of some known fact or judgement in order to expand our knowledge. In this case, they start from a premiss which is so minimal that it will not be questioned by a sceptic and draws out of it some a priori conclusions. They do so by looking for 'necessary conditions for the possibility' of this premiss to be true. If the premiss is true, then the necessary conditions must be also. In brief, the argument proceeds from a non-ambitious starting-point by plausible steps to a highly ambitious conclusion; namely, to some a priori knowledge.

On the other hand, they are employed in a straightforward anti-sceptical fashion. This type of transcendental argument is designed mainly to secure a judgement about something being the case. It proceeds by showing that any sceptic who attempted to question the truth of this judgement would exhibit himself as committed to its truth by virtue of the performative implications of his raising this criticism. He must accept the truth of the original judgement, since any denial would lead to a contradiction between what he says and what is implied by his rational act. (We will have to say much more about the nature of this implicit commitment shortly.)

It seems that a concentration on the explorational task is the hallmark of the Kantian tradition of transcendental arguments, while philosophers who follow more a Fichtean version of the argument give the weight to the foundational task.[1] I will call the first the 'explorational type', the second, for reasons given below, the 'retorsive type' of transcendental argument (or simply 'retorsive argument'). Let us turn to the explorational type first.

2.2. THE 'EXPLORATIONAL TYPE' OF TRANSCENDENTAL ARGUMENT

2.2.1. *The Structure of the Explorational Type*

A brief look at the *Critique of Pure Reason* (e.g. A 84 ff./B 116 ff.) will allow us to learn more about the explorational type of transcendental argument—and also why this type will hardly provide a basis for morality.

In his first *Critique* Kant introduces transcendental arguments in order to show that the 'subjective conditions for thinking have objective validity' (*CPuR* A 89). (For reasons of transparency, I do not follow Kant's own terminology of calling his argument 'transcendental deduction' because his use of the term 'deduction' is not quite ours.[2]) Kant's actual argument starts with a very minimal assumption; namely that we have experience. Then the argument requires an exploration of this starting-point through an analysis of the indispensable conditions for experience to be possible at all (cf. *CPuR* B 145). According to Kant the awareness of a world of independent, causally interacting, and spatio-temporal material

---

[1] Again, of course, a highly controversial claim. R. Walker has argued recently that Kant's transcendental reasoning can be interpreted as showing exactly this; namely, that even a sceptic must accept some premiss (1999: 21).

[2] Kant's use of the term 'deduction' originates from the legal usage of his time, where it meant the juridical defences of claims of right or legal entitlement, in answer to the *quaestio iuris* (cf. *CPuR* A 84/B116 ff.). In the legal context, it did not refer to any specific form or underlying argument; thus, it must not to be identified with 'deduction' in the modern use of the term (cf. Rosenberg 1975: 612; Henrich 1989). However, some philosophers have offered reconstructions of Kant's actual transcendental argument which render it 'deductive' in a stricter sense (e.g. Gram (1971: 22 ff., 1973: 254 ff.), and Wilkerson (1975: 110–11)). It is doubtful whether this is an appropriate interpretation, and it is not the way Kant thought of his own achievement.

objects is a necessary prerequisite for the possibility of experience. This reasoning is supposed to show a priori that certain categories find application in all experience.

We can express the explorational type formally as an argument from premisses to conclusions similar to *modus ponens*:[3]

q

q only if p (or: if q then p)

———————

∴ p

In this formal account, 'q' is supposed to be a judgement to the extent that some minimal fact exists or some state of affairs occurs. The second premiss, namely the 'transcendental conditional', spells out that p is a necessary condition for q to be the case (whereby 'p' is a judgement on some further fact or state of affairs). This conditional is decisive, although its exact nature is highly controversial—we will see shortly that there are many different interpretations of it. However, the function of the transcendental conditional is obvious. It is meant to show that someone who accepts q will find himself rationally committed also to accepting p.

2.2.2. The First Premiss of the Explorational Type

It is obvious that the strength of the first premiss is vital for the argument. If the starting-point can reasonably be questioned then this will affect the importance we give to the conclusion. That means that the first premiss cannot be secured inductively but must be, according to Kant's terminology, a judgement a priori. Since it makes a claim about the reality of some fact (for example, experience) it must be *synthetic* in addition. This seems puzzling and locates a great difficulty in this type of transcendental argument—it has to start from a premiss which itself must be regarded as a synthetic judgement a priori. Consequently, the argument which has been designed exactly for the purpose of establishing a priori synthetic judgements must presuppose at least one such judgement itself. Sullivan points to this difficulty with his remark that in a strict sense Kant's argument is not a '"proof" ... for there is no point in proving what we already accept' (1989: 301).

---

[3] This has been suggested by Hossenfelder (1988: 283), L. Stevenson (1982: 5), Walker (1989a: 59), and Lange (1988: 24–31).

We have argued above that no safe starting-point for claims to knowledge can be empirical or intuitive, and we have also to avoid the horns of the Münchhausen trilemma. Kant tries to escape from these traps by starting from a notion which seems so minimal and self-evident that it will not be questioned seriously by anyone. Even a sceptic should accept the notion as justified or as needing no justification—which will serve the same purpose. What exactly is this self-evident fact? Though Kant says much about it, he is not as clear about this point as one would wish him to be.[4] However, in general he calls this starting-point 'experience' (*CPuR* A 737/B 765). Since the exact interpretation of the starting-point is not decisive for the present purpose, we can take him to mean the fact that we have sensible experience of being aware of something in an intelligible way. (It includes for Kant concepts and a capacity to make judgements about one's experience.)

It is important to stress that Kant does not bolster up his starting-point by any further argument. We are left with the mere appeal to its immediate evidence. Prima facie this strategy does not appear to be too bad—there seem to be some facts (such as that we have experience) which will hardly be questioned by any sceptic and might therefore be taken for granted. Other apparently self-evident and non-presumptive starting-points which have been suggested in the philosophical literature are, to name just a few: being as such; the facts of self-consciousness or intentionality; the facts of language (i.e. that we use language); and the facts of knowledge (in particular, the most elementary experiential knowledge). Certainly, an appeal to self-evidence is not a justification of these first premisses, but it could well be argued that it is not particularly meaningful to deny them. It must be noted that sometimes (though not by Kant) arguments are added as to why some starting-point is supposed to be self-evident. These are mostly ways of reasoning that amount to what I called the 'retorsive type' of transcendental arguments, and I will discuss them below.

There is a hidden difficulty with this appeal to self-evidence. The sceptic will only accept the notion at the beginning if it is sufficiently weak and general. But weak starting-points might not yield interesting results. That is why many transcendental arguments start from more substantial

---

[4] There is an ongoing debate amongst Kantian scholars about this starting-point. Some alternative interpretations of it are, for example: the *possibility* of experience; self-consciousness or the possibility thereof; self-conscious experience; or the unity of the subject and the object in experience.

or specific first premisses, such as that we have experience that is derived from an external world, or that our experience is of objects in (three-dimensional) space and time. In the *Prolegomena* Kant seems to go so far as to take as his first premiss the fact that we have mathematical and scientific knowledge. These rich starting-points allow the arguments to proceed much faster—the *Prolegomena* is a rather thin book—but make them much weaker: the sceptic has ample room to question such a starting-point intelligibly. Against any opulent starting-point it might be argued, for example, that this is a mere contingent psychological fact (or feature of our contingent perceptional apparatus).[5]

We should keep this in mind, since it will be relevant for the use of explorational arguments for practical purposes. But let us look at the second premiss next and see how the argument proceeds.

2.2.3. The Second Premiss of the Explorational Type

There is little debate about what is required from the second premiss of the explorational type of transcendental argument. It must provide a valid conditional that proceeds from some hypothetically given fact q to some p by showing that p is a *necessary* condition of q. To ask for *sufficient* conditions would be futile as long as the sufficient conditions are not also the necessary ones (see Körner 1967: 320; Walker 1982: 19). In order to conclude from the premiss q that p, we must exclude the possibility that q leads to some other set of conditions z. But to do so means to demonstrate exactly this: that p is necessary for q. Only then is there a valid step from q to p—and only then does the whole argument work.

So what sort of conditional is it or should it be? Surely, we cannot look for any empirical conditional; for example, by asking scientists about the way human beings experience the world. Empirical research can never tell us anything about how things *must* be; it never tells us that no alternative is conceivable. It would amount to some psychological theory about us (as Hume would claim) or to some neurological theory (as some biologists would reconstruct transcendental arguments). This would not go beyond the claim that the type of experience human beings have is the experience which human beings happen to have. Some authors have thought that it would make a difference whether these empirical conditions are very specific (like the world-view of a certain

---

[5] Cf. e.g. Bennett's critical explorations of the possibility of experience of different structures (1966). See also Strawson (1966) and Walker (1982).

age) or about human nature in general (like our experience being of three-dimensional objects). Rosenberg, for example, argues (1975: 618): 'we can thus see Kant's categorical necessity as a species of natural necessity writ large'.[6] But this does not save the argument since in all these cases the conditional is only secured inductively—and whatever insight we would gain through induction, by definition we could not know a priori. The argument needs more in order to succeed; we are looking for a demonstration of some p being necessary for q to exist, that no other condition than p would be capable of making q possible. Only then can we assert that p on the basis of q (rather than p *or* z *or* some further condition). Robert Stern remarks rightly that this is a metaphysical enquiry (1999a: 3): 'if Y cannot obtain without X, this is not just because certain *natural* laws governing the *actual* world and discoverable by the empirical sciences make this impossible (in the way that, for example, life cannot exist without oxygen), but because certain metaphysical constraints that can be established by reflection make X a condition for Y in every *possible* world.'

Of course, if we had some privileged, direct insight into inseparable links (as, for example, Husserl and the phenomenological school might claim) then the problem of the conditional would be solved. We would be able to spot the condition of the possibility of q in an a priori fashion. But for two reasons that does not work. First, this phenomenological understanding of the second premiss would seem to make the entire transcendental argument superfluous. It could be replaced by direct insight, and the alleged 'argument' would be nothing more than advice not to trust one's phenomenological insight too easily. Secondly, we simply do not seem to have these a priori insights. The lack of direct access to the existence of things (or links between them) is the reason why Kant and others put so much hope in transcendental arguments in the first place. We want to *gain* some a priori knowledge (or at least not to presuppose too much of it, given that the first premiss is already a synthetic judgement a priori).[7]

---

[6] See Wilkerson (1975) who says that the condition must concern the most general level of human ability. K. Lorenz, the last incumbent of Kant's chair in Königsberg, also took this line, when he naturalized the Kantian categories as evolved structures of our epistemological apparatus—if Kant had known that this would be the coda of Königsberg philosophy, he might not have been amused.

[7] See Hossenfelder (1988: 288), Grundmann (1993: 262), and Niquet (1991: 138).

Let us look at Kant, although he does not say much about his methodology.[8] How does he proceed in the second premiss? The minimal information which is presupposed, namely that there is experience, is expanded by recognizing that the categories are required for its possibility (*CPuR* A 721/B 749; A 736/B 764–5; A 782; B 810–11). Without them, according to Kant, there simply could not be any 'experience of objects' (B 126). But what sort of impossibility is he talking about? As it stands, it is not sufficiently clear, and his examples do not answer this question either. The most famous one is the description of a boat which moves with the flow of a river. Kant argues that because we experience the world as necessarily causally structured we cannot deliberately inverse the order of our experience, thus we simply cannot perceive the boat first downstream and then upstream. With things that are not causally structured, like the parts of a house, we can start our observation at any point and move in any direction (*CPuR* B 237). Kant concludes that our experience seems in some way compelled to have a certain structure in time; it does not give us the freedom to let it be otherwise. As already said, he does not explain further in which sense the impossibility of an acausal experience has to be understood. And what he says does not seem very compelling: we can surely imagine what it would be like if boats did not follow the normal (causal) order of things—and it may be that some

---

[8] Kant says three things which seem to be relevant. First, he claims that arguments should never be indirect but always direct (*CPuR* B 817 ff.). This is rather odd because Kant himself uses indirect arguments to a great extent; for example, in his refutation of idealism. In addition, it seems impossible to reconstruct his transcendental deduction as a direct argument; after all, it infers the validity of the categories from the impossibility of experience without them. Secondly, Kant distinguishes at some point between a 'progressive-synthetic' and a 'regressive-analytic' way of arguing transcendentally (*KGS* IV. 271–2). The first seems to be a form which begins with a minimal notion and expands it further, and the second starts with a richer synthetic judgement a priori and analyses what is given with this judgement. Though the second way would be in accord with Kant's demand for a direct proof, it is hard to see how it could ever be made to work—what sort of rich notion could be accepted as a starting-point immune to sceptical objection? It might work for mathematics, where Kant thought he was entitled to presuppose some synthetic judgements a priori, but I cannot see where he hoped to find similarly rich starting-points for the categories. The third comment Kant makes refers to the transcendental conditional as not being merely analytic, but needing a *tertium* (*CPuR* B 194, B 765, B 811). The *tertium* in the suggested reconstruction of his argument is the 'starting-point'; namely, that there is experience or intuition. It still leaves the pivotal question open: whether the judgement which connects the starting-point and the categories, namely the second premiss, is analytic or synthetic (see the discussion above). Gram rightly argues that most of Kant's methodological comments do not particularly assist our understanding of his project (1978: 25 f., 51). For an extended investigation of Kant's methodology of the first *Critique* see Baum (1986).

drugs actually enable us to experience things in different orders. Simply not to call this imaginary experience an 'experience' at all would, of course, be begging the question. So we are left with the original question of whether it is not a contingent matter of fact that our experience is the way it is, and of how we find its necessary features or conditions—if, indeed, there are any.

It seems that the best, and probably the only, strategy is to show that a judgement of the kind 'q and non-p' would be contradictory.[9] Then, according to Kant's terminology, transcendental conditionals would be 'analytic' judgements, that are defined as those 'whose truth can always be adequately known in accordance with the principle of contradiction' (*CPuR* A 151/B190). And, indeed, some authors interpret the status of the second premiss as analytic.[10] According to an analytic interpretation, the argument would start from a rather imprecise definition of a certain q and the conditional would give more clarity about what the concept involves by carrying out the a priori analysis leading to p. Walker offers several arguments for this reading of the transcendental conditional in the *Critique of Pure Reason*, the main one being apagogic (1982: 14–23; 1989a: 59–60): since Kant knows only synthetic and analytic judgements, the only possible alternative is to understand the conditional as *synthetic*. But then Kant would face a dilemma. Either the judgement would be synthetic a posteriori and thus deprive the conclusion of its a priori status—or it would itself be a priori. In this case, however, we would have to *presuppose* the validity of a (further) synthetic judgement a priori (= the second premiss) in order for the transcendental argument to work. The entire enterprise would become questionable and easily challenged by the sceptic. It seems that within Kant's typology of arguments the analytic reading is the only suitable interpretation.[11]

---

[9] Strawson follows a similar line of thought when he sees the relevant kind of 'if p, q' connection as a unique type of logical relation. He defines this 'entailment' (as he calls it) as follows. ' "S(1) entails S (2)" = Df "S (1) and not S(2)" is inconsistent' (1952: 20). He argues that we have to ask whether it is consistently possible to think S(1) and to deny S (2) simultaneously.

[10] See Röd 1977; L. Stevenson 1982; Walker 1982, 1989a.

[11] It is very difficult to ascertain what Kant himself thought about the status of the second premiss, since he says little about it. Most of the authors who desire to show that this analytic interpretation is inadequate (like Grundmann 1993; Niquet 1991: 140 ff.) argue against the possibility of a successful analytic premiss in general, rather than offering objections to this being an adequate interpretation of Kant.

The Promise of Transcendental Arguments · 39

According to Frege's clarifying account (1961: § 3), the truth of an analytic judgement is based on logical laws and definitions alone; this judgement can be reduced to a substitution instance of a logical law by means of definitions. Does a focus on definitions help us to see what is going on in the transcendental conditional? Obviously, it cannot be centred around a definition that simply mirrors the way we *happen* to use the term 'q'. Then, transcendental arguments would be nothing but a posteriori linguistic exercises. The only plausible path is to look for an a priori analysis of what q *is* beyond the contingencies of our linguistic conventions of using 'q'. But what could this mean? It is highly controversial whether concepts are apt for this kind of investigation or whether this reflects a fundamental error about the way language works, as Wittgenstein has eminently suggested.[12] And there is always the danger of stipulative definitions that are not good bases for synthetic judgements a priori. It is exactly this error that Kant accuses the tradition of making: 'The procedure of metaphysics has hitherto been a merely random groping, and, what is worst of all, a groping among mere concepts' (*CPuR* B xv). Kant is right to object that we do not have such telling definitions simply at hand (cf. O'Neill 1989: 14).[13] But if we do not have them, how shall we come to acquire them? The pivotal task of the analysis must be to find out whether there must be some *indispensable* (and not merely stipulated or contingent) feature, or necessary condition, for something to be regarded as experience. And that means that we are back to our original question.

So let us leave the discussion of the interpretation of Kant and stay with the problem. In what sense could the transcendental conditional be understood so that it did give us a 'necessary condition' which is neither contingent nor stipulative? If the necessity is indeed one of thought (as it

---

[12] According to Quine (1951), there can be only tautological analytic judgements in the proper sense. Lange (1988) attempts to build a transcendental argument on an analysis of the extension of a word, in order to avoid Quine's famous objection. However, this would also lead to merely empirical judgements; how else can we find out what the extension is? See also Grundmann's critique of this approach (1993: 241–5).

[13] It seems that it was exactly this problem which in one of his few comments on the method of his transcendental argument allowed Kant to remark that its reasoning is *not* analytic. He criticizes traditional metaphysicians because they tried to gain knowledge by mere analysis of concepts—a procedure Kant calls 'useless' to the task of metaphysics (*CPuR*, B 23). And Kant is surely right that his transcendental argument could never work if it were analytic in this sense, i.e. by starting from the *conventional* usage of terms. For Kant's understanding of the meaning of words see also Beck (1956), and Grundmann (1993: 231–2).

must be in order to be a priori), and not just a matter of custom or habit, then this would mean that we cannot think coherently about our experience if we reject p. If p is rationally necessary, then any coherent understanding of q will include p. We can express this as a negative test: are there any features of experience which we *cannot intelligibly think away*? We can leave it open *why* we might not be able to dismiss p when we think about q—whether the rejection of p would lead to straightforward contradictions (as the analytic reading suggests) or whether its absence is ruled out in some other rational way (an example given by Kant is that we cannot think of a figure enclosed by two straight lines; see e.g. *CPuR* B 65). If we came across some such indispensable features, then we would have found a well-justified transcendental conditional.

In the case of experience, there is a very likely candidate: experience seems only possible if there is a subject of experience. If we think it away, we are left with an incomprehensible notion. Experience cannot happen without a subject because it is always the experience of a subject. (Or possibly of several subjects. It does not seem in the same way unintelligible to have several subjects linked to an experience as it is to have an experience without any subject.) Contrary to what Kant says, a universal causal order of things, in the way we normally imagine it, does not seem to be a necessary condition. It is possible to imagine a world in which things are ordered in a different fashion, while it is unlikely that anyone could convince us that he can imagine a world in which experiences take place without subjects. A sceptic who claims its possibility would have moved beyond intelligibility.

At this point, an analysis of what intelligibility amounts to seems required—but the difficulty is that we can only hope to demonstrate that our analysis is correct to someone who has already (implicitly) accepted our understanding in the first place. Any attempt to make 'intelligibility' intelligible presupposes that we know what it means to be intelligible. So again, the second as much as the first premiss of the explorational type of transcendental argument is ultimately based upon some self-evidence.

It is obvious that this account of the second premiss merely points us in a direction, and does not offer us a well-paved avenue. But although there are difficulties left, they do not make the explorational type of transcendental reasoning futile for the purpose of expanding our knowledge. Things are different if they are used for the purpose of practical reason. I will argue next that it is doubtful whether they could *ever* serve for justifying some source of normativity.

2.2.4. The Insufficiency of the Explorational Type for Practical Reason

Our enquiry is about transcendental reasoning providing a firm basis for normative judgements. As outlined above, explorational transcendental arguments start from some minimal basis (which no one would want to challenge) and proceed by exploring this. In whatever way the concrete argument is designed, it seems apparent that the starting-point cannot be too minimal to promise any interesting conclusions. We have already mentioned this obvious quandary: the more substantial the first premiss is (one that claims, for instance, that there is experience of a certain kind), the more information we can expect the conclusion to provide. But it is also true that if the first premiss is made too substantial it will hardly be regarded as impossible to challenge it.

This problem is hard to deal with in the context of theoretical reason—but it is much worse (and probably irresolvable) in that of practical reason. The main reason is that, in order to avoid the naturalistic fallacy, the starting-point would have to be *normative* if we want to conclude some normative p (like a demand or value). Otherwise, there would be a strong tension between a descriptive first premiss q and a normative conclusion p. It seems that no transcendental conditional can bridge the gap between the two. As Phillips-Griffiths sums up this point: 'A transcendent justification of any ultimate moral principle, that is to say one which shows the principle is necessary because of a fact standing outside morality, is impossible' (1957/8: 114).

We can illustrate this problem by looking at the demanded self-evidence of the starting-point. We have said above that the first premiss is supposed to be true; that means that something is assumed to be the case. Normative notions, however, are not referring to something (actions, values—whatever) which *is* already realized in all cases, but they refer to something that *ought to be*. So how could something which only ought to be turn out to be the necessary condition of something which is said to be self-evidently the case? One might object that we can imagine empirical cases where 'good' causes have neutral effects (a healthy constitution enabled Napoleon to sleep less than four hours a day). But this cannot serve as a paradigm for the transcendental argument. First, because even in this case there is no valid conclusion from the neutral effect to the goodness of its cause (living on little sleep does not tell us that it is *good* to have a healthy constitution). Secondly, and more importantly, the step from q to p is not a causal one, but supposed to be a necessity of thought. So even if, *per impossibile*, the conclusion could be made to work for Napoleon, nothing would follow regarding the transcendental conditional.

However, there is one possibility we should consider. Let us assume that there is some self-evident, and, as far as we know, neutral starting-point q. And let there be some p that turns out to be the condition of q's possibility. If, for whatever reason, p cannot be made intelligible other than as being a *normative* notion, then the argument would work. But, of course, this 'if' is substantial—what kind of reasoning can show us that we must think of some p in this normative way? It seems that this requires something like a *further* transcendental conditional (of the kind: 'we can only think of p if we consider it to be normative'). This further reasoning would have to be encapsulated in the transcendental conditional from q to p. I do not see how this route of argument can be excluded *tout court*, but there are no plausible examples of it. (It should be noted that this possibility does not speak against the point Phillips-Griffiths makes. In this case, p would not be regarded as good *because of* q—i.e. not 'because of a fact standing outside morality'—but for other reasons.)

A moral realist could, of course, think of an alternative way to salvage the explorational type of transcendental argument. He could look for a self-evident *normative* starting-point. That would cure the problem directly. But it is unlikely that he would ever succeed in finding it. None of the starting-points discussed above seems to fulfil this criterion—why should we regard, for example, experience, self-consciousness, or language as normative notions? Even if we accept their reality, it seems possible to question their normativity in an intelligible way. And if someone thinks he has found some starting-point that must be regarded as normative, then the sceptic is not likely to consider it as self-evident. After all, this kind of notion is exactly what some transcendental reasoning is supposed to establish and not to presuppose.

It is worth looking briefly at Kant's *Groundwork*. Kant, according to a common interpretation, starts from the notion of freedom of the will—his q. He continues to analyse a free will as being a will which is self-governed by maxims which are universalizable—this would be the transcendental conditional. Thus the condition, p, for the will to be free, would be for it to accept and act upon these universalizable principles, or, in short, that it be an ideal will governed by the moral law. In this reading, the starting-point would be a 'not-fully-clear' notion of a free will and the conditional would show what it really involves; namely, that this will has to accept the categorical imperative. Looking backwards from the conclusion to the first premiss, one would have to understand that the (truly) free will is and always has been this good will.[14] But this seems covertly to build something more into the starting-point. The freedom granted in the beginning was substantially weaker than the ideal of freedom under the moral law. The sceptic would surely protest that it is not this ('true') kind of freedom that he granted, and would withdraw his prior affirmation. The argument seems to employ 'free' only in an equivocal sense in the first and second premiss. It is unclear how a proponent of this freedom argument could demonstrate that someone who has accepted freedom in the weak meaning as a starting-point has *thereby* accepted the rich notion of freedom found in the conclusion. The transcendental argument itself will not show this, because it was its (normative) conclusion which caused the sceptic to distinguish between the two sorts of freedom in the first place. Whether or not this is Kant's argument, it is obviously flawed.[15]

Admittedly, all this does not prove that practical reason could never install a successful explorational transcendental argument in this manner. Someone might offer such a minimal normative notion from which the argument could begin—there is no reason to exclude this

[14] It should be added that Kant tried, but each time with little success, to develop the argument for the categorical imperative from different starting-points. Although his main tenet is that only experience is given as the *tertium* for any transcendental reasoning (e.g. A 737/B 765), there is a rudimentary and covert attempt to find a different *tertium* for practical reason in the *Groundwork* (KGS IV. 447). It remains, however, undeveloped. By the time of the second *Critique* Kant had certainly realized that his attempts to found the categorical imperative transcendentally were vain (cf. KGS V. 42 ff.), and he finally abandoned the project. We find a 'total reversal of positions' (Ameriks 1982: 211) in Kant's avowal that 'there is not so much hope of succeeding with a deduction [i.e. transcendental arguments], i.e. the justification of its objective and universal validity . . . as was possible in the case of the principles of pure theoretical reason' (KGS V. 46). However, this shift does not mean that Kant changed his central insight; namely, that morality must be seen as a transcendental branch of philosophy, because only as such can it provide the authority for its commands (e.g. V. 26, 42, n. 47). He hopes to preserve this even without any transcendental argument by calling the categorical imperative in the second *Critique* a 'fact of reason'. Here it seems that the categorical imperative is simply given and does not need any justification or proof—the ultimate normative framework is seen as an elementary 'fact' of which we are aware in a quasi-intuitive way (Beck 1960: 166 ff.; Ilting 1972: 125). But this will hardly do: we have discussed the problems of intuitive foundationalism above.

[15] Since Kant's *Groundwork* starts with the notion of the 'good will', it is unlikely that he did intend to provide a transcendental argument of the type outlined above. Even the third part of the *Groundwork* does not provide it. For this see Ameriks (1999).

44 · *The Grounds of Ethical Judgement*

possibility. But we must be aware of the huge burden laid on the starting-point: it must be normative, sufficiently substantial, but also so minimal that it could be seen as self-evident, even in the face of an armoury of anti-intuitionist arguments. Let us therefore turn to the retorsive type of transcendental argument (the 'retorsive argument') and see whether it has more to offer to the cause of moral realism.

2.3. THE 'RETORSIVE TYPE' OF TRANSCENDENTAL ARGUMENT

2.3.1. *The Structure of the Retorsive Argument*

Although Fichte (1971: I. 451 ff.) considered himself to be a true Kantian (and possibly the only one), he complains occasionally that Kant's first premisses are not sufficiently justified (*deduciert*) but simply taken as starting-points: 'Kant starts in the *Critique of Pure Reason* from the point of reflection, at which time, space and the manifold of intuitions are given' (1971: i. 411). In order to secure knowledge 'absolutely', a transcendental argument would have to show that there is something reason cannot question rather than merely appealing to the universal 'good will' whereby it might be accepted as granted. As an irrefutable starting-point for reason Fichte suggests the act of reasoning itself, since we cannot question reason's reality rationally without self-contradiction:

> All doubts and any denial of the possibility of a system of reason are based upon an assumption of heteronomy; upon the assumption that reason could be established through something outside itself. But such an assumption is thoroughly against all reason;—a contradiction to reason. (1971: iv. 59)

Both the demand for a starting-point which cannot be questioned and the claim that the act of reasoning itself will respond to this demand have been developed by several contemporary philosophers. Their reasonings are distinctively different from the explorational type of argumentation, and sufficiently similar to each other that it makes sense to see them as one category of argument[16]—although nearly all of them would miss the criteria for being called 'transcendental' by most analytic authors. Let us look at their structure more closely in order to see why it is plausible to regard them as 'transcendental arguments'.

---

[16] However, hardly anyone refers exclusively to Fichte (but see Hösle 1986). Some of them, e.g. O. O'Neill, understand their 'retorsive' reasoning as being truly Kantian.

Essentially, this type of argument is designed to show that some judgement 'r' is true because it cannot be rejected rationally. It does so by showing that any scepticism about r inevitably presupposes the truth of r by the implications of the very act or performance of sceptically regarding it. Thus, scepticism about the truth of r leads to a self-contradiction or inconsistency between what is *expressively* stated by the sceptic (the expressed judgement is '¬r') and what is *implicitly* expressed by his act of assertion (the implied judgement is 'r'). Affirming r also presupposes the truth of r by the implications of it being a rational act. The affirmative judgement can therefore consistently be raised since the same truth is affirmed expressively and implicitly. Given that the original assumption can only be true or false, it follows that it must be true, since it is self-contradictory to judge it as false.[17]

A prominent example of this kind of reasoning is to be found in Aristotle's refutation of scepticism concerning the principle of non-contradiction. In Book Γ of his *Metaphysics* (1005^b35–1006^a28) he points out that *any* sceptical rejection of this principle requires simultaneously that the principle be taken seriously and is therefore self-defeating. His main argument is that if the assertion of some statement 'a' would not exclude the assertion of 'non-a', then any assertion someone makes would be compatible with any other assertion. But then there would be no point in asserting anything at all and the whole business of making judgements and thus of reasoning would be deprived of any importance. That is why the sceptic has to presuppose the principle under discussion. Or, to put it in a form that makes the transcendental character obvious: the necessary condition for the possibility of any intelligible sceptical assertion is that the principle of non-contradiction is valid. Therefore, a sceptic cannot deny the principle without self-defeat. Therefore, the validity of the very principle of non-contradiction can be seen as 'most certain' (*Met.* 1006^a5).[18]

---

[17] I will use the following terminology: A 'sentence' is a grammatical entity or form of words, independently of how or whether it is uttered. A 'proposition' is what is expressed by a sentence, its meaning. I will call a proposition a 'statement' if it can be true or false. 'Asserting', 'making a judgement', or simply 'judging' synonymously signify a speech act, i.e. the act or performance of affirming or denying the truth of something.

[18] Aristotle uses the argument for different purposes and on several occasions, but it seems that this kind or reasoning was already known and accepted by many of his contemporaries. Thomas Aquinas, a careful reader of Aristotle, also uses this argument (for both see Finnis 1998: 58 ff.). Kant establishes the principle of non-contradiction in a similar way when he argues that 'if the last logical ground for everything which can be thought' has been abol-

We can list some more examples of apparently undeniable judgements that are discussed in the current literature: 'something exists'; 'there is language'; and 'we can reason about truth'.

It should be noted that this kind of justification is apagogic. The judgement under discussion does not have a necessity deduced from any presupposed axioms, but it is seen to be true because it cannot reasonably be questioned and thus it cannot be false. As we might say more metaphorically: the argument 'retorts' or 'turns' the objection of the sceptic 'back' against himself (in Latin, *retorquere*). Thereby the scepticism is transformed into support of the assumption; and that is why the argument is called 'retorsive' in the Continental tradition that we follow here.[19] We consider it to belong to the family of transcendental arguments because its crucial step is, again, to look for the necessary (performative) condition for the possibility (intelligibility) of something (an act of reasoning). (We do not have to take seriously an arational sceptic's objection, as we have shown above, since it does not mean anything.)

Note, again: the argument is not looking for semantic conditions, because this would only allow us to show that a certain expression or judgement is or is not consistent within our linguistic conventions. Nothing much would follow from spelling them out. Nor is the incon-

---

ished, then 'nothing remains which could be thought' (*KGS* II. 82; see also *KGS* III. 142). For contemporary applications of the argument for the principle of non-contradiction see e.g. D. Mitchell (1964: 136) and also Walker (1982: 23 ff.), who is less optimistic than the others as to what the argument can achieve. It should be added that Aristotle's argument requires further reasoning. It works as it stands to refute someone who claims that 'a and non-a' is a logical theorem quite easily (G. Priest calls this person a 'trivialist'). It is more difficult for dealing with someone (a 'dialetheist') who only claims that 'a and non-a' might possibly be valid *sometimes* and for *some contexts*. However, he faces the problem of making sense out of this limitation. Where and how are we supposed to find or identify these contexts? And, most importantly, could there ever be any *argumentative* context where the principle does not hold?

[19] I argued above that the starting-point of explorational transcendental arguments might be seen as self-evident (p. 34 f.). Here, again, terminology varies. Both notions, 'self-evident' and 'apagogically justified', refer to a non-deductive argumentation (since we do not argue for, or deduce, self-evident propositions). The difference is that there are some cases when we simply take something as a given—what I call 'self-evident' starting-points—or accept something because of the impossibility of a consistent denial—the 'apagogic' case. In contrast to this terminology, J. Finnis sees the retorsive argument as a test for the 'self-evidence' of first principles. Following Aristotle, he does not interpret the anti-sceptical argumentation as a justification proper, but rather as the demonstration of the fact that no such justification is required: 'It stands in need of no demonstration and itself is presupposed ... in all demonstrations whatsoever. It is self-evident' (1977: 250).

sistency caused by some straightforward self-refutation of the proposition, independent of its being asserted (e.g. 'r is true and false.').

Formally, the retorsive type of transcendental argument can be accounted for as follows:

> The reasoning begins with selecting a judgement 'r' (here called 'original assumption' or 'starting-point') whose truth is to be secured by the argument (1). Then the actual argument begins with the principle of the excluded middle ('either r or ¬r') applied to the original assumption (2). two transcendental investigations of the related speech acts follow—the first speech act, symbolized by '¬r', being to the effect that it is not the case that r, the second speech act, symbolized by 'r', that it is the case that r. In both cases we look for a transcendental conditional: the necessary performative conditions of the possibility of a speech act are spelt out—(3) and (5). Then its consistency with the proposition is checked.[20] (Obviously, this transcendental conditional is quite different from the one in the explorational type above!) The first investigation shows that '¬r' is performatively inconsistent (4), the second concludes that 'r' is performatively consistent (6).[21] Finally the truth of r is concluded (7).

(1) Original assumption: r
(2) Either r or ¬r is true
(3) '¬r' only if commitment to r ('transcendental conditional')

It follows from definition of '¬r' and (3):

---

[20] According to Gaston Isaye the expression 'retorsive' is taken from *redarguitio elenchica*, and has been used by Thomas Aquinas in a similar way (cf. 1950, liber iv, lectiones 6–7). Cf. G. Isaye (1954: 205): 'Nous appelons "rétorsion" le procédé de discussion que saint Thomas nomme *redarguitio elenchica*. Il est essentiel à cette démarche d'être une *réponse*. Certaines objections sont ainsi faites que l'objectant, par le fait même, de son objection, *in actu exercito*, concède la thèse qu'il voulait nier ou mettre en doute. Porter l'attention de l'objectant sur la concession qu'il vient de faire implicitement, c'est retourner l'objection en ma faveur, c'est rétorquer, c'est faire une rétorsion' (quoted from Finnis (1977: 250), who also uses the expression 'retorsive argument').

[21] K.-O. Apel, one of the main proponents of retorsive transcendental arguments in ethics, speaks of a performative self-affirmation of the truth of r and regards this self-affirmation as a second criterion of its truth (1976b: 71). In more traditional language we might put it as follows: A positive judgement with the *content* that r will find a further affirmation of r by the implications of what it is, i.e. by its *form*, since the affirmation *qua* rational endeavour implies r as its necessary condition. This comes very close to a point Fichte makes about absolutely secure knowledge in *Über den Begriff der Wissenschaftlehre*: in the case of any such judgement, form and content must be in accordance (1971: i. 51 ff.; cf. Hösle 1986: 238).

(4) '¬r' cannot be asserted consistently
(5) 'r' only if commitment to r ('transcendental conditional')

It follows from definition of 'r' and (5):

(6) 'r' can be asserted consistently

It follows from (2), (4), and (6):

(7) r is true

(Since the transcendental conditional is the central element of the proof (the original assumption (1) does not function as a premiss of the argument, so it can be left out, and (2) is a logical law), we can also simplify the scheme and write:

(i)   '¬r' only if commitment to r

It follows from definition of '¬r' and (i):

(ii) '¬r' cannot be asserted consistently
(iii) 'r' only if commitment to r

It follows from definition of 'r' and (iii):

(iv) 'r' can be asserted consistently

It follows from (ii) and (iv):

(v) r is true

This amounts to saying:

'¬r' only if r
'r' only if r
_____
∴ r)

Two clarifying remarks about this kind of transcendental argument should be made. First, it is obvious that any good argument must withstand sceptical objections. To consider them is therefore on the whole a useful way to throw light on the proposed reasoning and might make the covert defects obvious. Leibniz compares this kind of critique with the radiation of the early sun, which promises further clarity and insight (1996: i. 197). But the role sceptics play in retorsive transcendental arguments is much stronger: here scepticism, or rather its impossibility *itself*, provides the grounding. By showing that no consistent scepticism (concerning the original assumption) can be put forward, it demonstrates that it is literally 'irrational' to refute the judgement in question. Thus, the sceptic does not point the spotlight on to weak spots of the transcendental argument but rather on to the weakness of his own. This shows the impossibility of any counter thesis to the starting-point. (Of course, there can also be sceptical objections of the 'normal' type against retorsive arguments—when, for example, someone suspects that there have been mistakes in the concrete reasoning leading to the conclusion. But they are not decisive.)

Secondly, we should note that a positive retorsive argument must be sharply distinguished from a mere lack of counter-arguments to a suggested judgement; the latter can never provide more than a relative certainty. As we know from Popper (1984), the search for counter-arguments is used in science in order to investigate whether something can be falsified. In practical philosophy it can be found as well—Korsgaard calls this the 'negative test of sufficiency', which means that something is seen as justified 'as long as there is no extrinsic reason why not' (1986b: 487).[22] Although it might be an appropriate description of how we actually proceed in ethics in many cases, the fact that something is the best explanation at a given moment does not make it justified, since which account turns out to be the best depends merely on the situation (and on the known alternatives). Retorsive transcendental arguments are different in that they aim to show that we cannot even conceive of a reason raised against a particular judgement, now or at any time to come. The point is that any scepticism, even a sceptical position we have not yet thought of, would be self-defeating by the very nature of its being a rational scepticism. That is why the status of the resulting claim to truth is a priori—quite independently from experience we know that we cannot judge it to be false.

2.3.2. Where Does the Retorsive Argument Start?

What are appropriate original assumptions? Since the argument centres

---

[22] Similarly, Charles Taylor (1989: 58–9) introduces the weaker 'best-account principle', which he sees as the most appropriate method for practical reason. It is noteworthy that Taylor himself implicitly acknowledges the insufficiency of the principle he advocates when he tries to establish further 'transcendental reasons' for the necessity of values (cf. M. Lane 1992).

around the performative features of, or conditions for, sceptical reasoning, it will have to start with a judgement about the very features or conditions that qualify an intentional event as a rational act of assertion. These conditions can be more or less general, but in order for the argument to lead to substantial results (a priori knowledge) they must be non-empirical and must be necessarily implied by all possible ways of raising sceptical doubt about them. These conditions or features can be spelt out as presupposed judgements about something being the case. Examples which have been given are: 'there is truth'; 'rational beings are capable of recognizing the truth in principle'; other suggestions include: 'reason is a process'; or 'reason is an intersubjective enterprise'; 'reason must follow principles that allow interaction and communication': But also 'something exists' is a likely candidate—after all, a sceptical assertion must also 'exist' in order to be taken seriously.

At this point it might be useful to compare the differences between the explorational and the retorsive type of transcendental arguments. There are three respects in which they differ: First, the starting-point—in the explorational argument it does not have to be something linked to the act of reasoning, while this is essential for the retorsive argument. Certainly, the starting-point of the explorational type could *equally* well be some such aspect of reasoning. 'Experience', for example, is not merely a physical stimulation of sense organs but our (potential) awareness of something; that is, a form of knowledge.[23] But it is important to see the difference: for the explorational argument this is not essential; any other fact would do, so long as it were accepted by everyone (including the sceptic), and so long as it allowed further exploration through the transcendental conditional. For the retorsive argument, on the contrary, the reference to something that is linked to reasoning is essential, since it can only function if it starts from scepticism about the rational enterprise of (or of some aspects of) making judgement itself. (Because of this, the retorsive type of transcendental argument is sometimes also called 'reflexive': reason reflects upon itself.) Secondly, in the case of retorsive arguments, the starting-point is exactly that which is finally

---

[23] There is a further sense in which any starting-point is a rational matter. No argument, not even the explorational one, operates simply with facts but with judgements about facts (so the starting-point for Kant is not the entity 'experience', but a (rational) judgement to the extent that we have, or that there is, experience). This is trivial and necessary, since arguments are investigations of the relation of judgements, not of causal connections between facts or entities.

concluded to be true, while the explorational type tries to stress the divergence: p is only an aspect of q, its condition. Thirdly and finally, retorsive transcendental arguments offer a very different and unique reading of the transcendental conditional.

A crucial question is, of course: how we are supposed to find out what these conditions or features are? This task is twofold. Using the traditional terminology: on the one hand, we have the problem of critique; on the other hand, the problem of topics. We have to test a possible candidate r_x, but we also need a way to arrive at original assumptions, i.e. possible candidates, in the first place. Can they only be detected by our creative imagination—or does a method lead to a complete series r_1 to r_n? G. Isaye, for example, argues that these starting-points have to be found by 'intuition' before they can be secured by retorsive arguments (1953: 43). Others, most notably Hegel in his *Wissenschaft der Logik*, tried to develop the complex methodology of 'dialectics' in order to come to a complete list of first principles that can be secured transcendentally (at least according to a certain reading of Hegel). This is an important and much-debated issue, but not something we will discuss in this book. For the present purpose it is enough to concentrate on the critical aspect; only if the retorsive argument works at all should we continue to ask for more systematic ways of coming to original assumptions. To investigate the problem of topics would require a different book.

2.3.3. *The Transcendental Conditional as the Second Step of the Retorsive Argument*

The function of the transcendental conditional is to spell out those performative conditions which accompany the sceptic's objections, and which he has to admit when he reflects upon his own objection. 'Performative conditions', sometimes also called 'pragmatic implications' (C. K. Grant 1958), have to be taken in a wide sense: they are *all* of that which alone makes some reasoning intelligible. Here, the retorsive argument makes use of the speech-act theory, but it remains independent of some aspects of the theory (for example, that linguistic acts are prior to mental ones). Judgements are not entities like tables or the City of Westminster, for example (at least as we commonly take them to be), but mental performances; they need to be asserted in order to be. If the sceptical objection were *not* asserted and raised in something like a speech-act (at least in thought) it would not seem to make sense to speak about a sceptical challenge at all. This, however, does not mean that a real, talking sceptic has to attend the case: it is sufficient to see the objection as an open question, put forward by 'a voice of my own intelligence' (Finnis 1977: 253).

Since all the weight of the argument rests on the inconsistency which this conditional is supposed to detect in the sceptical objection, it is obvious that it is the Achilles' heel of the retorsive argument. For it to work, the performative conditions must be realized as *necessary* for any intelligible negation of the original assumption by a rational being in any circumstances. That means that no *contingent* performative conditions will suffice for the argument. Obviously, that excludes merely empirical conditions, such as the fact that we *qua* organisms need oxygen in order to make judgements. But we have to be aware that not all judgements which are undeniable for non-empirical reasons are also universally valid. There can be contingent conditions that characterize particular judgements, which cannot be denied by anyone in this particular situation without self-contradiction—but can be asserted by someone else or in a different situation. We can distinguish three different levels of performative self-contradictions:[24]

(1) Some judgements are only about themselves, like 'I am speaking English'. It cannot be denied consistently in English assertions (like 'I do not speak English')—but it can easily be questioned rationally in any other language. Here the search for a self-contradiction would exclude (contingent) scepticism about the truth of the statement at *some* moment. But the validity of this result is strictly bound to its circumstances. Scepticism at this level has sometimes been called 'pragmatically self-refuting'.[25] It seems obvious that the conditions of this level are too weak to justify any principles of great interest (although it is the same structure of contradiction; namely, between what is asserted by someone and what is implied by his act of assertion).

(2) There are general, undeniable judgements which I can make about myself, such as 'I am alive' or simply 'I am'. Their range is quite wide, their truth lasts for a lifetime—'seventy years, or eighty for those who are strong' (Ps. 90: 10). Judgements at this level owe their undeniability to

[24] See Hösle (1990: 176 ff.) and Passmore (1961: 58–80). I am following Hösle's distinction of three levels.
[25] See Finnis (1977: 250–1) and Mackie (1964). NB: According to the taxonomy of authors like Apel, Hösle, and Kuhlmann, the term 'pragmatic inconsistency' refers to self-contradiction at level (3) and *not* at level (1).

their reference to the *self* and not to any universal feature of all reasoning. But it seems that a transcendental argument based upon them would arrive at a scope which is too limited for the purpose of moral realism. Although it is true that all arguments must be raised by *some I*, there is not *one single I* which is the necessary condition for *all* arguments. Thus, there is a relativity to the particular agent at their centre that makes it questionable whether we can base any transcendental argument upon them that aims at universal judgements (cf. Stroud 1968: 213).

(3) There are judgements which cannot be denied, no matter what the situation or the person (be he human, Martian, an angel, or the serpent) who makes them—for example, 'it is possible to present an argument' or 'something exists'. Whatever the context is, any sceptical denial of them is performatively self-contradictory. Apel calls their negation 'pragmatically self-refuting', Finnis says 'operationally self-refuting', but I will stick with the term 'performative'. Judgements of this kind are the most promising ones in the quest for secure knowledge in practical matters. We have to look for judgements that are relevant to practical reason and that cannot be denied intelligibly—because of the performative self-contradiction to be found in any act of negating them.

How do we know what is performatively implied by a rational scepticism? One might want to object that 'performative implications' function as a sort of black box to which we (covertly) attach all the features we want to result from the retorsive transcendental argument (cf. Berlich 1982: 274 ff.). It seems that the argument only works if we have some knowledge of what it implies merely to reason, prior to any transcendental reflection about it. But this is not an implausible requirement. After all, we must see ourselves as having some understanding of reason *qua* being rational persons, since otherwise we would not even know whether we question this privileged access in any rational way. The awareness of what reasoning implies is something 'internal' to itself. That is, what it is about cannot be separated from what it is. And any intelligible reflection about it is—at least in a minimal sense—already rational.

That is why reasoning has often been intimately connected, even identified, with the 'I' (for example by Fichte). And, indeed, our access to reason has a great similarity to the privileged access we have to our 'selves'. But there are important differences to be aware of. If I know that I am, I still have not established any knowledge about other minds, nor do I really know what it means for someone else to be himself. But by knowing what reason is I seem to know what *a* 'reason' means *for everyone*, since reasons are independent of the person who raises them. To give a reason for something is, very roughly, to say why everyone is entitled to assume that this something is the case (when we talk about 'our' reason, we mean the capacity to do so). Of course, there are also reasons which take circumstances into account—but even they must be stated in such a way that everyone in the same circumstances must see them as reasons. Otherwise they would not be 'reasons'. So this knowledge transcends my individuality in a way that my knowledge about the fact that 'I am' does not.

Does the retorsive argument offer prospects for practical reason? Are there normative performative implications of reasoning? Aristotle never applied the argument to moral norms and very few philosophers have done so since. Thomas Aquinas was probably one of the first to use them for moral philosophy, and we find some retorsive arguments in the practical philosophies of German Idealism. But the most elaborated and, indeed, promising applications were developed in the late twentieth century. In the next two chapters I will concentrate on two very recent applications of the retorsive argument which I consider to be the most powerful. But before doing so we must rebut some more general objections which have been put forward against this kind of methodology.

2.3.4. *Some Objections to the Retorsive Argument*

First, one might suspect that transcendental arguments are pierced by the first horn of the deductive enterprise, the *petitio principii*: Does the argument simply presuppose the very principle which it sets out to prove? This criticism has been raised many times (e.g. Gethmann and Hegselmann 1977). But there are two related factors which allow the retorsive argument to escape from this threat. (1) Retorsive arguments do not conclude deductively from an axiom the validity of the assumption which functions as its starting-point. There is a significant difference, in that the first principle is said to be a necessary performative presupposition that everyone who reasons at all must have already accepted, prior to his activity. So the argument does not proceed *progressively* from a principle but is meant to discover *retrospectively* some principle as the undeniable, performative condition of all reasoning. (2) This leads to the second factor showing why transcendental arguments are not axiomatic: while the validity of a *petitio principii* can be rationally questioned from an external standpoint *outside* its axiom, this questioning stance towards the original assumption is impossible to hold (or turns out to be impossible). That is exactly the point of the retorsive argument; we cannot rationally occupy an external relation to what is involved in reasoning (cf. Hösle 1986: 239).

The last point (2) leads directly to a further objection. Is the result of the retorsive argument relative to our way of reasoning, or, as it has been put, to our conceptual scheme? This is Körner's argument. He claims that the transcendental conditional could only work if it showed that some condition is 'uniquely necessary' (1967). By that Körner means that there are *two* tasks for the transcendental argument: the first, to demonstrate that some r is a necessary condition for our reasoning, and the second, and more important, to demonstrate that no alternative way of reasoning is possible (i.e. that our conceptual scheme is unique). Körner sees the second task as being beyond what could possibly be achieved and thus detrimental to all transcendental arguments (1967: 321–2; cf. also Rosenberg 1975: 618). According to him, we can never defend the uniqueness of a conceptual scheme, because this would require a standpoint which is not accessible to us. We cannot defend it from 'within' our conceptual scheme (because it does not allow us to say anything about schemes outside the one we are 'in')—and we cannot do it from 'outside' our conceptual scheme (because we cannot get there). All we could prove is that we do employ the conceptual scheme we do employ.

But this is not an overwhelming objection. The proponents of retorsive transcendental arguments have rightly replied that there is, in fact, no meaning we can give to radically different, 'alternative' schemes (Schaper 1972: 108 ff.). We can neither think of them (impossible by definition because our thinking takes place in our conceptual scheme), nor can we translate them into our way of thinking (for then they will no longer be truly alternative schemes (cf. Davidson 1973; Rorty 1972)).[26] Any translation would require a shared conceptual (meta)scheme, which then would be the ultimate scheme. In brief, there is simply no intelligible way in which we might contrast our conceptual scheme and its principles with

---

[26] It must be noted that Davidson interprets this point as an argument against the possibility of raising the question (which he sees as fundamental to the transcendental enquiry) as to whether there could be an alternative to our conceptual scheme (see also R. Geuss 1983). This, however, is not an exhaustive account of the aim of transcendental philosophy, because it excludes the ontological claims usually made in this area.

other conceptual schemes—and no intelligible way to demand a proof of the uniqueness of our scheme. Körner is right to state that there is no intelligible standpoint outside our conceptual scheme, but he does not see that he himself has tried to do the impossible and to utter a criticism from this very viewpoint. His objection cannot really be made intelligible, and there is no way we could even know what it meant to take a non-intelligible criticism seriously. To put it differently: It is exactly the purpose of the transcendental conditional to show that some feature is an indispensable condition of any form of reasoning (or conceptual scheme) that is intelligible to us. Thus, the *successful* argument for the necessity of some features of our conceptual scheme is at the same time the justification of their being irreplaceable—and therefore unique in the required sense (Aschenberg 1982: 291). Körner's argument is not an objection against the method in principle, but rather a rejection of particular unsuccessful transcendental arguments.

There is a family of objections to the effect that we cannot conclude the truth of r from the impossibility of asserting '¬r'. We might distinguish a psychological version of this objection (i); a version that sees a mere *ad hominem* argument at work (ii); and a criticism of the principles of logic employed (iii). Let us look at each of them in turn.

(i) The objection can take the form of a general reluctance to accept the retorsive method as decisive. Some dissatisfaction seems to remain if we have nothing more than a merely apagogic basis for the conclusion that r; we might want an assurance of its truth of a more obvious kind. But this is not convincing for two reasons. First, it only makes sense to demand a stronger (or even different) form of evidence for first principles if we can explain what this would amount to. But since deduction is surely not the kind of evidence that we can expect for first principles (otherwise they could not be 'first'), the 'glorious summer' which we possibly could hope for, the call for 'more' evidence, seems vacuous. Secondly, if this apparent oddity of apagogic arguments is primarily mirroring our *psychological* expectations, then it is hard to see how this uneasiness itself should be used as an objection at all. After all, it is possible to explain away this 'winter of discontent'; it might result from the fact that we are not used to retorsive reasoning, since it neither plays a major role in our daily life nor is this kind of transcendental argument dominant in the philosophical tradition. There are many thoughts that would be strange and odd to anyone unfamiliar with them; and, similarly, many contingent conditions might have to be fulfilled in order to understand this type of retorsive argument properly. As Freud reminded us, not even our reasoning is immune from being distorted by our wishes, attachments to, and fixations on different ideas and expectations. And the history of science is full of examples. Consider the scientists and clergy of the Medici court who rejected Galileo's offer to look through the telescope. But this unease might pass away after thorough and open-minded engagement (if the argument or methodology actually works).

(ii) Even if it were not in doubt that the argument gives full (psychological) certainty, we could still wonder whether we are (methodologically) entitled to conclude the objective truth of r. Kant holds that we are not. At least, that's what he says when he rejects apagogic arguments in the first *Critique* (A 789–90/B 817–18):

> the apagogical proof, on the contrary, can produce certainty, to be sure, but never comprehensibility of the truth with regard to its connection with the grounds of its possibility. Hence the latter is more emergency aid than a procedure which satisfies all the aims of reason.

Though Kant never says it very clearly, it seems that he suspects that retorsive reasoning leads to a mere *ad hominem* rejection of scepticism.[27] Whether or not he did suspect this, this objection is worth looking at and has been raised against retorsive arguments by several authors.[28] They admit that the argument shows that the sceptic undercuts his own position by denying something; and that he might indeed face the dilemma of either remaining silent and abandoning any claim to intelligibility or granting the very point he wanted to question. But, so the objection goes, this does not show more than something about *him*. That is why the whole argument would boil down to some *ad hominem* rejection of scepticism. The sense in which the expression is used here is that a reasoner says something which contradicts things that his behaviour

---

[27] Walker (1999: 17) sees evidence for this in *CoPR* A 739/B 767. NB: Kant's dismissal of apagogic arguments is probably the reason why many proponents of the explorational type do *not* call indirect arguments 'transcendental' at all (e.g. Bennett 1979: 51).

[28] e.g. Aschenberg (1982: 373 ff.). Another author who seems to have something like the *ad hominem* objection in mind is H. Jonas (1979: 149). He claims that the inconsistency in the denial of a certain judgement does not imply that one would have to acknowledge its authority. Brink (1989: 119) writes in the same spirit that there can be coherent scepticism concerning methodology; the self-justifying strategy (like the retorsive argument) would only be successful on the basis of a further, unjustified assumption; *namely*, that a belief which one cannot avoid having is thereby justified.

58 · *The Grounds of Ethical Judgement*

implies, so that we do not have to take *him* seriously. Nothing more would follow from this; certainly not the truth of r.

But this objection misses what is aimed at by retorsive arguments. They are designed to show something different and something more: not that an individual sceptic has refuted himself by asserting his scepticism, but that a judgement cannot be denied *independently* of the situation or the person who asserts it. Thus, the inconsistency is neither that a speaker is unreliable or insincere, nor that he says different things at different times, but that there is an inevitable inconsistency between a sceptical proposition and *any* rational act of asserting it (cf. Finnis 1977: 251 n.). Retorsive arguments take the performative conditions of all conceivable reasoners into account (including non-human beings among such reasoners). They are therefore not *ad hominem*, at least not in the way the term is used in the objection, but refer to any scepticism of this kind—they are '*ad objicientem qua talem*' as G. Isaye has put it (1954: 209). That's why they do allow us fully to reject ¬r—and thus to conclude the truth of r as the only possible alternative.

(iii) Is there indeed no other possibility for r, other than being false or true? The retorsive argument presupposes the validity of classical bivalent logic; in particular, the principle of non-contradiction in connection with the principle of excluded middle (*tertium non datur*) according to which contradictories (like r and ¬r) cannot both be true and cannot both be false. Without the principle of excluded middle, r might be neither 'true' nor 'false' but could have a third truth-value; for example, 'possible' (as Jan Lukasiewicz has suggested). In this case, the truth of r would not follow from the falsehood of ¬r, but only that r is *either* 'true' *or* 'possible'.[29]

There are two ways to answer this objection. The first one is to limit the result of retorsive transcendental arguments to the validity of classical logic. This is not a severe limitation—after all, if moral realism can be justified under the domain of the laws of classical logic, much will have

---

[29] Although both principles are usually linked (as they are in classical logic), there are logical systems that try to hold one without the other. L. E. J. Brouwer's intuitionist school of mathematics, for example, denies the principle of excluded middle in some contexts (in reasoning about infinite sets) but affirms the principle of non-contradiction. The converse is held by G. Priest, who has introduced a kind of inconsistency under the name 'dialethism'. According to Priest, we might construct a logic in which contradictories can be both false and true at the same time (so the principle of non-contradiction does not hold) but where there is no third option (so the principle of excluded middle is valid).

been achieved. To do more, that is, to argue for the correctness of classical logic itself, is not the purpose of an ethical enquiry. That is also the reason why we will take the principle of non-contradiction, as well as the principle of excluded middle, simply for granted for the subsequent investigations.

However, one might want to answer (iii) in a different way; namely, by using retorsive arguments in order to show that even a sceptic who is sceptical about classical logic is implicitly committed to its correctness: he can argue against these principles (and for alternative logical systems) only from *within* classical logic. There is no other standpoint that is intelligible to us (or to him). As mentioned above (p. 45), Aristotle has already suggested some such transcendental argument to the effect that the principle of non-contradiction must be regarded as valid. A similar argument can be used to show that the sceptic is also committed to the principle of the excluded middle. Let us see how this argument works. The Lukasiewiczian sceptic questions the methodological thesis (1): 'x is necessarily true if x cannot intelligibly be denied'. He would hold the opposite thesis $\neg$ (1) instead: 'x is not necessarily true if x cannot intelligibly be denied'. Can this sceptical judgement be consistently asserted? It seems that the methodological sceptic is committed to the truth of $\neg$ (1) rather than (1), since otherwise his objection would lose its point. But then his assertion implies that either (1) or $\neg$ (1) is true—which is, of course, an affirmation of the denied (1). Can he make his scepticism self-consistent by saying that he only holds that (1) is false but not that $\neg$ (1) is true? If he argues that $\neg$ (1) is 'true or possible' (and thus that (1) and $\neg$ (1) could both be false), then his scepticism seems, at least prima facie, in accordance with the propositional content of $\neg$ (1). This manoeuvre, however, does not help, because it would force him to admit that the status of *this* second-order methodological judgement, as we might call it (namely of '$\neg$ (1) is true or possible'), is not true but, again, only 'true or possible'. And so on, iterating eternally. It seems unclear what to make of this methodological claim; a claim that must be put in endless 'meta-level' brackets of the 'true or possible'. Is he claiming anything at all? And can the status of his claim be made intelligible? And even if he succeeds in giving an intelligible account of it, he will have to explain the status of this account in the very same way. Is the account meant to be accurate—or merely 'true or possible'? It seems that in order to be intelligible he would have to accept the principle of the excluded middle at least at some level; namely, the level where he claims that this infinite regression exists.³⁰ It is hard to see how he could escape from inconsistency.

Obviously, this is only a rough outline of an argument, not a fully delineated one. But it should be sufficient to show the manner in which the correctness of classical logic might be defended by retorsive arguments. It will have to be shown that there is just no room for scepticism about such basic principles 'because there is no place to stand where we can formulate or think it without immediately contradicting ourselves by relying on it' (Nagel 1997: 62). To do more than sketch this manner of argument would require a different kind of book.

Let us turn to another objection that can already be found in Fichte (who rejects it, see 1971: iv. 16) and was renewed by Stroud in his classic 1968 essay. Here the inference from the impossibility of ¬ r to r is not questioned, but the strength of the resulting knowledge is. Though Stroud mainly formulates the objection in a narrow sense—he directs it against two particular transcendental arguments by Strawson (1959) and Shoemaker (1963)—it can easily be stated more generally. Stroud's objection goes as follows: Even if a transcendental argument shows us how we must judge something to be, we could still doubt whether it gives us any knowledge about how things *really are*. Transcendental arguments remain, according to Stroud, internal to the thoughts or conceptual schemes of people and cannot yield results about how the world outside our thoughts and beliefs must be. In other words, the result of transcendental reasoning would seem at best ontologically neutral towards the world, and perhaps entirely independent of it. 'One can become haunted', as Michael Williams puts this criticism (1977: 101), 'by the picture of one's belief system incorporating all sorts of internal relations of justification while, as a whole, floating on the world with no point of contact'. Only if we presuppose that reality must be ultimately constructed in a way that is intelligible to us do we have to accept that the necessity of our thinking reveals the structure of the world.³¹ Thus,

---

³⁰ For a similar application of the retorsive argument against scepticism concerning classical logic see G. Isaye (1952) and V. Hösle (1990: 152 ff).

³¹ It must be mentioned that Kant attends to Stroud's problem, by connecting the transcendental arguments he uses with his transcendental idealism. We have, according to him, a firm set of synthetic judgements a priori which tell us how we must structure experience, but they tell us nothing about how things are 'in themselves'. Kant's subjective-idealist solution (which is not entirely acceptable, for a number of different reasons) would bypass Stroud's objection. If things 'really' (i.e. phenomenally) were the way that we think them

the protagonists of transcendental arguments, says Stroud, face a dilemma. Either they accept that the argument shows substantially less than they thought. Or they subscribe to a 'verification principle' (1968: 247), which says, roughly, that everything is in fact the way we believe it to be. But if they choose the second option, then the weight of justification is no longer carried by the transcendental argument but by this (dogmatic) principle. Although Stroud grants that transcendental arguments might be able to refute the rather harmless sceptic who denies that we have a certain conceptual scheme, he sees the more sophisticated sceptic as unmoved by the argument. This sceptic accepts that everyone, including himself, is committed to a certain conceptual scheme, but he asks for the credentials of the verification principle, querying whether there is in fact a reality that corresponds to his and our necessary beliefs.

Let us analyse this objection. The obstinate sceptic seems to make the following claim: 'I see that I must believe r, but is it really *true* that r?' Consider a schizophrenic who hears an inner voice telling him stories; he might indeed ask himself sceptically: 'I am compelled to assume that there is someone talking to me, but is there really someone?' Yet there are some crucial differences to Stroud's sceptical questions. First, the necessity is of a different kind—transcendental arguments show that there is no rational way to reject some beliefs, while the schizophrenic is merely confronted with an unavoidable experience (a *psychological* compulsion). He can still imagine rationally what it would be like to hear no voices. Secondly, there is a meaningful way to check the truth of beliefs resulting from a mental disorder: by comparing them with other evidence to the contrary. The transcendental argument does not allow for an independent checking of its results—the Münchhausen trilemma has shown that there is no other rational way to establish them. These differences tell us why Stroud's sceptic aims for the impossible: he must believe x by force of a 'must' which spells out that there is no reasonable alternative—and he cannot picture his epistemological situation 'from sideways on' (McDowell 1996: 34). Stroud's objection cannot be formed

because we think them to be like that (and nothing about their noumenal reality could be said), then the problem would be solved. This is why some philosophers who argued on Kantian lines became idealists (like Fichte) or, more recently, coherence theorists of truth (cf. Hintikka (1972: 1974), who—if I understand him rightly—interprets the entire transcendental argument in an idealist way when he says it provides a kind of 'maker's knowledge'). However, to defend the results of transcendental arguments against Stroud's objection simply by presupposing such a theory of truth must be eschewed as begging the question.

rationally. Whenever someone attempts this sideways move (as M. Williams in the quote above) it is *he* who 'enters' the point of view *with his thinking*. If it is impossible not to think in a certain way, then we cannot 'think' that the world could be different from how we must think. We can conclude that there is no additional, unjustified principle of verification as a presupposition of retorsive transcendental arguments.

But Stroud's objection can be reformulated as a warning: we must always pay attention to the possibility of mistaking contingent (psychological) conditions of our thinking for necessary ones. A starting-point of a transcendental argument must not remain in any way relative to the contingent situation of the rational agent and the way he sees the world. Stroud simply spells out what we are looking for. As William Stine puts it (1972), every successful transcendental argument is itself a verification. If the argument works, it is meant to show exactly this; namely, that—by mere force of reason—we must take certain things truly to be the way that we consider them to be, quite independently of us. The conclusion of a valid transcendental argument is *that* x, because we must believe x—rather than the tautological outcome of (merely) believing in x, because we must believe x. Stroud's demand for a verificationist principle has, however, much more force when we look at explorational transcendental arguments. They can be reconstructed in such a way as to deliver a hypothetical conclusion: when we accept their starting-point, then they lead to an insight we must also accept. Hence it is possible that everything we are logically obliged to think, given the starting-point, may be contingently false.

However, Stroud's objection can also make us alert to an ontological problem. Even when we must think that reality is the way we must think it to be (because we cannot think it to be otherwise) an explanation seems to be required of how it is possible that our thinking matches the way reality (outside our thinking) is. Stroud has pointed to this aspect of his objection more recently:

> how can truths about the world which appear to say or imply nothing about human thought or experience be shown to be genuinely necessary conditions of such psychological facts as that we think and experience things in certain ways, from which the proofs begin? It would seem that we must find, and cross, a bridge of necessity from the one to the other. That would be a truly remarkable feat, and some convincing explanation would surely be needed of how the whole thing is possible.(1994: 234)

This is not itself an objection but, rather, a puzzle. Again, it is not salient to the concerns of this present book; it is enough here to mention this puzzle and proceed (I will turn back to it very briefly in Sect. 6.4.3).

There is a final objection that we should turn to. It might be argued that the retorsive argument is in no better a position with regard to the threat of the naturalistic fallacy than is the explorational argument. Our main task is to find a methodology for practical reason, and thus to ground normative principles. Retorsive arguments will only achieve this if we find some r that turns out to be normative—the transcendental conditional cannot add normativity to an otherwise neutral original assumption without begging the question. Thus, the naturalistic-fallacy objection can be reformulated into a demand for a successful retorsive transcendental argument. It will support moral realism only if it can be shown that even the sceptic presupposes some normative r *qua* raising his sceptical objection. This seems particularly hard to deal with because of the two different sceptical objections possible: a rational sceptic might accept the undeniable constitutive role of some r—and yet still question whether this has anything to do with normativity. He could concede that, for example, the laws of logic are indispensable to him as much as to any rational agent, but he could still wonder whether there is any *obligation* to be rational and thus to subscribe to their authority. This kind of scepticism will be the most problematic for proponents of the retorsive argument.

2.4. A VERY SHORT CONCLUSION

Let us summarize the discussion of this and the last chapter. Transcendental arguments seem to be the most promising candidates in the philosophical endeavour securely to establish first principles. We have discussed why alternative methods will not work, especially in the context of practical reason. Two types of transcendental argument have been distinguished, of which the retorsive type turns out to be, for the reasons above, most promising. Yet we will not be able to ascertain whether this method actually succeeds unless we find a concrete argument of this type which withstands criticism. Let us see why several recent attempts to establish ethical principles in this way cannot meet this challenge.

CHAPTER 3
The Argument from Discourse

3.1. THE PROJECT OF JUSTIFYING ETHICS

Although Karl-Otto Apel had forerunners in this field, he was the first to offer an elaborate and advanced version of a retorsive transcendental argument for normative principles (*Letztbegründung*).[1] His project aims to re-establish rational ethics and to cast off relativism. The main line of his reasoning is given in the title of his ground-breaking 1973 paper, 'The *A Priori* of the Communication Community and the Foundation of Ethics: The Problem of a Rational Foundation of Ethics in the Scientific Age' (quoted, in what follows, from the 1980 translation). In this article he calls it the paradox of modernity that, on the one hand, modern science and technology have given mankind enormous capabilities of destruction which create urgent needs for a universal ethics, yet, on the other hand, that the same *forma mentis* has destroyed all hopes for arriving at a universal morality by rational means. Science accounts only for induction and deduction as rational procedures and leaves no space for the foundation of normative principles. 'A universal, i.e. intersubjectively valid ethics of collective responsibility thus seems both necessary and impossible' (1980: 229).

---

[1] For a detailed account of the history of the argument see Kuhlmann (1985: 254 ff.) and Hösle (1990: 159 ff.). In the Anglo-American literature, an argument of this structure can be found in Royce (1969), Peters (1966), and Phillips-Griffiths (1957/8; 1967), and more recently O. O'Neill (1989). C. S. Peirce, who has been very important for the development of Apel's philosophy, offers a similar, but more limited, argument. It will become obvious how this idea is expanded by Apel (cf. Hösle 1990: 99 f., 110 ff.).

Apel suggests a transcendental argument to solve this dilemma. It runs roughly as follows: Whenever we argue, even in any form of sceptical reasoning, we are implicitly committed to aim at the truth. Since this cannot be denied consistently, we must regard this aim as all-binding. Apel then equates truth with consensus of a universal discursive community. From this he concludes that commitment to truth implies the commitment to the authority of all the (normative) principles that constitute a universal discursive community. The most important principle is 'respect towards all other agents'; we owe it to them because they are participants in the discursive community.

In order to examine Apel's reasoning critically we will have to look at it in more detail. (Since Wolfgang Kuhlmann (1985) has advanced this transcendental argument in many important respects, it will prove useful to refer also to him.)

3.1.1. *Our Commitment to Aiming at Truth (First Step)*

Already Thomas Aquinas argued transcendentally in order to show that even the sceptic has to admit that there is truth (or more precisely that it is possible to make true judgements): 'Truth is known through itself', Thomas writes, 'because everyone who denies that there is truth, withdraws from this negation. The reason being that if there is no truth, then it would be true that there is no truth'[2] (*ST* liber 1, q. 2 a. 1 obi. 3, quoted from 1932: 12). In other words, the sceptic's negation of truth would contradict itself if it were true. So it cannot be true.

While Thomas puts his whole argument in one sentence, Apel is much more elaborate about his reasoning. Drawing upon J. Searle's and J. L. Austin's speech-act theory, he distinguishes between illocutative performative aspects of arguing and propositional ones. The important point is that some of these illocutative performative aspects are unable to be circumvented; they are necessary performative conditions and thus are as firmly grounded as reason itself. The ones most central for Apel are the implicit commitments to the possibility of true judgements and, equally important, to our own ability to make true judgements by way of reasoning or arguing (1980: 265–6).[3] While the sceptic denies the possibility of

---

[2] 'veritatem esse per se notum; quia qui negat veritatem esse, concedit veritatem non esse. Si enim veritas non est, verum est veritatem non esse'. (See also a similar argument in Thomas' *Summa contra Gentiles*, liber 2, caput 33, Amplius.)

[3] Cf. Kuhlmann 1985: 232 ff.

true judgements, he still makes a claim to truth by contributing to the debate. Whatever the arguments are which he brings forward, he must intend his contribution (for example, the claim that there is *no* truth) to be possibly right or at least nearer the truth than his proponent's claim (that there *is* truth). Otherwise, his reasoning would fail to be an intelligible contribution (1980: 265). Thus, any attempt by a sceptic to reject the two central commitments leads to a performative self-defeat in which he annuls the propositional content of a speech-act through what is implied by its performative enactment. The sceptic suffers from an inconsistency between what he expresses at different levels.

And there is no point *outside* the argumentative situation and its conditions from which the sceptic could raise his doubts in an intelligible, rational way. As Apel argues, even the extreme sceptic who refuses to raise any objection affirms this result. Either:

(*a*) he would regard his silence as the right or correct response to the discourse. Then the act of non-participation is meant as a (speechless, yet still communicative) contribution to the debate. Popper (1958: ii. 284) talks about the implicit 'argument' of refusing to argue. In this case, he would also make an implicit claim to truth.

Or:

(*b*) his non-participation is not intended to mean anything in the context of the investigation. Then, it is what it is; namely, nothing meaningful. To remain silent *in this sense* is no argument. This sceptic would not raise any argument and can therefore not be seen as a consistent sceptic—he is no sceptic at all. Apel refers to Aristotle's remark that his relevance can be compared with that of a vegetable (1976b: 126).

Apel adds that our commitment to truth cannot be *affirmed* without already presupposing its rightness (1976b: 71; see (5) and (6) on p. 48 above). Someone who uses an argument (like the suggested transcendental one) in order to justify the claim that we can come to true judgements is himself presupposing this possibility as a performative condition of his reasoning being intelligible. Hence an affirmation of truth-seeking is consistent with what is expressed at both levels.

According to Apel and Kuhlmann, this also explains why this argument is *not* a deduction: the justified principles are not deduced (or reduced) from other judgements which are either outside or different from them, because they are precisely the conditions under which deduction makes sense. The argument states that there are no optional, alternative ways to argue, and that is why the principles adduced are not ad lib—the sceptic cannot choose one form of reasoning rather than another (for example, one which does not allow for deduction). A claim to this end (like Keuth 1983) simply does not make any sense or is, once again, self-refuting: our reasoning is only meaningful within its principles and cannot relativize itself by talking about the possibility of alternative concepts of reason which might not 'aim at the truth'. Any attempt to do so would performatively affirm the validity of the very 'way' of reasoning under attack (Kuhlmann 1985: 232 ff.). The sceptical objection that there might be alternative forms of reason cannot be put forward in a performatively consistent way *within* a rational discourse—and how else could it be raised? This dubious objection is directed against the one standard which alone could make doubts intelligible (ibid. 88).

From what has been said before it is obvious that Apel's argument is of the retorsive type. It does not rely on any external starting-point but is designed to show that some judgements are undeniable. Any attempt to anchor such judgements already presupposes them. For Apel and Kuhlmann these judgements can be discovered by virtue of a 'transcendental reflection' and are thus the 'a prioris' for any reasoning. In order to see how this result can be expanded to a more substantial ethics we must turn to their understanding of 'reason' as a discursive process.

3.1.2. *Commitment to Truth as a Commitment to Universal Consensus (Second Step)*

For Apel reason is a discursive enterprise; it always happens in a real 'communicative community' (*Kommunikationsgemeinschaft*). This intersubjectivity has a transcendental status; without it there cannot be any reasoning. Further, Apel argues that truth as the implied aim of all reasoning is ultimately constituted by the consensus of a *universal* community of reasoners, the 'ideal communicative community'. This means that by being committed to the truth the agent is also committed to aiming at this universal consensus.

Apel offers two central arguments for this transcendental role of universal intersubjectivity. The first is about truth: A judgement must be regarded as true when no further objection against it can be thought of—and that is the situation of a universal consensus. Apel's second argument is based upon Wittgenstein's philosophy of language. Words get their meaning only through being used by a community of people. And since language is the precondition for any reasoning, this also shows the uncircumventable status of intersubjectivity. That is why Apel talks about the implicit goal of 'the "intersubjective unity of interpretation" *qua* understanding of meaning and *qua* consensus of truth' (1980: 267). Let us look at the two arguments in some more detail.

Apel's consensus theory of truth (1976a: ii, 311) originates in the philosophy of C. S. Peirce. Peirce holds that individual evidence alone can never be a sufficient criterion for truth and that we need to conceive of truth as the agreement of a community (Peirce 1931–58: v. 265). Since truth is no metaphysical entity, but rather a predicate of substantial judgements put forward by a reasoning subject, and since we can have no direct access to truth, the only assurance of the truth of a judgement is the absence of further meaningful objections to it. According to Apel, this is the case if there is an undisputed agreement about a judgement; that is, everyone freely agrees with one another and is motivated to accept the judgement only on the basis of good arguments. But while Peirce limits this insight to truth in scientific matters, Apel expands it to any rational enterprise (even to rational agency—see below). He argues that there cannot be any 'reason' to limit this conception of truth to science, because a limited understanding would itself have to refer to the consensus in order to be justified and not arbitrary (cf. 1980: 277). The impossibility of a rational self-restriction also explains why the consensus has to be *universal*: any attempt to be satisfied with a real community[4] can only be justified by transcending this community—it will have to be argued that no objection outside the ones that have been raised in the community is possible. But this can only be done by appealing to the universal community. That is the reason why any participation in the real community anticipates the ideal community. This comes very close to a point made by O. O'Neill (who argues in an Apelian fashion): 'if reasoning cannot gain authority beyond the circles within which it guides communication—if its authority is, so to speak, retrospectively established rather than antecedently given—then private "uses of reason" would seem to be without any general authority, hence not really uses of reason at all' (1989: 37).

---

[4] For aesthetic reasons, I do not use 'communication community' to translate Apel's expression 'Kommunikationsgemeinschaft' but rather 'intersubjective community' or simply 'community'.

When Apel states his linguistic argument for the universal community, he, again, refers to Peirce. According to Peirce, understanding is not a relation between an object and a subject alone, but needs a further component, namely a sign, which is a representation that stands for something. There cannot be any epistemological approach to the world without language. Going beyond Peirce, Apel adds a fourth component; namely, the *co-subject* who alone makes this use of signs and the process of interpretation meaningful and the subjects capable of coming to the truth (1989). A second point of reference is Wittgenstein and his argument against the possibility of a private language (a language which can be understood by no one but the speaker alone; cf. Wittgenstein 1982: § 243). In the same way in which there cannot be a private language, Apel says, any private form of reasoning is impossible, since reason requires language. Wittgenstein, however, does not argue for the need of *universally* shared practices or rule acceptance. But Apel tries to expand Wittgenstein's argument when he contends that there must be one universal language-game, because we could not otherwise communicate between different language-games (1976a: ii. 319 ff.). And whenever we interact with someone we have already acknowledged (performatively) that we can communicate and hence that there is indeed a shared language-game. This explains why the intersubjective community has to be thought of as being universal: *everyone* seems to have the communicative capacities and must therefore be regarded as a virtual participant in this ideal community (cf. 1980: 259).

Apel, Kuhlmann, and others come to the same result: the anticipation of universal and discursive cooperation in an ideal community is the necessary performative condition of any reasoning.

3.1.3. *Categorical Norms for Reasoning and for all Actions (Third Step)*

Apel's step towards a general and categorical ethics starts from his conception of reason as a discourse. His argument runs as follows: since we necessarily argue as a member of and with regard to a universal community, we have thereby already accepted those rules which govern the public language and the rational cooperation of human beings. The most important of these rules is that everyone engaged in the discourse must recognize and respect all participants as persons. This is the crucial point of the 'humanitas', as Apel puts it, which is presupposed in any act of understanding (1976a: ii. 385). Again, Apel has been inspired by Peirce. Based upon his interpretation of scientific truth as an ultimate consensus of the scientific community, Peirce concludes that there must be an ethical imperative for scientists: they have to transgress their egoism, to 'self-surrender', and to strive for 'transsubjectivity' (1931–58: v. §§ 354 ff.). Though Peirce comes to principles very similar to the normative requirements of Apel, he limits their domain to the scientist and does not develop a general ethical system.

Let us look briefly at the way Apel argues for a much wider scope for the imperatives. It is at the starting-point of his retorsive transcendental argument (and where else could it be?) that Apel goes far beyond Peirce. He transcends the scientific arena when he writes that the 'highest point' (i.e. 'r' according to the account in the last chapter) is general 'human argumentation' which includes all forms of reasoning (1980: 267). To make a judgement about anything, be it affirmative or sceptical, as much as to raise questions (ibid. 271) or to doubt, are all forms of participation in the discourse. But Apel goes beyond even that: Someone who merely wants to use words, or to think in an intelligible way (ibid. 275), has already entered the realm of intersubjective, discursive rationality, since it alone gives meaning to what he does.[5] Apel seems to make an even stronger claim, in that the discursive situation is not limited to the explicit (outer or inner) use of language but also includes meaningful actions as such. He states that 'everyone, even if he merely *acts* in a *meaningful* manner—for example takes a decision in the face of an alternative and claims to understand himself—already implicitly presupposes the logical and moral preconditions for critical communication' (1980: 269). As far as I can see, Apel offers two arguments for this extreme expansion of the discursive situation. First, he says that even a self-reflexive awareness of one's actions requires some minimal use of language; secondly, that (intelligible) actions are special ways of making claims. According to

---

[5] Kuhlmann, following Apel, characterizes the starting-point as 'everything, which deserves the name "thinking"', including 'every kind of argumentation or rational consideration, independent of the kind of question under discussion, be it theoretical, practical, or technical, independent of the degree of explicitness of the argumentation, i.e. whether the consideration is expressed and detailed or whether it can only be reconstructed *ex post*. Further, it is independent of the quality of the reasons considered, so long as it is governed by our interest in finding a right answer and so long as serious claims to validity are raised. Obviously, it is also independent of whether they are raised in the presence of and in interaction with some addressee or whether they are made in *de facto* solitude, in the sole conversation of the soul with itself' (1985: 147).

Apel, to act is a performative expression of the agent's intention that his behaviour should be approved or accepted by the whole community. Thus, whenever we act in an intelligible way we aim performatively at the universal consensus. This does not necessarily mean that everyone ends up having the same interests, but that the interests people have are compatible with those of others.

Kuhlmann is more careful on this point; he speaks only of 'manifold links' (1985: 204) between actions and argumentation (although he claims that it is sometimes impossible to distinguish between them sharply). His main reason for applying the argument from discourse even to actions is indirect and different from Apel's. According to Kuhlmann, right actions are necessary in building up the ideal intersubjective community. He argues in two steps. First, since many practical conflicts are intimately linked with the ideal discourse and therefore have an impact on the possibility of a consensus even in theoretical matters, the solution of these conflicts is a precondition for the functioning of the community (ibid. 205–6). Secondly, since it is possible that *any* practical issue could have an impact on the discourse, the sum of everyone's interests has to be considered under those rules which alone allow harmonious cooperation. On this basis Kuhlmann expands the argument from discourse to the wide range of all intelligible human activities. He concludes that the authority of the uncircumventable normative principles is not limited to a specific theoretic discourse, but includes any interaction of human beings with each other and the world.

What exactly are these normative principles and rules that are supposed to have categorical authority? Apel distinguishes three types of a priori norms. The first guides behaviour in the real community (i); the second is the demand to help realize the ideal community in the present situation of a real community (ii); and the third is about actions in the ideal community (iii). These three amount to, as he calls it at one point, a 'minimal ethics' (1976a: i. 357). Since all the demands are universal (valid for all rational beings) and symmetrical (no one is in any privileged position), Apel sees them as *moral*. And since they are not empirical preconditions—they are 'rather . . . the precondition for the possibility of every discussion of hypothetically posited, empirical preconditions' (Apel 1980: 270)—they must have unconditional, 'categorical' authority (ibid.). Let us look at these three types more closely.

(i) The norm for the real world we live in is the search for a consensus in theoretical as much as practical matters whenever our aims, interests, or needs might collide with those of others. That means, first, that we have to respect others; that is, to treat them as ends in themselves—because only then can communication happen at all. Centrally, there is an obligation to cooperate without using any force. Secondly, when we act we must regard ourselves as accountable to the community. It means that 'all human needs—as potential claims—i.e. which can be reconciled with the needs of all the others by argumentation, must be made the concern of the communication community' (Apel 1980: 277/8). Thirdly, however, we should never forget that all this takes place in the real world. This requires a realistic consideration of the actual situation in which we act and an enquiry into what means are adequate within this context. It is, for example, not always a promising strategy to act as if one were respected by everyone else. To demand this from the agent would be unfair and absurd and to behave towards others in this way (for example, towards suppressors and towards highly aggressive people) might even be counter-productive and diminish the chance of any communication. Ethics demands different behaviour in a world that is far from ideal. Sometimes one can only choose between alternative *strategic* uses of reason,[6] when the situation does not allow us to use reason truly communicatively.

(ii) There is, according to Apel and Kuhlmann, a gap between the actual discourse taking place in the world and the ideal community. Because our participation in the real discourses of our non-ideal world implies commitment to the consensus of the ideal community, the ultimate aim is to set up the preconditions for this ideal community. As stated above, we cannot behave as if this ideal situation had already been realized, but we should not be satisfied with simply establishing real communications in the real world; we are under an obligation to pave the way for the ideal. And as soon as parts of the ideal community have been realized we will have to protect them: 'take care for the preservation of those conditions of the possible realization of the ideal community which already exist' (Kuhlmann 1985: 214).

---

[6] Partly following Horkheimer, Apel distinguishes four forms of reasoning (1979). One concerns causal connections; this is the way science operates. The second is the 'technical' use of reason (with the two subclasses 'instrumental' and 'strategic', the first regarding subject–object relations, the second subject–subject relations). The third is hermeneutic reasoning, i.e. the ability to understand and communicate. Finally, there is an ethical (or communicative) use of reason by which reason arrives at norms.

(iii) Once the ideal community has been achieved, things will be different. The ideal community is the situation of equal opportunities and absence of suppression by force. Here strategic demands will have come to an end and the main duty will be to uphold the ideal, fair situation without suppression, where all agents treat all others as ends in themselves.

But there is, according to Apel, not only 'minimal ethics' with its three types of moral norms but a further set of obligations. Apel argues that all the institutions and regulations which can be agreed upon in a rational discourse find thereby also a rational justification: the notion of fair discourse lays down the criteria of what can be accepted as a rational claim or interest. Whatever is justified by recourse to the community does not have the strong justification of minimal ethics, but derives its justification indirectly from the authority of this community. The justification of the derived claims and norms is weaker than that of minimal ethics, since the community is not yet ideal. In some ways this conception of justification is comparable to contractual theories that are based on the idea that interests can be justified only on the basis of fair agreement (esp. Rawls 1972).

Thus, Apel arrives at his twofold ethical system: the a priori norms of minimal ethics (which alone are interesting for the project of moral realism) and the a posteriori norms arising from the discursive community (cf. 1998: 246 ff.).[7]

---

[7] It is here that the *Universalpragmatik* of Habermas (1982) comes very close to Apel's practical philosophy. Habermas is also concerned with a *reconstruction* of the *Universalisierungsprinzip* as the crucial underlying principle of a rational discourse, or, as he calls it, the 'formal feature of argumentation' (1973b: 241). But for him a rational justification comes into it only as the *result* of a fair discourse, hence on the second of the two Apelian levels. Habermas rejects any request for a further or stronger justification of (fundamental) moral demands as a 'pseudo-problem' (1973a: 151–2). In opposition to this, Apel's point is that it cannot simply be assumed that the underlying structures resulting from phylogenetical and ontogenetical development are unquestionable *rules* for reason. Habermas's solution takes things much too lightly. For the task of philosophy's justification of norms *is* a serious problem which cannot be reduced to a sociological analysis of how people happen to behave when they argue. Apel wants to show that they *must* reason in a certain way (cf. Wimmer 1980: 48–59). It should be noted that this criticism is more relevant to the early Habermas; in more recent years he is inclined, partly as an answer to Apel's objections, to accept some normative input even at this most fundamental level.

3.2. MORAL REALISM AND THE ARGUMENT FROM DISCOURSE

Obviously, if Apel's and Kuhlmann's retorsive transcendental argument works then they have shown that we must accept some fundamental moral judgements as justified. Hence moral realism based upon this argument will have found a solid basis at least for the truth thesis; that we can make some moral judgements and determine their truth-value. Apel and Kuhlmann avoid getting too involved in these questions and refrain from saying anything about the truth of moral judgements—only about them being 'right'—but if we take the consensus theory of truth seriously then these 'ultimately justified' judgements have to be called 'true'. They are true since no one can *possibly* deny them rationally. The ideal community would have to acknowledge them unanimously, and more readily than any other judgement (cf. Ch. 1 n. 4).

The third claim (see Sect. 1.2)—that there is a correspondence between a person's motives and his moral judgements—might also find support if we look at the specific role the will plays in this argument. Even the sceptic has demonstrated that he has been *motivated* to reason, by raising doubts, and these doubts themselves might form a bridge to the motivation required for further acceptance of the norms which are constitutional to any 'ideal' reasoning. It is less clear what exactly the 'moral facts' are supposed to be which are postulated in the second claim of moral realism (see page 4). However, we would most probably have to describe them as facts about reason; hence, reason itself would be seen to be normative, as the most elementary moral fact.[8]

So it seems that moral realism could find a basis—if Apel's argument succeeds. I will discuss this in the subsequent paragraphs and will maintain that the argument as it stands is inadequate. Its failure, however, is at a very high level. It can show that everyone is committed *qua* rational being to some normative, non-empirical judgements about his reasoning. But these judgements are not yet fully universal. As I will argue, Apel cannot demonstrate that they include *everyone* in the required sense. I will show first (3.3), that the argument can avoid the naturalistic fallacy and provide the basis for a normative judgement of some sort. Secondly

---

[8] The lack of reflection on the ontological implications of the argument from discourse has been criticized by Hösle, who himself argues for an objective idealism as the only sensible metaphysics underlying this transcendental reasoning (1990).

(3.4), a distinction between universal, objective (and thus 'moral') and more restricted normative judgements will be introduced in a short excursus. Thirdly (3.5), I will criticize the steps to universal intersubjectivity: neither the consensus theory of truth nor the argument from language works. Consequently, the argument does not ground a universal but merely a more restricted normative judgement that is not 'moral' in the full and relevant sense. After that, I will raise a related criticism: the resulting norms do not sufficiently protect those people who do not contribute to the discourse. Hence, the failure to establish full universality at the foundational level has its counterpart in the practical domain; the respect for other people as ends in themselves does not include everyone. Finally (3.6), some general conclusions will be drawn about the criteria any retorsive transcendental argument would have to fulfil in order to serve as a basis for moral realism.

3.3. HOW THE ARGUMENT FROM DISCOURSE ANSWERS THE NATURALISTIC-FALLACY OBJECTION

Both Apel and Kuhlmann demonstrate very clearly the manner in which their argument is supposed to escape the naturalistic fallacy. Basically, their answer is that the starting-point, 'reasoning' (rational action, etc.) itself, turns out to be normative if we reflect upon it. It is therefore said to be no wonder (read 'no naturalistic fallacy') that the principles which constitute reasoning are themselves normative.

It is again the retorsive argument which is designed to demonstrate this: even someone who wishes to deny the normativity of the conditions for rational discourse only does so *within* a discourse which already presupposes the normativity of these principles. In the very same way that we cannot question reason rationally, we cannot question the normative principles which constitute reason, because any attempt to do so only makes sense by applying these very principles. Here we find, as Apel emphasizes (1975), a fundamental contrast to Peirce's moral imperatives, which are merely hypothetical: they are only valid for a scientist if he wants to discover true results in scientific matters. But there is no obligation to become a scientist and to put oneself under these demands. Reason, in contrast to this, or the meaningful use of language (for

Kuhlmann and Apel these two concepts basically amount to the same thing) is supposed to provide a *universal* starting-point with unconditional categorical obligations.

Is the defeat of the sceptic compelling? One particularly tough form of scepticism seems not yet to have been dealt with: a rational critic who accepts the undeniable constitutive role of reason could question whether this has anything to do with morality. He could concede that, for example, the laws of logic are indispensable to him as much as to any rational agent, but he could still wonder whether there is any *obligation to be rational* and thus to subscribe to their authority. In other words, this sceptic may ask Moore's famous 'open question': Why should it be *good* to reason? As A. Phillips-Griffiths writes in the context of his reasoning (which is rather similar to Apel's argument): any argument of this type can only refer to the 'most rational morality', instead of being applicable 'to any morality'. It is only 'if we are rational that we must consider moral and other questions in a certain way' (1957: 116).[9]

As far as I can see, Apel develops his response in two steps. First, he rejects any alleged point 'before' or 'outside' reason from where a moral value might or might not be attached to reason (1). We are always 'within' reason and, hence, if we attach moral value to it this is not done from outside but from within. Secondly, Apel argues that by reasoning, an act of acknowledgement of reason's own value has always been performed: no one can contest consistently the *normativity* of reason (2). It follows that reason is necessarily a normative notion—we have to grant it this status *qua* being rational. And since there is no point outside reason from where we could question this—the result from (1)—the value is unconditioned and the related imperatives categorical. Let us look more carefully at the two points.

(1) Why should there not be a first voluntary act of being rational, a first act which might also be the acceptance of morality in a minimal sense? Let us remember Carnap's distinction between internal and external questions. According to him, external questions about the framework of reason as a whole are not capable of being answered rationally, because this would be an answer from *within* the framework. These questions can only be decided in a practical manner (1972: 259). In the

---

[9] Cf. e.g. Gram (1974: 309–12) and Wimmer (1980: 338). As Benhabib argues on these lines, a principle with 'normative content' must precede the argument itself in order for it to work (1990: 337–8).

same spirit, Popper says that any 'resolution to be rational' is itself an 'irrational decision' (Popper and Marcuse 1971: 38–9) and a pure 'act of faith'. If they were right, then any alleged normativity of reason would be a feature which has to be accepted voluntarily by *accepting* 'reason' in this act of faith. Normativity could still be a feature which is inseparably linked to reason, but it would be something we are free to reject by rejecting reason.

Apel's response is that this objection claims the impossible (1998: 221 ff.). There is no way we could make sense of a 'decision' to be rational without already presupposing reason:

> Any decision in the face of an alternative, which is as such comprehensible (and for whose moral necessity one even wants to argue), presupposes the point of view to be shared by the subject who must make a decision as much as by all other subjects in such a situation. It is the point of view of communicative, virtually argumentative reason. (Ibid. 236)

It is, Apel says, simply incomprehensible to speak about a meaningful choice 'before' any reason. Apel's response is compelling: there cannot be a 'choice' for someone who neither knows what the alternatives are (this already being an act of comprehension), nor what he or she 'wants' (to be aware of one's intentions needs some understanding), nor is able to weigh the pros and cons of accepting reason. In brief, it would be no decision at all, but, at most, something that 'happened'. Empirically, and anecdotally, the 'rejection' of reason only seems to happen in the tragic cases of encephalitic and other severely brain-damaged individuals. But this involves a medical condition, not a decision, and hence is not the basis for a philosophical objection. Whatever the physiological basis for rational beings might be, *qua* rational being they must see reason without alternative, to relativize it is transcendentally impossible. Of course, once someone *is* rational he or she might consider acting or thinking more or less rationally or even abandoning this form of existence entirely—Apel does not question the possibility of self-destruction for a rational being (1998: 236). But this would be different from Popper's 'irrational decision': someone who wants to escape from reason would still decide to do so 'within' reason and hence be, Apel says, under the demands spelt out by reason. It would be a case of moral disobedience but not a proof of the thesis that reason and its normativity is freely and pre-rationally chosen—this person simply 'relinquishes the possibility of both self-understanding and self-identification' (1980: 269).

(2) Reason, then, is not chosen in any pre-rational act. But in order to secure the basis of *morality* Apel and Kuhlmann must shore up the strong claim that there is something *good* about reason (or a certain form of reasoning) and that we gain this insight by reflection. Here their line of argument is an expansion of the first step; namely, that there is also no position from which scepticism *about normativity* could be consistently raised. They argue that whoever attempts to question reason's value meaningfully must do so by acknowledging the very value of reason and its rules performatively. Every act of reasoning, even a scepticism about the validity of these principles, is a wilful enterprise; we cannot 'go back on our will to argumentation' (ibid. 270). Thus, any refusal to accept the validity is at the same time *qua* wilful engagement an affirmation of their validity. Hence, the practical realization of reason is accompanied by a commitment to accepting the validity of its constitutive moral rules (ibid. 269)—but, as Apel makes clear, this does not mean that everyone who reasons is other than *morally* compelled to obey these rules to the fullest extent. There is no causal compulsion to do so; to act upon them fully requires a further wilful affirmation.[10]

But how is it possible to conclude something normatively *positive* simply from our being necessarily entrapped or imprisoned in some normative enterprise without (rational) escape? What appears to be good or bad could still be some ultimately neutral aspect of rational beings, which only appears necessarily to them to be normative (cf. Ilting 1994: 151–2). We might elucidate this by approaching it from a theological perspective. There might not have been anything good in God's creation of rational beings as such, but once they were there they had no alternative but to see certain norms as indispensable conditions for their existence. Has Apel made it sufficiently clear why subscribing to reason is more than the mere affirmation of a necessary condition for an otherwise *neutral fact*; namely, that there are rational beings? To answer this Apel would have to show at what point the reasoner realizes by reflection that his reasoning is a profoundly moral activity, that there is something good about him being what he is. Apel does so by arguing that any act of wilful, positive affirmation of the goodness of reasoning is always a condition for reasoning. Unfortunately, he does not say much more

---

[10] See also K. H. Ilting (1972/4; 1976; 1994: 355–6). This point is also made by Höffe (1979; and esp. 1982), Riedel (1979), and more recently G. Schönrich (1994). It is a difficulty which already concerned Kant in his *Religionsschrift*, where he deplores the limits of rational morality and asks for a first choice prior to anything else.

about this crucial step, although a detailed argumentation seems to be required about the way in which normativity enters the transcendental reflection. We will see shortly that some of the ideas of A. Gewirth are useful in making this point clear. For the moment, I will take it for granted for the sake of argument that the reference to the 'wilful affirmation' suffices as a defence.

3.4. GENERAL EXCURSUS: RESTRICTED AND UNRESTRICTED NORMATIVE JUDGEMENTS

There is still another and, as I will argue, irreconcilable, difficulty with the argument from discourse. It seems that even if Apel and Kuhlmann have demonstrated that reasoners are committed to some normative judgements, they have not achieved their aim fully: they do not arrive at *moral* principles. In order to make this objection clear, a short excursus regarding the criteria for a 'moral' normative judgement must be added.

What are normative judgements? For our purpose it is sufficient to consider only *practical*, action-related (and not aesthetic) normative notions; that is, ones that are in the widest sense connected with the idea of 'good'. What all normative judgements of the practical type have in common is the illocutionary force of expressing a favourable, positive appraisal of the states of affairs, purposes, or ways of behaviour about which they are made; an appraisal with practical implications. This means that these judgements must involve the practical dimension of recommending certain appropriate actions in so far as these remain to be realized.

Still, for the sake of clarity, we should not employ an understanding which is too limited in the first place: not all such judgements must necessarily be about *objective* values or norms in the sense that they are seen as binding *for everyone*. We can say rather that whenever someone affirms a preference this is a normative judgement, even if it is only the expression of a subjective positive evaluation. Normative judgements can range from those purely subjective in nature (for example, the pursuit of my pleasures), to ones more general (for example, patriotism), up to those which make a universal claim (for example, respect for other people). In this sense, we can use 'normative judgement' (equally 'positive value judgement' or 'norm') as a twofold assertion: (a) as a description of a state of affairs or course of events, and (b) as an expression of an *active pro-attitude* towards it which is seen as appropriate. Depending on the grade of generality of this judgement, this recommendation can be directed towards me, some others, or everyone.

It should be noted that it is precisely this demand for a practical pro-attitude which distinguishes values or norms from mere 'desires'. We can desire things without seeing anything (even subjectively) 'valuable' in them.[11] It is also important to note that this account remains neutral regarding the reasons *why* something is seen as normative and by whom. We can imagine normative judgements resulting from desires, emotions, or intuitions, reflecting simply our upbringing or resulting from rational insight. Since they can be subjective, they can be short-term as much as long-term and can contradict other normative judgements someone happens to make—and they would still be normative judgements. However, it is obvious that any (valid) rational normative judgement would require exactly this: that the norm it states be *consistent* with all other rational norms and that *every* rational being should accept its justification and thus it itself on the basis of its argumentative force. The account is also neutral towards the question as to what the alternative to this pro-attitude might be (in particular, it is consistent with there being no meaningful and rational alternative at all).

What are the characteristics of a 'moral' normative judgement? The most important feature seems to be that these judgements are made with the implication of being *objectively* binding and thus of having universal validity—that is at least the strict way in which I wish to use the term, following the tradition since Kant. Hence nothing can be called a moral 'good' proper if it is addressed to only one or merely a few people. Further, we commonly consider moral judgements not to privilege one agent. Hence a judgement of the type 'Everyone must do what Alexander says!', though apparently universal, is not moral. This aspect has also been expressed as the demand that moral judgements be 'just'; they must express symmetrical relations. An example *par excellence* of moral judgements are declarations of human rights: they are supposed to include and protect every human being equally (even those who do

---

[11] The practical dimension is also necessary in order to separate values from wishes. We must acknowledge the obligation to be led towards actions through positive values and not be satisfied by mere hope for their realization (as in wishing). Although it seems that wishes do have this aspect of a conscious approval that desires need not have, neither desires nor wishes have the required practical dimension. Since it is of no importance for the forthcoming investigation, I shall not try to explore this further.

not believe in human rights) and spell out demands which *should* be respected by everyone. (NB, human rights are not always presented as demanded by rationality: sometimes they are considered to be based upon some intuition or contract. So the criteria for 'moral norms' can be fulfilled independently of the foundation given to norms or values.) Closely connected is the modern (and, again, Kantian) demand that moral judgements must not dismiss people; they must respect everyone 'as an end' and never merely as a means. Finally, at least for a cognitivist moral realism, these judgements must be regarded as consistently valid, over all time, in all situations, and for all agents, and it is insisted that it must be possible to hold their validity consistently in the face of all other moral values.[12] This, of course, does not mean that they will always find some application (think of Robinson Crusoe, who does not have to care about human rights too much before Friday arrives), but it means that in all sufficiently similar situations their application does not depend on the particular agent or the recipient.

Although definitions can show consistent possibilities, they cannot grant the reality of anything. It might still be the case that we would never find a moral norm in the strict sense for which we can provide a rational justification. It is the task of this book to explore exactly this aspiration.

It is noteworthy that we might come across normative judgements which fulfil some but not *all* the conditions of moral ones (think about 'Everyone must do what Alexander says!'). It does not seem to make sense to call them 'moral', although it is difficult to find an appropriate label for them. As I will argue in the next section, the shortcoming of Apel and Kuhlmann is exactly that they only arrive at some such *restricted* normative judgements. They leave no doubt that they see the norms resulting from their arguments as 'moral' in the sense outlined above, since the crucial step to intersubjectivity is supposed to grant universal validity. But it is this step which I will question in the next section.

---

[12] To argue for moral realism without universality and mutual consistency of norms leads to a situation where it is simply impossible to recognize by any means (even intuition or revelation) what these individualistic 'norms' should be. It is therefore no moral realism at all (see Illies 1999). It should not be a surprise that the list of conditions for a moral normative judgement sounds very much like Kant's delineation of the different formula of the categorical imperative—after all, his practical philosophy is centred around the idea of moral realism and the *Groundwork* is an attempt to express what this implies in detail (even if Kant does not provide a satisfactory justification of the categorical imperative).

82 · The Grounds of Ethical Judgement

3.5. CRITIQUE OF THE ARGUMENT FROM DISCOURSE

3.5.1. *Shortcomings of the Consensus Theory of Truth and the Argument for a Universal Language-Game*

Linking the retorsive transcendental argument with the consensus theory of truth is surely problematic.[13] One might be tempted to reject it simply on the basis that there is by no means a universal consensus that *this* is the right account of what truth is—and as long as this is not achieved it cannot consistently be held that the consensus theory of truth is true.

In addition it might seem suspicious that Apel's ultimate justification, supposedly designed to achieve valid synthetic judgements a priori, does not itself rely on the consensus theory of truth. These judgements are seen to be true because of the rational justification they find through a retorsive transcendental argument, independently of what other reasoners might say, and of whether or not there is a consensus. The argument is designed to show that no objection can be put forward—which is much stronger than (and indeed different from) showing that no objection has in fact been put forward. It seems that Apel is reluctant to talk about the 'truth' of these fundamental principles, but I cannot see how he can avoid doing so. After all, if truth consists in a consensus without possible further objections then, as said above, *a fortiori* a judgement against which no objection is imaginable should be called 'true'. The fact that these norms are judgements of practical reason does not change their status, and to call them 'valid' instead of 'true' (1998: 252) does not make a difference.[14]

Further arguments are commonly presented against the consensus

---

[13] None of the arguments against the consensus theory of truth shows that mere evidence is a sufficient criterion for truth. The criticisms of correspondence theories by Peirce and Apel are very plausible. My own rejection of intuition as a source of knowledge, in Chapter 1, has some parallels. But to reject pure evidence as a criterion does not require accepting mere consensus instead.

[14] After all, Apel makes it very clear that his consensus theory is supposed to embrace practical judgements, since even when we make judgements about our interests, we are—Apel says—under the obligation to strive for *universal* consensus.

It is interesting to speculate why Apel is not very keen on speaking about 'truth' but rather about judgements being 'right'. One of the reasons might be that he is afraid of the metaphysical burden the truth thesis might carry.

theory that are still hard or impossible, to reject. The main one is that it can legitimately be questioned whether consensus is *any* criterion of truth: the majority, or conceivably everyone, might simply be mistaken about some matter. The consensus theorist would surely respond that 'mistaken' has no meaning in this objection. But this is taking things too lightly. For the consensus to be a criterion at all, the possibility of collective philosophical madness must be excluded. It is right that 'true' judgements are those against which ultimately no further (rational) objection can be raised. But the mere absence of objections may be the result of various and contingent reasons. It might simply be that no one happens to think of a further objection. That would not exclude the possibility that there might be one. (And, vice versa, it might be that even once the truth about something has been found someone continues to disagree with it.)

It does not help the consensus theorist for him to distinguish between a contingent and an ultimate consensus of a community, because he does not offer any criterion by which we might identify the latter. The response that we recognize the ultimate consensus by the fact that no further objections can be thought of (or by arguing that here the truth is found) is obviously circular. Mere consensus is simply an empty criterion—by itself it is not sufficient to identify true judgements. The norms which are supposed to be obeyed by the ideal community itself do not help: they offer at most a (formal) necessary criterion for the ultimate consensus, not a *sufficient* one. It is imaginable that even in an ideal community with full universal respect it still might arise that no one realizes that some crucial objections exist to a judgement which is universally made. If, however, the aspired to, truth-granting state of an ultimate consensus is specified by further, substantial criteria (like, *inter alia*, whether there is any evidence, etc.), consensus is no longer the sole criterion for its truth and it is hard to see what role it should play at all. (On occasion Apel argues that the consensus might be the decisive criterion in the case of conflicting judgements (1987; 1998: 112). But this faces the same problems.)[15]

---

[15] Apel strongly opposes any such interpretation. He understands the ultimate consensus not as an applicable criterion or 'touchstone' (1998: 270) for the truth, but as a regulative idea—a point, which can possibly never be reached, where all contributions and objections, all evidence and arguments have been brought forward and have led to consensus. It is, however, not clear what that might mean. Further, the fact that Apel regards ultimate consensus as a regulative idea does not establish that he has rejected the thesis that truth consists in such consensus.

Hösle objects rightly that the consensus theory is the attempt to solve the problem of the validity of the normative dimension by reference to a mere fact (1990: 100). This is never convincing regardless of whether the fact is a state of the external world (as some forms of the correspondence theory want it to be) or of our consciousness (as intuitionists claim) or whether it is an intersubjective structure like the collective agreement of a community (as Wittgenstein and, *ceteris paribus*, Apel and Kuhlmann claim). In each case it destroys the autonomy of reason—which would be devastating for any argument which is supposed to start from the uncircumventable status of reason.

Still, consensus will have to play some role. One would have to agree that a consensus *should* ultimately follow, once the truth has been found. Since we regard true judgements as universally valid, in the end every rational and well-informed participant in a community should agree upon them simply because of the cogent reasons which speak for them. So consensus is a possible *consequence* of truth. To this extent Apel is right. But if this is all he wants to claim then the consensus theory is no longer sufficient to link his retorsive transcendental argument to moral norms. If consensus is not itself something we must aspire to but only a consequence of the goal of 'truth', then it cannot itself be demanded categorically. As a consequence it is not analytically given with the notion of 'truth'; there might be many contingent reasons why some actual truth does not find universal acceptance. Apel cannot have it both ways. Either he claims that reason is simply identical with the attempt to strive for a state of universal free agreement and cooperation, or reason is the attempt to strive for truth, which consists in making properly justified judgements. If the first claim is true, any participation would indeed be identical with the endeavour to bring this state about. But this claim seems simply false or at least dogmatic. If the second claim is true, then respect towards others is *only* necessary to the extent to which they help to serve this aim—there is no further need to promote the truth and to make everyone agree with it. By reasoning I aim at the truth but not automatically at a state of universal knowledge of the truth.

This leads to a further possible objection to Apel's consensus theory with regard to practical judgements. In his twofold ethical system he argues that there are also derivative norms; they are based upon interests that are accepted by the whole community. But why should we assume at all that there is a consensus in these matters? As said above, it seems rational to demand that a consensus should follow from the truth—but it is by no means clear why this should be the case in questions of practical cooperation. The interests of people might simply be too selfish for them to be in possible concord with the interests of others. What guarantee do we have that the consensus is a possible regulating idea in this respect? There is no reason to assume that a consensus demands that people circumscribe their own interests to the extent that their remaining interests are acceptable to everyone. This is different in the case of theoretical reason, where the idea of mutually excluding truths seems inappropriate; truth is not dependent on contingencies. But it seems against all empirical evidence to assume that interests are not mutually exclusive.

As far as I can see, these objections to the consensus theory of truth cannot be answered satisfactorily within Apel's own terms.

What about Apel's arguments for a universal language-game? For a start, Apel does not show that Wittgenstein's argument is right, he simply presupposes it. This is rather unfortunate because of the deep controversy surrounding the validity of the private-language argument.[16] But even if we take the impossibility of private languages for granted, and also Wittgenstein's thesis that language-games alone can provide

---

[16] Kuhlmann (1985: 150–60) defends the contention that private languages are impossible. His argument runs as follows: (1) We cannot assume that there are things which cannot be recognized or thought in principle, because any such claim is either wrong or meaningless. If the claim means that that there is something whose existence can be checked in some other way, then the claim is self-contradictory and thus wrong. If, on the other hand, there is no criterion by which the existence of something might ever be checked, then the claim is meaningless: 'to exist' could mean anything. (2) The same is true for private languages. We can only talk about them in a meaningful way (for example, about their possibility or impossibility) if we can recognize them. To identify something as a language means to analyse it as a rule-governed way of behaving which, in turn, is only possible if we (in our language) can identify those rules that govern this behaviour. But then it follows that nothing can be identified as a language if it is not possible to translate it into a public language. (3) It follows immediately that we cannot judge the possibility of something being a private language without recognizing that it is a language in the first place. But then to claim meaningfully 'P speaks a private language' requires that other rational beings can analyse this allegedly private language and recognize it as a rule-governed behaviour. Hence it is no longer an inaccessible private language.

Indeed Kuhlmann is right that language as a 'rule-governed behaviour' requires that it must have some regularity (or at least some *regular irregularity*—which would be a rule of the second order). The person who uses this language might proceed in a very obscure way by changing the rules and generating new ones all the time. So long as these rules are transparent for him it must be possible *in principle* to give an account of these underlying regularities. However, there might be many practical difficulties which would make it impossible ever to find these rules and thus arrive at a translation—which jeopardizes Kuhlmann's argument for the present purpose. It could still be that we have nonetheless good reasons to assume that it is a language (cf. e.g. the Phaistos Disc and Linear A in Crete).

meaning, a serious problem remains concerning Apel's need for a *universal* language-game. According to Wittgenstein, meaning is only given to a community of speakers who share a form of life—but this is for him always a group much smaller than the universal community. In fact, Wittgenstein even considers this universal community impossible. Against this, Apel has argued powerfully (1965: 92; 1972a; 1972b: 320)—and Kuhlmann agrees—that there must be a transcendental universal language-game, because otherwise claims like the ones by Wittgenstein, which are supposed to be about all languages, would be impossible. This seems right, but it does not help, because it does not follow that *any* use of language is directed towards the universal community; only some very special discourse about all other language-games. In order to avoid the problems of a private language, in most cases it would be enough if only a large group of people so directed their language use. It is therefore not shown that every use of reason implies the acknowledgement of those rules that constitute a universal community (or language-game). There is a similar difficulty with Apel's supportive argument that any interaction with someone implies the acknowledgement of a shared language-game with that person. The problem with this argument is that I might simply refuse to interact with many people. Again, why should I be bound by rules of or for a linguistic community that I do not enter? The fact that I *could* enter it with every human being does not seem to carry sufficient weight. Only if there were a categorical demand that I should interact with everyone would I be obliged to follow the rules that are constitutive for this universal interaction.

In brief, it is not clear how Apel or Kuhlmann can derive their claim to *universal* rule observance in all forms of reasoning and acting from the mere fact that these activities are language-based.

3.5.2. *The Limited Scope of the End-in-Itself Formula*

There is a second problem which results from the first and which cannot be answered satisfactorily. I question whether Apel and Kuhlmann can show that we must treat *all* others as ends in themselves. Following the definition articulated above, it is a crucial condition of any system of 'moral' rules that it refers to everybody. Such a condition of universal respect is certainly seen by Apel and Kuhlmann as one of the most fundamental moral requirements. Let us examine more carefully the particular notion of respect which results from their reasoning.

According to Apel and Kuhlmann, without this universal respect reason's task would not be fulfilled. It is only in the ideal community of universal mutual respect that truth can be found. However, contrary to the conclusions its proponents wish to draw, it would seem that on the basis of the argument from discourse we have to respect others only *in so far as they are potential participants in this debate* and *not* because they must be regarded as ends in themselves. In other words, the need is not to respect *them* but to respect their *contribution* to the discourse.

It must be admitted that this is a special case of an instrumental use of respect. An agent who considers other people instrumentally in this way must see himself in the same light, and thus does not use only others for his own purpose but rather uses them as much as himself for a common end—consensus or the quest for the ideal community. But this does not change the fundamental structure; ideologists do exactly the same by seeing all people (including themselves) as instruments for the purpose of a common end.

Apel defends himself by contending that discourse only takes place when we treat others *as if* they were ends in themselves. But the crucial difference seems to remain. The objection could be raised at a second level: that the 'treatment of others as ends' would still seem *itself* to be instrumentalized, toward the aim of debate or discourse. And this, one might argue, would lend a rather cynical cast to the enterprise. I would endeavour to make other people believe that I respect them solely in order to use them (secretly) for another purpose at a *second* level. Apel attempts to counter this objection as follows: He claims that it is simply impossible to use someone as a means of discourse and simultaneously respect him as an end in himself. As he writes (1980: 262):

[It] is not Kant's argument—that even devils who can use their intellect can, in principle, behave 'dutifully'—which is relevant, but rather the argument that even devils must behave dutifully if they wish to partake of the truth . . . This means that the devil, inasmuch as he desired to be a member of the community of argumentation would for ever more have to behave towards its members (i.e. all rational beings) as if he had overcome egoism and, consequently, himself. The instrumentalist reservation that we assumed in his case loses its significance here since it cannot basically be verified.

Thus, according to Apel, the present objection is beside the point, since the nature of discourse requires exactly that we should respect the other person as an end in himself, and not merely exploit him as a strategic ally. Any (even hidden) strategic use would destroy the true debate. This is all morality demands and all it can *rightly* demand.

This argument is difficult to reject. It is indeed questionable whether one can find any *relevant* meaning that we could give to the (additional) demand that we must not only *treat* but also *regard* others as ends in themselves.[17] But even if we grant that it is sufficient to treat others as ends in themselves, the argument from discourse fails to show that we must indeed treat *everyone* and *on all occasions* as ends in themselves. This is so because whenever there is a conflict between the ultimate end of discourse and the notion of respect towards others, the discourse would have to come first. This has three unpleasant results.

First, the goal of an ideal discourse would tell us whom we should and whom we should not respect. If, as argued above, the proponents of the argument cannot show that *everyone* is an equal participant in the discourse, then someone who might never be a participant of any importance (so-called marginal agents) would *not* be sufficiently covered by this demand. There will always be some who simply cannot contribute anything to the discourse (such as severely mentally handicapped people). Why, to give another example, teach the stupid rather than putting all of our resources into educating the gifted? It is surely more likely that we might come to new and 'most important arguments and points of view' by supporting some rather than others.

Secondly, if the end is the participation in the discourse, the way we treat other people will depend on this end. Thus, we might have to treat others rather disrespectfully on occasion if it helps us to reach this consensus. A. Phillips-Griffiths is well aware of this problem when he writes: 'if one of the parties to the discussion were a less enthusiastic disputant than the other it would be rational for his fellow to beat him mercilessly until he agreed to carry on' (1957–8: 116).[18] In addition, we

---

[17] A critic of Apel could argue that it is insufficient to *treat* others as ends in themselves in all applicable respects without also *thinking* of them as such in some further way. But this will not do. The demand to 'think' of others will add nothing of importance if the 'treatment' of others includes anything whatsoever which can have bearing on actions and the discourse. Further, if Apel and Kuhlmann are right and any meaningful *thought* requires an orientation towards the universal intersubjective community (and to all others as its participants), then it seems superfluous to formulate the allegedly distinct demand to 'think' of others as ends in themselves.

[18] A. Phillips-Griffiths has proposed an argument for the justification of 'ultimate moral norms' (1967) which is very similar to Apel's and Kuhlmann's. His critique is mainly directed against his own approach and intended to mark its limits.

might ask why we should treat them as ends even if we know that it will not make any difference to our search for the truth. Why, for example, should we respect them in extreme situations where we are sure that this will not foster any further discourse? Consider the case of a comatose person who is going to die?

Thirdly, one might even wonder why anyone should respect anyone else in the ideal community. If all truth has been found, further respect for others will not serve any morally demanded end. If Apel claims that the continuation of this community in time is an important moral end, then this needs a further argument; it does not follow from the aim of truth.

Against this objection one might want to argue that we have to avoid the risk of the argument being based upon power or personal considerations *at any price* and that we can never be sure whether someone or some situation is of no importance to the discourse. There is, so this defence goes, no limit in principle and thus a *minimal* chance will always remain that the other person, even the marginal agent, might yet contribute to the discourse (cf. Kuhlmann 1985: 198, 206–7).

But this response is not sufficient. The argument cannot cover *all* other human beings in the same way. In particular, it will not include the weaker participants in situations where we have to make a choice between them and stronger participants. This is so because the 'risk' of losing some information can be absolutely minimal and, in some cases, even nil. To emphasize that we can never be sure is not a strong argument: in practice, we can be pretty sure or at least sure enough to ignore some people entirely. The able and participating people should therefore be highly privileged as long as our resources are limited (and as long as we are not in the ideal community). Hence it seems that it is exactly in those situations where moral demands are of the highest relevance, when we are dealing with people who cannot contribute anything, that the principle of Apel and Kuhlmann garners the smallest force. Those who need the special concern of moral demands seem placed at the very edge of discourse ethics.

To sum up: since they cannot demonstrate the firm link between (or identity of) reason and truth on the one side and *universal* consensus on the other, I cannot see how Apel and Kuhlmann's argument could serve as the basis for an ethics which establishes a universal, inclusive, and equal respect for other people.

3.6. GENERAL CONCLUSION: WHAT MORAL REALISM MUST ACHIEVE

In this chapter I have investigated the argument from discourse as an example of a retorsive transcendental argument in the service of moral realism. I have concentrated on Apel's and Kuhlmann's version, which I believe is the most fully articulated and at least partially successful. Starting from the notion of 'reasoning', they strive to justify *some* normative judgements which are necessarily implied by any use of reason—most importantly that there is truth and that every reasoner must aim at it. There is no way of rejecting this claim. Although it would have been desirable if they had made this point more clearly, I have argued that they can also show that rational reflection discloses that reason has a normative dimension to it. Every person (*qua* reasoner) is committed to an appreciation of truth as a worthwhile end (in some way and at least for him) which demands support. The argument does not fall into the naturalistic fallacy in any blatant way.

However, as it stands, the argument from discourse shows two closely related weaknesses. First, and most importantly, it cannot demonstrate that the normative notion of reason (and the retorsive transcendental argument starting from reason) is inseparably linked to *universal* intersubjectivity. Although the rational agent is committed to making some normative judgements, these judgements are not about a good for *everyone*. Secondly, the respect towards other agents is not based upon the direct attribution of value to *them*. They are only respected as participants in the discourse. In contrast to Apel and Kuhlmann, I can see many cases where—against our moral intuitions—instead of respect, disregard and scorn follow from their argument (where some agents are not relevant to the discourse). Given the definition above, these resulting judgements do not qualify as 'moral'. The argument from discourse might provide a basis for some 'normative realism', but it seems a rather odd one. We would have a *very* different form of ethical system than we had hoped for.

To make this point clear: I don't think that the *authority* of the resulting judgements is limited, as O'Neill argues in her version of an argument from discourse.[19] She restricts the authority of the resulting

---

[19] Structurally, her transcendental argument is of the retorsive type. The starting-point is secured by the impossibility of denying it: 'it cannot be questioned, because intelligible ques-

demands (though she calls them 'categorical imperatives') to those with a will to be rational and to cooperate with others, and sees the entire project as being 'anti-foundationalist' (1989: p. x). According to O'Neill, the authority of reason is self-imposed by autonomous participants in the debate and does not go further. Against this, Apel and Kuhlmann rightly argue that any such rational limitation of the authority is itself an affirmation of the authority of reason and thus inconsistent: every reasoner must grant reason—and thus all the normative implications of reason—full, categorical authority, even for those who have not yet become aware of it. The problem is rather that the *content* of these demands remains limited. All they can show is that every reasoner must evaluate his or her reasoning as being right or true, but they cannot conclude that this implies a universal respect towards all other reasoners *tout court*. Their basis, albeit categorical (since uncircumventable), is too weak to support a *moral* imperative.

A final comment must be made. One might want to defend the step towards universality by recourse to some further argument. After all, 'truth' is not an abstract entity or good, but a property of a propositional formula—truth (and falsity) is predicated of judgements (or propositions).

tioning presumes the very authority it seeks to question. Although the great architectonic is a plan for a human edifice, it is not one we can coherently reject; were we to do so we would be left disoriented nomads, condemned to solitary and thoughtless silence' (1989: 42). According to O'Neill (and very much in accordance with Apel), reason is ultimately seen as communicative and thus 'reason's authority must . . . be seen as a practical and collective task, like that of constituting practical authority' (1989: 18). She sees reason as a self-grounding process, which can be understood as a form of debate which receives its authority recursively by its intrinsic openness towards criticism. Full authority, for O'Neill, is only achieved if the potential criticism of all people is included—and this is the step towards intersubjectivity. Here the criticism raised against Apel and Kuhlmann is also applicable: it will not lead to a situation where it is necessary to respect *all* other people.

It should be noted that O'Neill herself sees her argument as a version of Kant's (called an 'explorational transcendental argument' above). This is unconvincing for two reasons. First, it seems implausible to build on to Kant's irreflexive transcendental philosophy a retorsive argument. Reason as a self-grounding process is not his understanding of 'Vernunft' (cf. Aschenberg 1978: 319). Secondly, it might further be questioned whether O'Neill's reading grasps the way Kant understood 'practical reason'. In general, he conceives the role of the other participants in a debate more as a method to *check* the results of reason, rather than to ground them or its authority. He frequently notes that it is the subjective touchstone of objective truth to ask whether something can be communicated with others and whether other rational beings have to agree (*CPuR* B 848). For Kant, this possible agreement is the consequence of something being true, but he denies explicitly that it is the *foundation* of truth or of knowledge. (For an interpretation of Kant similar to O'Neill's see W. Hogrebe 1974: 187–99.)

Thus, one might argue, to evaluate truth implies the evaluation of the *reasoner* who is capable of making true judgements *simply because there can be no truth without him*. If the argument from discourse shows a categorical orientation towards 'truth' on the side of any reasoner *qua* reasoner, then, so one might argue, this result can also be expressed as a categorical demand to respect oneself as the necessary (transcendental) condition for the 'support' of truth. An argument by analogy can be added. With respect to judgements and truth no one seems to be in any privileged position. Hence we must respect others as much as ourselves—'for how could he think that he alone has any claims?' (as R. S. Peters writes in the context of his similar argument (1966: 171)).

The difference between this argument and Apel's reasoning is obvious: he sees reason as a discourse, which is ultimately an enterprise of universal participation. That means that from the possibility of reason and truth we conclude the demand for a consensus, which entails the demand for universal respect. The present argument would proceed from reason and truth directly to the required respect of reasoners, first at the individual level (a single reasoner understands the importance and value of *him* making true judgements) and then, by analogy, at the universal level. If this argument can be used to support universal respect, it would no longer require any understanding of reason as a *discourse*. We would have gained a very different retorsive transcendental argument. A. Gewirth has proposed an argument for a fundamental moral principle, which goes some way in this direction. We will now examine his argument in some detail.

CHAPTER 4

The Argument from Agency

4.1. GEWIRTH'S ATTEMPT TO FOUND ETHICS ON THE IMPLICATIONS OF AGENCY

4.1.1. *A Short Survey of this Chapter*

In this chapter I wish to turn to a further transcendental argument, which has been developed by Alan Gewirth in recent years.[1] His 'Dialectically Necessary Method', as he calls it, is designed to provide a justification for fundamental moral principles on the basis of the implications of human agency. According to Gewirth, all agents are committed to making some judgements 'on the basis of what is necessarily involved in their actions' (1981: 44). Gewirth's aim is not to detect factual judgements about the structure of agency, but right from the beginning to detect judgements about the way agents must place positive value in the world. The methodological core of his proof is that to deny certain agent-related evaluations is only possible, as he puts it, 'on pain of self-contradiction' (ibid. 26–7).

In order to investigate whether Gewirth provides a basis for the foundation of moral realism, I shall proceed as follows. In this section (4.1) I will give a brief account of what I consider to be his reasoning. This will partly be a restructuring of the argument in the light of our investigation, and so the argument will be presented in somewhat modified terms. In Section 4.2 I will investigate whether the argument from agency is a promising basis for moral realism. A short analysis of the structure of the argument follows (4.3), as a preparation for a criticism of his achievements (4.4). Ultimately, it seems that Gewirth fails to solve a

---

[1] Mainly in his book *Reason and Morality* (1981) and in many articles thereafter (e.g. Regis (ed.) 1984). Two excellent monographs on Gewirth's argument have been published in recent years: Beyleveld (1991) and Steigleder (1992a). They provide an extensive bibliography of Gewirth's works and publications about his ethics up to 1992.

problem that is very similar to that of the argument from discourse. Or so I will argue.

4.1.2. Preliminary Remarks about Free Agency as Gewirth's Starting-Point

What is a free action? For Gewirth 'action' must be understood as freely chosen, intentional behaviour—it is done in order to achieve a purpose voluntarily selected by the agent (1981: 22, 26–7). Thus, whenever someone chooses and realizes a course of affairs for purposes he wants to attain, we can consider him to act. These two structural aspects, the voluntary and the intentional character of actions, are called by Gewirth the 'generic features' (ibid. 25) of his description of action. It will soon become clear that it does not matter that it will not always be possible to give a clear and uncontroversial account of a particular action. Actions are not always sharply distinguished from each other or categorized; they can overlap, be incomplete, and consist of different, more elementary ones. A neutral and all-satisfying account of what we actually do (or let happen) at a certain moment is presumably impossible. But it is not necessary for Gewirth. In a similar way, the freedom for and within particular actions will hardly be understood completely. Notwithstanding these inevitable unclarities, for the present purpose it is sufficient to presuppose the rather minimal understanding of free intentional actions: someone is considered to act intentionally when he does something for some purpose but could have done something else (cf. ibid. 27).

Since actions are intentional events, they must be performed consciously, at least in a minimal sense. Although sometimes one acts without any conscious reflection, at least some awareness that one is the subject of an action is needed in order to pursue an end. This does not imply that we therefore have any 'experience' of ourselves, but we must see that the actions are in some way connected with us as their origin. In a Kantian fashion, one could say that some 'I act' must be connected with any action very much in the way the 'I think' is present in every experience (more accurately, in every synthesis). We are, as we might express it, in the privileged position of being the point of reference of what we do.

This notion of being the subject of one's actions is closely connected with our view of freedom; it is important that we understand ourselves as able to act freely. The degree of freedom that we attribute to agents will obviously differ from situation to situation, but this does not matter. As said before, it is sufficient to employ a minimal understanding of freedom: all it means is that one acts in a certain way and could have done otherwise (problematic as this logical predicate is) or could have chosen not to act at all. (This point is not explicitly stated by Gewirth, but given with his argument; cf. Steigleder 1992a: 121 ff.)

This definition of free agency also marks the starting-point of Gewirth's transcendental argument. It can be stated as follows: 'We are free prospective purposive agents'—or, as Gewirth's puts it: 'I do X for purpose E' (1981: 49).

One might ask whether this is indeed indubitable. This question can be raised in two ways: do we *act* at all? And, more specifically, do we act *freely*?

How can the first thesis, that we are agents, be secured? For the most part, Gewirth argues that he is a 'foundationalist' with regard to this starting-point—he simply considers it self-evident and logically necessary for an agent to see himself as such (1984: 192–3). According to Gewirth, this 'foundationalism' is unproblematic, since the first claim is not itself a moral principle. This reading would bring Gewirth's reasoning close to the explorational type of transcendental argument. However, there are also some rudimentary apagogic arguments that foster this first claim. We have no choice, Gewirth says, but to be agents. Although we can choose our particular action, agency in general is not something that could be rejected, because even omissions are, according to Gewirth, actions if they are a chosen form of behaviour. This does not mean that human beings act all the time, but that their status is not ad lib—to have the disposition to act (which means to be agents) is indispensable (1981: 111 ff.). Beyleveld (1991: 118) in his elaborated defence of Gewirth's argument speaks about a 'phenomenological necessity' and writes: 'We can't categorically know that we are PPAs [prospective purposive agents]. However, the phenomenology of our ... agency makes it, in practice, impossible to assume that we are not' (ibid.).

What about Gewirth's second claim about the *freedom* of agency—are we 'free' agents? One might defend it rather pragmatically on the basis of the purpose of the philosophical investigation. Gewirth describes exactly the kind of action that is relevant for practical philosophy: he is interested in free behaviour as the addressee of practical precepts. No philosophical investigation in ethics makes sense unless we take it for granted that we are such self-determining agents. If there are other forms of behaviour, which are done out of compulsion without showing both or either of the two essential features, they are simply not under the authority of rules and norms. As Beyleveld notes: 'Within the context of the question guiding his enterprise, Gewirth's definitions of agency and related concepts are not arbitrary, but logically necessary' (1991: 68).[2] In addition, there is strong practical evidence for considering ourselves free agents: we have no choice other than to see ourselves in this light whenever we must act. Obviously, this basis of practical evidence is not an *explanation* of what reasons and free agency are and how they operate. But independently of the rather metaphysical debate about their ontology, there seems to be a sufficiently clear meaning which we can give to freedom as self-determination in contrast to compulsive agency.[3] So even if Gewirth cannot give an irrefutable justification for the inception of free agency, it seems fair enough to take practical reasoning (namely, that it is unavoidable to see ourselves as such when we act) as a sufficiently strong foundation.

---

[2] See also Steigleder 1992a: 123. Does this take things too facilely? From the fact that practical principles need these addressees, it does not follow that they exist. The entire enterprise could simply be vain (see also R. Trigg's criticism of Gewirth's argument (1980: 151)). The freedom of agency, namely that anyone could have acted otherwise, might be questioned as our common illusion, which merely mellows the firm reign of causality in the world (cf. Pothast 1987). There is, so the determinist says, ultimately always compulsion and never freedom. But this objection goes far beyond the domain of our investigation. Hudson remarks quite rightly that it would be 'less than fair' to dismiss Gewirth's argument on the basis of his account of agency: 'At the very least, Gewirth is entitled to raise the issue of what follows if the generic features of action are what we normally take them to be' (1984: 112).

[3] It should be noted that it seems possible to defend Gewirth's argument even within the limits of an ontological determinism so long as a sufficiently strong distinction between self-determination and coercion etc. is maintained. This has been done by Beyleveld (1991: 69, 118). This attempt is not absolutely unique in moral philosophy. There are some interesting philosophical systems which, although they accept the categorical distinction between reasons and causes, still consider it possible to connect a rational moral realism with a full determinism. They see no contradiction between the features of reason and the validity of strict, determining laws underlying the world (cf. e.g. Leibniz). The main difficulty of these systems is whether they can provide a meaningful notion of 'responsibility' within the ultimately determined world. The strength of these approaches is that they have few difficulties with the motivational thesis of moral realism, i.e. the question of how 'reasons' should be of physical importance within an energetically closed world. If causes and reasons do not belong to two entirely separated realms, their correspondence will be more transparent.

4.1.3. The Positive Evaluation of the Ends of our Actions

As already mentioned, Gewirth tries to analyse implicit evaluations which accompany our self-understanding as free agents. The first positive value judgement which Gewirth identifies is that every agent must place some value on the end of his actions. This follows from the free intentionality of every action. It allows us to conclude that the agent has not only favoured one state of affairs in comparison with others but has also *practically confirmed* this choice by performing an action leading to this end. Thus, the action itself is the realization of a practical pro-attitude towards the chosen end. This pro-attitude can also be seen as an implicit value judgement of the agent. Gewirth pinpoints this result by stressing three essential aspects of actions, all of which demonstrate that it is appropriate to talk about an underlying positive value judgement. First, every action reveals a *selective attention* towards an end. Secondly, it shows a *directedness of an agent* towards something as an aim. And, thirdly, it expresses the agent's *active interest* in achieving the aim (1981: 40). There are, of course, actions which do not have a distinct goal. In such cases, the agent places value in the action itself if he performs it and could have done otherwise. Hence, the analysis and the connected argument would work as well (cf. ibid. 27).

Actions are crucially different from being mere preferences and the difference lies precisely in the fact that they are practical. There are forms of expressing freely chosen preferences other than acting, such as desiring, wishing, or wanting something, but they lack the additional element of the *practical affirmation* of a choice. This is also why actions can be construed as implicit positive value judgements without at the same time falling into the same trap of a naturalistic fallacy as J. S. Mill did in his foundation of utilitarianism (at least on a certain reading). Gewirth does *not* argue that because we desire something we therefore see the state of affairs manifested by us acting on our desire as (objectively) desir*able*. By being *freely chosen practical* realizations of some states of affairs, actions express a restricted amount of practical approval at the moment of action. This aspect of a wilful practical affirmation alone allows us to see how a value judgement could be involved. We have approved of some desire and have decided to act upon it.[4]

---

[4] NB: 'approval' is here used in a very restricted sense—we can surely act upon a desire (and thereby approve of it) though we disapprove of this desire otherwise. That's why Gewirth can reject the critique of Bond (1980a, 1980b), who argues that 'To desire, even to crave a thing, is not necessarily to see it as good' (Bond 1980a: 44).

However, as Gewirth writes, the reach of this judgement is limited. It is only that the agent (implicitly) regards the object of his action as 'having sufficient value to merit his trying to attain it' (1984: 204). Nothing more has been shown so far. We can express this result as a normative judgement from the I-perspective:

(1) *I make at least a restricted positive value judgement about the end of my particular actions.*

(It should be mentioned that this, as well as the following judgements, with the exception of judgement (9), is my reconstruction of Gewirth's reasoning and not stated by him explicitly.)

The result can also be remodelled as a descriptive judgement about agents:

(2) *Everyone who acts freely and intentionally makes at least a restricted positive value judgement about the end of his particular actions.*

Gewirth's analysis is highly accurate about what has been achieved: the agent does not see anything objectively 'good' in his end but makes a more modest evaluation. That is why the following critique by B. Williams does not jeopardize Gewirth's argument:

In any ordinary understanding of *good*, surely, an extra step is taken if you go from saying that you want something or have decided to pursue it to saying that it is good, or (more to the point) that it is good that you should have it. The idea of something's being good imports an idea, however minimal or hazy, of a perspective in which it can be acknowledged by more than one agent as good. (1985: 58)

Since judgements (1) and (2) remain strictly within the standpoint of the agent, Gewirth does not have to bother about this allegation. All he has concluded is that the agent must make a normative judgement about the end of his actions in the most minimal sense; he must see it as of positive value *for him*. At this point, Gewirth's argument does not need to introduce any external perspective.

It is important to emphasize that the result is independent of any theory of *how* things can have the character of being values or *why* they are seen as such by the agent. That is, an implicit positive value judgement of this type can be based on all kinds of reasons or even on no reason at all.[5] An agent might hold as a reason either the search for plea-

---

5 This is of, of course, a question of terminology. One might call desires or impulses and

sure and the avoidance of pain, or a more highly thought-out reason. The judgement is not yet about objective values or goods and therefore not open to an attack such as Moore's open-question test. As Gewirth writes, the value need not be moral, but will vary according to the criteria upon which the agent acts.

Further, it must be added that nothing can be concluded from one particular implied value judgement of an agent about other particular judgements he might make implicitly or explicitly. The value judgements implied in an individual action are independent of one another in the same way that actions are. It is therefore possible that action-based value judgements of different actions of the same agent might be contradictory. In addition, these restricted evaluations might contradict additional and separate, stronger values that an agent actually holds (cf. ibid. 51). It is by no means asserted that the agent must see his purpose as 'good' *tout court*, absolutely or in the light of further criteria. In this case, we might despise someone or even ourselves for such a weakness of the will; that is, in not doing what we otherwise consider to be good. And we would not consider either him or ourselves to be a consistent 'moral' agent if either he or we acted in this way. Some overall consistency of one's positive values seems to be a necessary part of any characterization of a 'moral' agent (cf. G. Taylor 1985: 108–41). Yet, despite this, he or we would still be proper 'agents'.

In addition, the thesis does not imply that it is always possible to identify the exact underlying valuation. The difficulty of this analysis is closely connected with the general problem of giving an exact account of 'action' or 'purpose' (cf. Anscombe 1957; Searle 1983). The purpose of an action can be the action itself or some outcome, such as, for example, pleasure arising from a satisfied desire or from the performed action itself. Furthermore, valuations can be mediated: some end of an action might be valued because it leads to a further, indirect end—or something is merely selected as the better of two rather unpleasant alternatives. In many cases we will find overlapping or muddled evaluations, rudimentary ones, or irrational, inconsistent ones (e.g. when something is done because the agent wrongly assumes that it serves a certain end). All of this is possible but does not jeopardize the results (1) and (2).

---

even the capricious motivation (e.g. 'I just want to do it, full stop.') the *reason* to have chosen this action. Given this (odd) terminology, then every action is by definition reason-based. In the present context, however, reason is used in the richer, traditional sense.

It must be emphasized that for judgement (2) to be right it is not necessary that the agent be aware of judgement (1), nor that he makes judgement (1) explicitly against what Bond seems to assume (cf. 1980a: 44). All that is required is a minimal awareness of acting consciously, in so far as one sees oneself as the determining subject of the action. This is enough to conclude (2); namely, that the *implied* positive value judgement is structurally (and undeniably) part of every intentional action.[6] Gewirth writes:

> To the extent to which such practical thinking is attributable, and to some extent necessarily attributable, to the agent who performs actions ... to the same extent linguistic expressions or judgements are also attributable to him. This does not mean that he necessarily speaks aloud or mutters to himself vocally, but rather that in acting and thinking as he does the agent uses or makes judgements that can be expressed in words. To say that they are expressible is not, of course, to say that they are actually expressed. (1981: 42)

But what about someone who acts intentionally to achieve evil? This person seems to regard his purpose as bad and is moved by exactly *this* feature of his action (cf. Puolimatka: 1989, 58–9). Gewirth can discard the case of the diabolical as well. Even here, the diabolic agent must see something worth pursuing in the end, something positive to this extent. Although he might consider the end as evil in the light of different criteria, the fact that he has chosen to act upon it reveals that he pragmatically attributes a positive value to the support of this evil. A similar point has already been made by Plato in his *Meno* (77b ff.). He rejects the possibility that someone might do something because he aims at something which he disregards.

---

[6] That is why Heslep's (1986) objection that Gewirth's argument would not cover the case of capricious actions misses the point. Heslep argues that on occasion agents can have a purpose for no reason, or arbitrarily. And, as he objects (ibid. 382), though these desires might not compel the agent to behave in a certain way but are freely chosen, they do not involve any esteem and thus no evaluation of the purpose of the action. This objection misreads Gewirth's argument: the case of capricious actions does not create a counter example because his argument does not presuppose reasons reflected upon for choosing actions in the first place. His aim is to look for implicit value judgements 'made' pragmatically by choosing a certain purpose. For this pragmatic dimension it does not matter why some purpose is selected. Obviously, not every agent has proper reasons for his purposes, and sometimes they will only be 'reasons of caprice' (as Heslep calls them himself ibid. 387)). In all these cases, the agent has still decided to act for some purposes and thereby subscribed to judgement (1) pragmatically. His action reveals the preference of the chosen end over all alternatives— whatever the pursuer might think about its value otherwise (cf. Beyleveld 1991: 71–4).

Unsurprisingly, Gewirth's result has many prominent philosophical antecedents, which also state that agents see some good in the purpose for which they are acting. However, other philosophers are not always so conscious of the limits to the evaluation as Gewirth is.[7] Gewirth's further contribution is to emphasize that the positive value judgement owes its self-evident character to the fact that it is included in the notion of agency. To act *means* to support some end practically—and 'to support some end' can be reformulated as the practical expression of a pro-attitude. Judgement (1) simply translates an aspect of a meaningful event (an action) into meaningful words. Gewirth himself calls the inference 'true by virtue of meanings' (1981: 173) and labels it as 'analytic' (ibid. 171–7). He argues that this is possible because in the case of their agency 'persons can conceptually understand extralinguistic properties and make linguistic classifications based on that understanding' (ibid. 174–5).[8] Thereby the presupposed definition of agency is not seen as arbitrary or merely conventional, but as an appropriate account of what agency really is. As he writes: 'The analysis of the concept of action is not to be regarded as yielding results that are merely "conceptual" as opposed to "real"' (1981: 29).

Gewirth defends his result against Hume's important prohibition as follows: A normative judgement from the I-perspective remains restricted in its validity and is therefore only about what 'seems' good to the agent. It is not an assertoric claim about what 'is' good. 'The position is hence not subject to attack from the usual version of the "open question" test: even if E is someone's purpose, something he wants or values, it still makes sense to ask whether E is good. For the test to apply here, it

---

[7] Aristotle works in the *Nicomachean Ethics* with a similar idea when he argues that all our activities aim at happiness, which is later interpreted as a good. But he does not always distinguish sharply between something that a subject sees as good and some objective good. The scholastic tradition followed Aristotle and held that: 'omne appetitum appetitur sub specie boni'. Leibniz writes: 'Il y a toujours une raison prévalente qui porte la volonté à son choix . . . Jamais la volonté n'est portée à agir que par la représentation du bien, qui prévaut aux représentations contraires'—the will is always moved to act by the idea of something being 'good' (1996: 274). Kant, to name just one more, also ascribes to an implicit positive evaluation, though in different terms. He insists that every action must be free and intentional, hence have an end (e.g. *KGS* V. 385) and that this end is not neutral for the agent (cf. *Religion*, *KGS* VI. 7 f.). Here he is close to Gewirth in not assuming an objective evaluation.

[8] Cf. G. Lycan (1969: 140), who criticizes Gewirth on the basis that any analytic reading would make his result 'stipulative, or definitional, or otherwise purely linguistic (true by convention)'. That this is not necessarily the case, because it depends on the source of the 'meaning' of words, has been argued by Gewirth and by Beyleveld (1991: 116–18).

would have to make sense to ask whether E *seems* good to the person whose purpose it is' (ibid: 51). And, Gewirth says, *this* question has been answered by his argument. So there is no point in raising it further.

4.1.4. The Necessity to Evaluate one's Freedom to Act

The next, crucial step in a Gewirthian analysis is to show that the present result leads to further and much stronger positive value judgements; namely, that every agent *necessarily* places positive value in his *general freedom to act*—a very big step from the rather modest first result, whose scope is strictly limited to the moment of acting. The reasoning for this contention can be divided into two parts:

(3) While I act I must make a positive value judgement about the freedom to perform the action.

(4) I must make a positive value judgement about my freedom to perform actions in general.

Let us turn to Gewirth's argument for judgement (3). He writes:

The agent's positive evaluation extends not only to his particular purpose but also a fortiori to the generic features that characterize all his actions. These features hence constitute, in his view, what I shall call *generic goods*. Since his action is a means of attaining something he regards as good, even if this is only the performance of the action itself, he regards as a necessary good the voluntariness or freedom that is an essential feature of his action, for without this he would not be able to act for any purpose or good at all. The freedom thus valued consists both in his controlling each of his particular behaviours by his unforced choice and his longer-range ability to exercise such control. (1981: 52)

Gewirth's argument proceeds in two steps. The first step states that we have not only a pro-attitude towards the *ends* of our actions but also to the *performance* itself (i). In the second step Gewirth argues that freedom is an 'essential feature' of any acting.[9] That's why it would be incomprehensible not to transfer the value which we place in the action to the freedom to act (ii).

---

[9] The freedom to act is not itself freely chosen (as we can learn from Kant's struggle in the *Religion*, *KGS* VI). It is a meaningless redundancy to say that we are free to act freely. Thus, we do *not* affirm freedom's value by taking a practical, freely chosen pro-attitude towards our freedom in the same way we take a pro-attitude towards the ends of our actions. Freedom is the crucial feature for acting: if we are not free to act in a certain way, we cannot perform the action. And it is *thus* that we cannot place positive value in an end, and an action as the chosen pro-attitude towards this end, without placing the same value in the freedom to have been able to act in the particular way.

His argument for (i) goes as follows: the same reasoning which allows us to detect an implicit value judgement about the end of an action must also hold for the action itself. If we affirm some state of affairs through a certain action, then the chosen practical pro-attitude itself, i.e. the action, is also approved of to the same extent. If someone has drunk a glass of Muscat to enjoy its taste, then he had at one stage also a pro-attitude towards the act of drinking, because otherwise he would not have done it. This does not mean that *all* possible pro-attitudes towards valued ends are necessarily seen as having positive values. We can disapprove of some means although they may help to bring about a state of affairs which we value—concrete means are not analytically given with any end, as Kant reminds us; we only know them empirically (*KGS* IV. 417). However, if someone does act then this pro-attitude is obviously itself chosen as an appropriate means, used by the agent for achieving his aim. One might object that people often choose means they despise as the only ones possible to achieve a certain end. But even then the action as a means has been seen as sufficiently appropriate to serve the end at the moment of acting because it has been preferred to the alternative of remaining passive.

What about the second step of the argument (ii)? According to Gewirth the freedom to act is evaluated positively whenever we act since *an action is a practical exercise of freedom*. Thus, if judgements (1) and (2) show that we place positive value in the particular pro-attitude (i.e. the end of our action and also the action which we perform) then we can also express this as placing positive value in the particular exercise of freedom (or in having been free to act in a particular way).[10] At this point, it is important to demonstrate that Gewirth's result is not based upon circular reasoning. One might object that an implicit value judgement was detected as the normative structure of actions *because* of it being a freely chosen practical pro-attitude. But do we then conclude from this value judgement that the freedom to perform the act (which has been

---

[10] Korsgaard suggests a related argument (1986*b*) as a reconstruction of a Kantian reasoning. She identifies the freedom of self-determination as the only possible 'source of value' (ibid. 449) for all things to which we attribute real worth: 'we regard some of our ends as good, even though they are obviously conditional; there must be a condition of their goodness, a source of their value; we regard them as good whenever they are chosen with full rational autonomy' (ibid. 500). The deficiency of her argument is the insufficiently strong first premiss: the fact that we place positive value does not of itself simply make the value-placing faculty unconditionally good. It is here, in the more detailed analysis of what is involved in evaluations, that Gewirth's approach is more convincing.

the reason why the action has been valued in the first place) is retrospectively evaluated as well? In other words, freedom seems to give positive value to actions, and seems to be seen as such a value itself because we place this value in actions. This apparent circle, however, misses the point of what the present analysis is supposed to do. There is no circular transfer of positive value from freedom to actions and back to freedom; the task of the analysis is to detect *implicit* value judgements which are present in both. In Gewirth's version of the argument, freedom serves as the crucial indicator for them. We can identify a value judgement implicit in our actions because they are freely chosen. Then we infer from the normative structure of actions that this normativity must also *include* the freedom which finds its expression in the action—hence all these value judgements are implicitly made when someone acts (cf. 1981: 42–7). The possibility of expressing this structure in different value judgements results from the different ways of looking at actions. One can focus upon the end of the action, or upon the action as a particular performance, or upon its being the practical expression of freedom.

What is Gewirth's argument for the generalization of the evaluation of freedom as expressed in judgement (4)? Judgement (1), which we make, is always only within the strict limits of the affirmation, both performative and normative, of the particular action. Judgement (3), as Gewirth argues, is different in an important respect. It is made *whenever we act*—it is universal to all actions. Although to perform an action p implies only placing value in the particular freedom to perform action p, we can abstract from the particular actions and see the general 'voluntariness or freedom' as the 'generic feature' of all actions. This has important consequences for the value judgement (3). The positive evaluation is, according to Gewirth, universal and indispensable for us *qua* agents. It follows directly from the universality of agency—it is, so to speak, the common denominator of all actions. As Gewirth writes: '[T]he agent . . . regards his freedom as intrinsically good, simply because it is an essential component of purposive action and indeed of the very possibility of action' (ibid. 52). Thus, we must make judgement (4), because we must consider ourselves as purposeful agents.

According to Gewirth, the litmus test of the validity of (4) is that, for any consistent agent, this judgement is practically undeniable. There is no performative possibility for agents to refuse to accept this value of freedom and agency. If every action expresses a positive value judgement about freedom, then the only way to avoid implicitly making this judgement seems to be to *cease to act*. But to *freely* choose the practical option of no longer acting freely is, in essence, a practical confirmation of the positive value of freedom. Gewirth illustrates the impossibility of an 'escape from freedom' (ibid. 53–4) with the example of people who put themselves in the hands of a totalitarian institution: 'The persons are still agents at the point where they intentionally give up . . . control' (ibid.). Imagine someone who comes to the conclusion that the freedom to act or to be a free agent is not worthwhile, and who places positive value in being unfree. He could only express this either by arguing against the implicit judgement which he makes (if he does not stop being an agent) or by freely choosing to stop being free (for example, by committing suicide). But both ways of placing value in non-freedom are, once again, *qua* act, practical confirmations of the positive value that they are supposed to deny. Even agents who have succeeded in giving up their freedom entirely do not disprove the argument. The crucial point is that they cannot value anything any more. 'They cease to be agents', as Gewirth writes rather laconically (ibid. 53). The notion of placing value in something becomes meaningless if one is no longer free to do so.

It must be noted that Gewirth travels in several ways beyond judgement (4) above. He argues that agents have to value not only their freedom but also all those things which are 'generically' necessary for freedom, most of all the well-being of the agent. The indispensability of these generic necessities is due to them being the 'most general and proximate necessary conditions of all his purpose-fulfilling actions, so that without his having these conditions his engaging in purposive action would be futile or impossible' (1981: 65). That is why judgement (4) is expanded to:

(5) *I must make a positive value judgement about the freedom to act and about my well-being as the condition for this freedom.*

This step is not without its own problems. Principally, there is difficulty in offering a convincing account of and necessary conditions for freedom (cf. R. Brooks 1981: 293; Mahowald 1980: 447). However, we can disregard these difficulties for the time being, since this is but a small point with respect to our present argument.

Judgement (5) is, as Gewirth makes very clear, still a 'dialectically necessary judgement' (1981: 152) in that it expresses what everyone must judge as a positive value. Judgements (4) and (5) must be 'logically' accepted by every agent (1981: 195) on the basis of his agency. It is, as

Gewirth emphasizes, not an 'assertoric' judgement (1981; 43–4) about what *is* good in an objective sense. That is why this step is supposed to escape the naturalistic fallacy too. The same is true for the next and highly important step.

4.1.5. The 'Prudential-Rights' Claim of Agents

Gewirth draws the conclusion—and this is crucial for his argument—that we necessarily make an ought judgement about our freedom, which he sees as identical with holding that one has a claim to a right (of a special type) to one's freedom and well-being.[11] Let us see how he proceeds. The first judgement to look at is the following:

> (6) *If there are threats to my freedom, etc., then I necessarily regard my freedom to act and my well-being as something which ought not to be restrained.*

This judgement is supposed to follow from the strict necessity to evaluate freedom and well-being spelt out in judgement (5), in addition to the condition that my freedom and well-being might possibly be threatened in the world. What is Gewirth's reasoning for introducing an 'ought' from the I-perspective? Basically, he infers (6) indirectly by arguing that *not* to connect the evaluation with the 'ought' would implicitly state that I *need not* have the freedom to act—which in consequence would contradict the necessary value judgements I make as an agent in general.

Gewirth's argument seem more transparent when we look at what it means to 'value' something. As argued before, even the most restricted positive evaluation can be expressed as the judgement that a pro-attitude towards some state of affairs or course of events is regarded as appropriate. This pro-attitude must have practical implications: in contrast to mere desires, a positive evaluation recommends certain supportive actions of realization or preservation. Thus, any claim of the kind that 'it is acceptable if all practical pro-attitudes to some E are made impossible' contradicts any simultaneous positive evaluation of E (E being someone's purpose: see above). This explains why to accept negative interference with the conditions of agency rebuts judgement (5) and why I cannot see it as 'permissible' (1981: 80) that someone else might interfere

---

[11] At this point, Gewirth's own argumentation is not always clear; he employs a variety of intermixed arguments. In the subsequent reconstruction of the main gist of his reasoning I follow mainly Steigleder (1992a: 159–233).

with my freedom and well-being. In brief, I must regard it as strictly unacceptable and thus it ought not to happen.

Gewirth goes further and argues that we must see ourselves as having a 'prudential right' to be free. It seems that we can put Gewirth's argument to this end as follows: I must categorically oppose any negative interference with my freedom or well-being, because I affirm this freedom implicitly whenever I act. Thus, for me my freedom and well-being are necessary goods and I must regard them as demanding a general pro-attitude. To express such a demand is to talk about a 'right'; according to Gewirth we are entitled to regard ourselves as having this right:

> (7) *As a prospective purposive agent I regard myself as having a right to freedom and well-being.*

(Following Gewirth, I will use 'to claim to have a right' synonymously with 'to regard oneself as having a right' and will call judgement (7) a 'right-claim' on occasion.)

On logical grounds judgement (7) can be stated by every agent. The agent has to recognize that he can make judgement (7) because he is an agent; thus, agency is a sufficient reason for all other agents to make the same judgement. The result can be expressed as judgement (8):

> (8) *All prospective purposive agents regard themselves as having a right to freedom and well-being.*

Gewirth contends that the basis for this claim to a right is still within the limits of the restricted value judgement of the agent perspective and therefore undeniable. It is not yet shown, so Gewirth argues, that 'agents have rights' (in an objective sense), but rather that 'each agent must *claim* or *accept* that he has rights' (1984: 206). Thus, *the agent* must see all others as being obliged to respect his freedom. It has not been shown that *anyone else* must see himself as being so obliged towards this agent; judgement (8) merely states what everyone must regard himself being entitled to.[12]

---

[12] Once again, Gewirth does not argue that everyone will claim (6) or (7) *explicitly*. There will surely be people who, rather, claim the opposite—like the radical sceptic, who sees it as impossible for anyone to claim rights, since there cannot be any. But this person would count as a clear case of inconsistency; he fails to see the judgements that his agency involves. That is why S. K. White's criticism has no force (cf. 1982: 282 ff.). More difficult seems the radical solipsist, who would see any such rights-claim as meaningless, since, according to his worldview, there are no other agents towards whom a right might be claimed. But even he should accept (6) or (7) if a further conditional (which he considers as never to occur) were added: *If*

Let us look more closely at the transfer from positive evaluations to judgements about rights. In a useful discussion of Gewirth's argument Steigleder (1992a: 166) distinguishes three different types of rights. There are 'legal rights' which are established within a political system—something which is obviously different from Gewirth's right-claims. There are also 'moral' rights. But for two reasons Gewirth's rights are not of this type. First, because the content of (7) does not transcend the interests of a subject, and, secondly, because a moral right must make a claim to universal acceptance—something which is not stated in judgement (7). The third type of right is very special and the one which Gewirth employs. There are 'claim rights' or 'prudential rights' of the individual raised *towards* everyone—but not demands *for* everyone in the sense that all others from their point of view must accept them (at least without further reasoning). Thus, only half a step has been made to universality: the individual agent must see his claims as addressing everyone else, but it is not yet demonstrated that everyone else must see himself as a rightful addressee of these demands. Obviously, it might be questioned whether 'right' is an appropriate term for this very special type of claim, but the peculiar definition itself is no substantial reason to reject judgement (7). And Gewirth defends his labelling as follows: 'Rights', he says in *Reason and Morality*, have several variables, of which the most important one is that they need a 'justifying reason or ground . . . by virtue of which the right is had' (1981: 65). Since everyone's claims for freedom are 'the most general and proximate necessary conditions of all . . . purpose fulfilling actions' (ibid.), they provide, according to Gewirth, a sufficient justifying reason for the corresponding right-claim (cf. 1984: 210). The agent necessarily affirms his (necessary) positive values; an affirmation which must be seen as so strong that he *cannot* admit any exceptions. Hence he must regard himself as having a right, not because this right is well justified through other reasons but because he cannot accept any threat to his freedom (in particular, any inhibiting interference of others). The impossibility of consistently accepting such a situation seems to be equivalent to regarding oneself as having a right.

Still, one might wonder—and this criticism has been levelled quite

there are threats to my freedom from other agents then I necessarily see my freedom to act and my well-being as something which ought not to be restrained by them and for which I have a (claim) right. Gewirth does not have to worry about him too much.

frequently against Gewirth[13]—whether this step is an illegitimate move from the agent perspective towards others, by me claiming that *they* are obliged. And, indeed, although the *reasons* for the positive evaluation and the subsequent obligation and right-claim are linked to me as a subject, the *content* of this judgement, the resulting right, is not. *For me* the 'ought' is addressed to everyone who can endanger or fortify the positive value, *i.e.* to me and equally to all other agents. (If I am in the relevant situation, then the 'ought' can be expressed as a self-regarding obligation—in cases in which it addresses others, I see it as their obligation towards me or (in the sense above) my right towards them.)

Let us look at Gewirth's response. He argues that at this stage the agent is not declaring that his insight provides a reason for others (this will follow in the next step of the argument), but 'merely' that he has sufficient and categorically compelling reasons to claim that others should not interfere. By this agent-relativity—indicated by the label 'prudential' rights (though a rather misleading terminology)—judgement (7) is meant to gain something akin to the indubitable certainty of 'for-me-it-seems' claims. This is not establishing an ethical subjectivism of any kind, since the authority of rights is not based on our free, subjective decision, but results from the necessary judgements individual agents must make. After all, these right-claims are made implicitly even by an agent whose subjective ethical system is entirely different.

4.1.6. The Universal Right to Freedom

From judgement (8) Gewirth proceeds to a supreme principle of morality and of all practical reason, the 'principle of generic consistency'—a principle with great resemblance to the categorical imperative (cf. Gewirth 1993):

> (9) *Act in accord with the generic rights of your recipient as well as of yourself.* (1981: 135)

Let us briefly develop Gewirth's reasoning. His first supportive argument comes along as a kind of clarification of what it means to necessarily claim a right. When I make a claim of this kind, then I do not claim it conditionally. I do not merely think of my situation *as if* I had a right to freedom and well-being, but I conclude that I actually have a right (1981:

---

[13] Cf. e.g. MacIntyre (1985: 66–8), B. Williams (1985: 59–60). See also the collection of critical papers edited by Regis (1984).

112). We might put Gewirth's argument thus: There is no gap between my necessary judgement that something ought to be respected and my self-understanding of having the related right. I could not make any reservation about the objectivity of the content (the 'ought') of the judgement, because this would be meaningless from my perspective. As we might put it, I cannot take the Stroudian distance of saying that although I must regard myself as having a right, I do not know how things really 'are'. Gewirth's transcendental reasoning is supposed to show that we must think ourselves to have a right without any such reservation.

Gewirth's second supportive argument runs as follows: Other agents are capable of actions as well, and we must accept that they can make claims about having rights in the same way we do (see judgement (8)). It follows that we must accept them as *having* rights in the same way we regard ourselves as having them. Otherwise, as Gewirth says, the agent would face the 'pain of self-contradiction':

For on the one hand in holding, as he logically must, that he has the rights of freedom and well-being because he is a prospective purposive agent, he accepts that being a prospective purposive agent is a sufficient condition of having these rights: but if he denies the generalization, then he holds that being a prospective purposive agent is not a sufficient condition of having these rights. (Ibid. 112)

In brief, if I must see the justifying reason as strong enough to judge unconditionally that I have a right in my own case, then I must see it as strong enough for all other agents' unconditional claims to this right as well—and I am obliged to respect their right-claim as rationally justified. That's why, according to Gewirth, I—as much as everyone else—can no longer act as if my claims are in any privileged position. Every agent must accept a 'normative limitation' (Steigleder 1992a: 198) of his rights because he cannot see them as overriding the claims for freedom and well-being of others. As Gewirth writes, 'it requires the agent to take favourable account of the interests of persons other than or in addition to himself' (1981; 112). Hence if there is a conflict between the actions of one person and those of another, then agents ought to strive for a practical solution which grants to both the maximum freedom possible. The resulting obligation can be summed up as the 'principle of generic consistency'.

Gewirth makes it very clear this judgement is a 'moral principle' because 'its criterion is not his own [i.e. the speaker's] interests or prudential purposes but rather the interests or prudential purposes of persons other than himself the speaker. He thus has to accept a judgement that he must favourably consider the prudential purposes or interests of persons other than himself' (ibid. 147). Gewirth shows in great detail how this principle is an apt basis for a far-reaching ethical system; but since these discussions are not important for the foundational question, we can ignore them.

4.2. MORAL REALISM AND THE ARGUMENT FROM AGENCY

The argument from agency is meant to avoid the naturalistic fallacy. The final step towards universality is supposed to be performed on logical grounds alone, normativity having entered the argument at a much earlier point; namely, when the agent realized the evaluations implied in his agency. These are first at the modest level of his individual ends or purposes, then it is argued that they include the freedom to act (the evaluation becomes stronger, since necessary), and, ultimately, they are expanded to a strict normative principle. The step to necessity as much as to the wider areas is performed by a kind of exploration of what the original evaluation actually involved, not by adding some normative judgements—at least that is how Gewirth sees it. The final step to judgement (9) is made through a universalization—and the result is able to withstand Moore's challenge by giving a firm reason *why* we must see it as morally good that everyone has the freedom and well-being required for agency. We conclude this, according to Gewirth, simply by expanding logically the (not yet moral) evaluation that we are compelled to make in our own case.

With regard to the respect that we owe to others Gewirth's reasoning is more successful than the argument from discourse. Everyone would have to be valued so long as he is (and because he is) at least a potentially purposeful agent. Thus, all agents have rights (whether or not they are aware of them) on the mere basis of what they are, not for any end they serve. Although, according to Gewirth, we recognize the rights of others only because we recognize our own in the first place, we must see and respect their positive value in a manner independent of their contribution to our interests. We are obliged towards others because of the value to be found in their agency; the individual degree of rational self-determination or awareness is irrelevant for the rights agents have. And, since they rely upon the implications of agency and not on any explicit judgements made by anybody, they include every person as long as he is capable of some such actions, even in the most restricted sense.[14]

We can conclude that if Gewirth's argument works it will be a very good basis for moral realism. To my knowledge, this point is not explicitly discussed. Beyleveld, however, is very clear about the consequences of Gewirth's argument with regard to truth. He writes that Kant's reasoning leading to synthetic judgements a priori 'is strictly analogous to Gewirth's claim that *if* we suppose that we are PPAs [purposeful prospective agents] then there are certain propositions that we must consider to be true of ourselves' (1991: 118). And, indeed, if Gewirth's justification works then the resulting moral judgement should be seen as *true* (at least, there is no reason why a fully rationally justified judgement should not be called 'true'). Further, its truth would be independent of the evidence for it (the second thesis of moral realism): Though, according to Gewirth, the origin of our *knowing* the principle of generic consistency is that it results from our necessary self-understanding, the *source of normativity* is agency (and its implicit structure), not our reasoning about it. Freedom is not constituted as a moral good or right through our mutual recognition. As Gewirth states (1981: 44): 'It is important to note, however, that it is not the Dialectically Necessary Method that determines the generic features of action and hence the general standpoint of agency itself'. Thus, the first and second theses of moral realism seem to find a possible basis. And since the entire argument is deeply connected with what practical commitments agency (a state of being motivated to do something) involves, even the motivational thesis would probably find support through the argument from discourse.

So if Gewirth were to succeed, moral realism would find a good basis. I will argue that he does not, but in order to do so we must look at the structure of his reasoning in some more detail.

---

[14] Cf. Gewirth (1981: 124) and also Beyleveld (1991: 251 ff.), who defends this point powerfully against Ben-Zeev (1982: 653 ff.) and D. B. Wong (1984: 201).

4.3. THE STRUCTURE OF GEWIRTH'S ARGUMENT

Gewirth does not seem to consider his reasoning as transcendental but rather to result from some premiss (our agency) and strictly deductive reasoning (cf. 1991: 23 ff.). However, it seems that he employs not one but, rather, several methodologies and that they include elements of both types of transcendental reasoning.

Let us try to distinguish between the different steps of his argument. The starting-point of the argument and its first stage follow the explorational type of transcendental argument. (Beyleveld rightly parallels Gewirth's methodology and Kant's transcendental reasoning—see 1991: 68–9, 117–18.) Gewirth begins with a commonly accepted notion of agency (a notion, however, which finds some further support through practical reasoning), and the argument proceeds by spelling out the analytically given aspects of agency in the second premiss (i.e. judgement (1)) and then comes to a conclusion (judgement (2)). Our status as free agents is mainly introduced as self-evident and only rudimentary arguments attempt to secure it further by some indirect reasoning. The generic features of this agency are detected by exploring what appears to constitute the necessary structure of action. 'The statements the method attributes to the agent are set forth as necessary ones in that they reflect what is conceptually necessary to being an agent who voluntarily or freely acts for the purposes he wants to attain' (ibid. 44). Thus, the transcendental conditional, the second premiss, is formally of the analytic type. It is not an investigation of the pragmatic-performative conditions of making or denying some judgement. But with regard to its *content*, the second premiss resembles the pragmatic version of the transcendental conditional, since it analyses what the features of actions are—hence of pragmatic-performative entities.

One might wonder whether this accords with Gewirth's 'pain of self-contradiction', which seems to indicate some retorsive, apagogic reasoning at the heart of his justification. I think Gewirth's expression is simply misleading. At least in its first stages, Gewirth does not argue that to deny something contradicts *itself* in a strict sense, i.e. it does not contradict the denial. He argues rather that the denial would contradict the agent-nature of the person in general. Agency provides 'an objective basis or subject matter against which ... moral judgements or rules ... can be checked for their truth and correctness' (ibid. 26). It only happens to be that *we are* this 'objective basis', and this is why, when we do not accept the generic features, we contradict our*selves*. (By contrast, for the argument from discourse the litmus test of whether something can be denied without self-contradiction is the performative dimension of the denial itself, thus an argument *qua* practical enterprise.)

Judgements (4) and (5), on the other hand, which state our necessary positive evaluation of freedom, are demonstrated by a retorsive, apagogic proof very much like the one Apel offers. Gewirth argues that the evaluation of freedom cannot be denied because any (practical and implicit) denial would itself be a further practical affirmation of this positive evaluation. Here we find a proper 'pain of self-contradiction': the (implicit) denial is, *qua* act, at the same time an (implicit) affirmation. (This aspect of Gewirth's argument is worth emphasizing: he mainly tests *implicit* claims or judgements against the point of reference.[15])

Judgement (6), the connection of freedom and the 'ought', seems, again, to be an analytic conclusion: necessarily to evaluate something positively *means* to acknowledge the necessity of a pro-attitude. The latter necessity can be expressed as an 'ought'.

Judgement (7) is also based upon analytic reasoning. If someone does not consider himself to have a right, then this would *mean* that others may interfere. But this would be at odds with the necessary judgement (6). Therefore, rights cannot be denied consistently.

The step towards a universal judgement about rights, the final stage of the argument, is very important. Here the results of the dialectically necessary method turn into an assertoric judgement; that is, into a moral principle which is said to be objectively valid. This time, Gewirth's reasoning might remind us of Thomas Nagel's famous argument for the possibility of altruism (1978). The universalization seems possible because of the nature of what a reason is—it gives a general, agent-independent condition for something being the case. Since agency justifies me making a right-claim, it allows everyone to do the same and I have to accept their claims as being equally well founded as my own. If Q is a sufficient reason for Z_1 claiming P, then it must be true for all Z_n that if Q then they are entitled to claim P. That is why Gewirth argues

---

[15] It does not mean that Apel and Kuhlmann never test implicit judgements. Apel, for example, argues that an action is a performative expression of one's intention that the intersubjective community (see Chapter 3) should approve this behaviour. (see page 70 f.)

on occasion that this step must be made 'on pain of irrationality' (1981: 161).

It seems a great weakness of Gewirth's own understanding of his methodology that he calls different tests for validity all equally the 'pain of self-contradiction'. As far as I can see, Gewirth detects this 'pain' *whenever* he sees a conclusion as invalid—for whatever methodological reasons.[16] At the heart of his reasoning, however, is a transcendental conditional. This becomes quite transparent when he characterizes it as a

> method of argument which begins from assumptions, opinions, statements, or claims made by protagonists or interlocutors and then proceeds to examine what these logically imply. It will be in this sense that my method is dialectical . . . The Dialectically Necessary Method begins from statements or judgements that are necessarily attributable to every agent because they derive from the generic features that constitute the necessary structure of action. The method I shall use here will be a dialectically necessary one, since it reflects the objectivity and universality reason achieves through the conceptual analysis of action . . . As dialectical, the method proceeds from within the standpoint of the agent, since it begins from statements or assumptions he makes. (Ibid. 43–4.)

If we replace 'generic features that constitute the necessary structure' by 'necessary conditions for something being the case'—as we might well do, given Gewirth's account of these 'generic features'—, this shows the closeness of his method (or at least of some of the steps of the whole argument) to transcendental argumentation as accounted for in Chapter 2. After all, the Dialectically Necessary Method is supposed to state that something must be the case if something else—here purposeful prospective agency—is to be possible.

The novelty of Gewirth's argument is the interesting distinction between assertoric and dialectically necessary judgements: the first type concern what is the case objectively, while the latter 'reflect judgements all agents necessarily make on the basis of what is necessarily involved in their action' (ibid. 44). They are made from 'within the standpoint of the agent' (ibid.). But what does this mean exactly? Gewirth makes some general remarks, that the 'dialectic' investigation of agency provides more 'directness and security' (ibid. 160) for its conclusions. Let us see why. What are the features of these judgements which make them more apt to withstand error? There seem to be two aspects of this dialectical

---

[16] Similarly, he uses the term 'logical implication' invariantly for different forms of inference.

approach from 'within' by which we are supposed to arrive at this result—one with regard to their content, the other with regard to their form. First, they are not only made *within* the individual standpoint, but also *about* the standpoint of the subject himself who makes the judgements. This seems to grant him an extremely self-evident starting-point, something especially important in such delicate matters as normative judgements. An 'external observer' is, as Gewirth says, more likely to go 'beyond the evidence by illicitly moving to a value conclusion from a limited factual premise' (ibid.). Secondly, there seems to be a *form of justification* (of normative judgements) which is only accessible to the subject. At least initially, it seems that some reasons in Gewirth's explorative analysis are only compelling for the subjects themselves: 'the method is restricted to what every purposive agent is logically or rationally justified in claiming from within his standpoint' (ibid.). However, it transpires that the justificatory force of this reason is seen as *not* strictly exclusive to the subject—the crucial step from (8) to (9) is only possible if everyone else accepts the subject's reason as binding upon everyone.

In principle, there is nothing wrong with this form of justification or kind of reasoning. Transcendental arguments are supposed to spell out what the subject must think and conclude that such is the case. It is the ambiguous first aspect of the standpoint 'within' which constitutes the Achilles' heel of Gewirth's argument. I will argue that the value judgement the subject must make is crucially underdetermined and thus not strong enough to lead to right-claims. But let us look first at the starting-point of his argument.

4.4. CRITIQUE OF THE ARGUMENT FROM AGENCY

4.4.1. *A Short Comment on the First Steps of the Argument*

Although Gewirth's starting-point 'I do X for the purpose E' is mainly introduced on the basis of self-evidence, it seems quite strong. The fact that there are also non-purposeful, unfree, irrational forms of behaviour is no powerful objection, since it bears no relevance to his argument. Any such unfree 'actions' would be outside the reach of the categorical moral demand.[17]

The necessary evaluation of E, resulting from the first stage of the

---

[17] If a sceptic were to go further and claim that *all* allegedly free actions might be deter-

argument, also withstands criticism. It is no valid objection that the agent had no choice but to do something and that in many situations even his passivity could rightly be considered as a kind of acting. Evaluations and necessity are not mutually exclusive. This is also true for the more substantial judgement (3); namely, that every agent must see a value for him in his freedom to perform the action he is performing. He has affirmed the practical realization of this freedom (or self-determination) by having performed it. Thus, Gewirth's conclusion about the evaluation of freedom seems valid. Moreover, a short retorsive (and quite Apelian) argument can be added to show that any fundamental objection to judgement (1) is impossible. Even a sceptic who opposes (1) fulfils the criteria of having a positive pro-attitude to the end of his action; namely, his rational engagement. He has revealed a selective attention towards an end in his action since he argues rather than being mute or doing something else. Further, he is directed towards making a (sceptical) contribution as an aim and, also, expresses his active interest in achieving this aim. Thus, all criteria for an implicit positive evaluation are met (cf. Gewirth 1981: 40) and, therefore, this restricted normative judgement from the I-perspective cannot be denied consistently by any agent. *Ceteris paribus*, the same argument can rebut objections against judgement (3), about the evaluation of freedom, because even a sceptical objection is a practical realization and, hence, a positive evaluation of the very freedom to act. The sceptic needs freedom in the sense of 'self-determination', since he must judge himself as being able to act (i.e. to make judgements) on the basis of insight or of reasons—otherwise his judgements are not rational objections and contributions to the discourse at all.[18] Whether this self-determination is 'freedom' in any stricter (metaphysical) sense need not worry Gewirth, or us, too much.

---

mined events outside our control, then Gewirth could simply state his entire argument in the form of a conditional, saying '*If we are able to act purposefully and intentionally* (and thus if we are able to act upon the principle of generic consistency) then this principle is absolutely binding.' This would not transform the categorical demand (9) into a merely hypothetical imperative: the conditional would only be about the *applicability* of the principle and not touch its absolute authority.

[18] However, this additional indirect defence might reach a limit: a sceptic could still protest that this would only show the validity of judgements (1), (2), and (3) *for acts of reasoning*, but not for all actions *tout court* until it has been demonstrated that they are free in the relevant sense. This is right, but would not have to bother Gewirth too much: his argument would still suffice to show that judgements (1)–(3) are valid for all self-determined actions, no matter what belongs to this privileged group.

The notion of self-determination is sufficiently strong to make acting upon the moral principle possible, and that is all Gewirth has to be concerned with.

Hence I think that there are good reasons to follow Gewirth up to the necessary positive evaluation of our freedom to perform the actions that we perform (the transcendental argument I will develop in the next chapter uses this result). But judgement (4), claiming that I necessarily place value in my freedom to perform actions *in general*—and not only to perform the present action—goes substantially beyond this result by abstracting further from the particular action. Here, I think, the first flaw in Gewirth's argument is to be found.

4.4.2. *A First Shortcoming: Particular Actions and Agency in Time*

Gewirth offers several arguments why the result can be expanded from the particular action to the generic features of agency in general. The first group of such arguments is supposed to show that the evaluation of freedom is something like the common denominator of all actions and takes place whenever I act. Freedom—and well-being as its necessary condition—are at a 'high level of generality' (1981: 59); they are 'second-order abilities to retain and expand [the individual's] first-order abilities to act to fulfil his purposes' (ibid. 60). Since I have no choice but to act so long as I exist, and since whatever I do I thereby evaluate these conditions, the generality of this evaluation seems to follow. The second group of arguments is retorsive. There is, according to Gewirth, no performatively consistent possibility to reject this general value of freedom and agency, since any attempt to do so is, again, an implicit affirmation of the positive value of freedom. Although I think that these two lines of argument are both successful and irrefutable in principle, they show less than Gewirth hopes for. There are doubts about their range, and Gewirth would need to find further arguments to support his claim. Let me explain.

It is correct to say that whenever I act my action implies an evaluation of freedom and, hence, that this evaluation is inevitable for me as an agent. But the evaluation is still less general and more strongly linked to the particular action and the time of acting than Gewirth requires it to be. Principally, it does not of itself extend into the *general* future. Gewirth's claim that the 'freedom thus valued consists . . . [in the individual's] *longer-range* ability to exercise such control' (ibid. 52; my italics) is simply stating too much. My present action does not imply that there is anything valuable about my future freedom to perform further, different actions. It requires an additional argument that the special kinds of values which result from the dialectically necessary method belong to the grand family of *timeless* values. The (contingent) evaluation of the end E of some action has no logical bearing on future ends I might have, and neither does the evaluation of the present freedom have a logical bearing on my future freedom. Gewirth seems to assume that this alleged timelessness is a straight consequence of the fact that we necessarily make value judgements. But this is wrong. The necessity only concerns the *making* of the judgement. It does not carry over to the *content*, in the sense that it does not automatically include freedom in all respects; not every form of freedom is necessary. Gewirth's retorsive supportive argument begs the question; it does not prove his point unless his claim is already accepted. And if I do *not* grant that implicit judgements about my freedom have necessary implications about the future, then there is nothing inconsistent in positively evaluating the state of being a robot, slave, or even corpse at some time to come. Somebody who, for example, sells himself into slavery must be regarded as free from any 'pain of self-contradiction', since at the moment of making this deal he is free and affirms his freedom in doing what he does. Why should the special deal he is engaged in (and all the other actions he does) imply not only the evaluation of the freedom to participate in this sale but also to perform different, future actions? Surely, at any time to come he will evaluate positively his (then *present*) freedom as long as he acts. But this is a different issue. The fact that I will evaluate something in the future is not the same as evaluating it now for all times to come. To claim more is smuggling some stronger understanding of value into the result than is justified on the basis of the dialectically necessary method. At this point, we must take Gewirth's method more seriously than he seems to do himself.

As far as I can see, there are two ways in which Gewirth does or might reply to this objection. The first is that we are not simply present but also prospective agents.[19] As such, at any given moment an agent evaluates not merely his present freedom but the purposiveness which accompa-

---

[19] For this reading see Hudson (1984: 126). There is a further argument Gewirth offers. According to him, the agent necessarily values the 'increase in his level of purpose-fulfilment' as well, 'since it directly reflects the conative nature of his action, that for the sake of which he puts forth whatever effort enters into his action' (1981: 56). But this is not very convincing. Although it might empirically be correct that this cumulative moment could be found in most practical efforts, it is surely not analytically implied in willing something or acting for a purpose.

nies his actions (1981: 58 ff.). Purposiveness, even more than freedom, is by virtue of what it is a form of being directed towards the future. So it seems that Gewirth's argument is that we necessarily evaluate something at any moment of action which *transcends* this very moment. Hence to evaluate purposiveness connects the present with the future.

But this defence is not sufficient. Although it is correct that purposiveness analytically includes some transcendence beyond the present moment, this move is not unlimited. It ends exactly at the point of having achieved the end or particular purpose. Of course, if it takes a long time to achieve his purpose then the agent must evaluate his freedom for a long period into the future—but there is no compulsion (or indubitable obligation) for anyone to have long-term or even life-covering purposes. Even if it is likely that agents have among their purposes many that extend quite far into the future, and even if there will be overlapping purposes (new purposes start before all the old ones have ended), so that a patchwork of purposes will stretch to the end of the agent's life, this is merely an empirical matter of fact. It need not be the case. We need a philosophical argument as to why one should not say rather modestly: 'Take therefore no thought for the morrow: for the morrow shall take thought for the things of itself. Sufficient unto the day is the evil thereof' (Matt. 6: 34). Gewirth would only succeed if he could show that *this* thought is impossible; namely, that there is a contradiction in the notion of having merely very short-term purposes. But he cannot.

The second reply which Gewirth might consider is to question the view of the subject that seems to underlie this objection. If there are no intentional moments connecting the agent over time, this would ultimately lead to his atomization into a bundle of acting mini-subjects with a short duration, and a distortion of personal unity. And it surely is very difficult to see oneself in this light. But we need more than phenomenological support for conceiving ourselves as agents who persist in time. It is not necessarily so: some schizophrenic people lack this capacity and still act. It does not seem *logically* compelling to take this strong view of oneself as a unity with regard to the future; after all, we all live with the notion of our finitude, with the consciousness of being mortal. Although Kant's transcendental reasoning against Hume's bundle theory is apt to reject his radical version of a non-unified self at any time, a further argument is necessary to support the conclusion that the unity *should* be directed towards the future in the substantial way that Gewirth's argument requires. On the contrary, one might argue—as I will do in the next chapter—that to care for one's own future state of being an agent is already a moral demand rather than a transcendental presupposition of being an agent. As pointed out earlier, we see something *good* in being an agent who reveals a unity of his evaluations over time, who acts with consistent, long-term (good) purposes. So this second defence requires more. Gewirth would have to show either that it is *impossible* to see oneself as particularized in time, or that our state of being such a united agent must also be seen as *good*.[20] As it stands, his argument shows neither the first nor the second.

4.4.3. A Second Shortcoming: The Basis for the Claim to Objectivity

Gewirth's progress from (5)—'I must make a positive value judgement about the freedom to act and about my well-being as the condition for this freedom'—to the claim about how others ought to act (6) and about claim-rights towards them (7) is not sufficiently argued. It would be justified only if, on the basis of Gewirth's argument, I were entitled to regard my freedom as an *objective* (positive) value. Without this subject-transcending status I am not entitled to make any 'ought-' or 'right'-claims which affect other subjects. But this objective status is not provided by the dialectically necessary method: it is not only crucially underdetermined with regard to the expansion of the valuation in time, but also with regard to the relevance it might have to others.

Let us look at Gewirth's reasoning at this point in some more detail. To do so, I will divide the movement from (5) to (6)—i.e. to 'I necessarily regard my freedom to act and my well-being as something which ought not to be restrained'—into several smaller steps. Then the argument would read as follows:

(i) I must make a positive value judgement about F (F = freedom to act).
(ii) I must judge pro-attitudes towards F as appropriate.
(iii) I must judge that F ought not to be restrained.

---

[20] Many if not most philosophers would agree for different reasons that there is some human self-interest in and thus evaluation of this state of being an agent in general. Spinoza's *conatus* might be an example as much as the instinct of self-preservation which modern science identifies as underlying all our actions. And even B. Williams, never one to accept too much too easily, concedes: 'it might still be true that I should see my freedom as good' (1985: 59). But we need more than affirmations: moral realism has to show why we must accept this evaluation.

(iv) I must judge that F ought not to be restrained by me or *by anyone else*.

In brief, (i) to (iii) boil down to different expressions of the same judgement: all of them are about me necessarily placing value in F. As outlined in Chapter 3, a value can be considered as a state of affairs towards which an active pro-attitude is seen as appropriate. And from the necessity of a pro-attitude the necessary rejection of interference follows—as long as it is limited to what the agent considers as *his* obligation. The problem is Gewirth's step from (iii) to (iv). The evaluation of (i), which I must make, is simply silent with regard to what type of value it is, especially whether it is binding for anyone else but me. Implicit judgements are, by their very nature, while not empty yet not *fully* determined. Of course, they leave room for interpretation, but any such interpretation must be carefully argued for. All we know is that it must include me because I have affirmed it through my acting—but this does not provide by itself a reason for others to acknowledge the authority of my claims.

Let us look at Gewirth's argument for (iv). According to him, it follows because I *could not imagine* a situation in which anyone would be allowed to interfere with what I necessarily evaluate. But this is either false or circular, or less substantial than Gewirth hopes. Let us look at the three possible readings of the impossibility of imagining such interference. Following Steigleder's distinction above, the first is a legal one. But if the 'ought' is interpreted in this way, it is simply false that I could not imagine a situation where others may legally interfere. I can easily picture some state officials (like Orwell's thought police) putting me in chains and being entitled and obliged to do so by some law. I might not wish this, or might not approve of it, but it is possible and could be legal. The second reading of the 'ought', in terms of a moral right, leads to a circular argument. If Gewirth claims that I cannot see it as *morally* permissible that others may interfere with my freedom and put me in chains, then this would require me to accept a substantial moral principle—e.g. 'It is immoral to restrain those things which I necessarily evaluate'—*prior* to the dialectically necessary method. Without further argument this would obviously beg the question. Let us turn to the third reading, the one which Gewirth actually seems to have in mind, the 'prudential-right' interpretation. Here the rationale behind the prohibition (iv) appears to be that I consider any negative interference to contradict my necessary value judgements. But why should there be a clash?

The value judgement I must make is simply not explicit about whether it is a value only for me or also for others; its scope (and hence the scope of the obligation) remains crucially underdetermined. I cannot rule out the possibility that the value is exclusive to me; I simply do not know. (If positive values express an ideal state of affairs, there might well be ideals for smaller groups of people or even for only one person; for example, me.) Gewirth has not shown a contradiction with respect to my agency when I claim that my freedom is a necessary value for me but not for others.

It should be added that the fact that I *must* evaluate something does not determine range. It only expresses that I cannot but have a certain relationship to that thing (a positive attitude), but not automatically that I must think that it is good in a full and objective sense. Gewirth, in contrast, seems to conclude exactly this; namely, that since I *must* make a normative judgement, this must address *everyone*. I do not argue that some Stroudian gap reopens between what I must judge to be the case and what really is—but that I am not entitled to the substantial judgement Gewirth hoped for. Objective validity does not follow, not even 'within the standpoint of the agent'. (The term 'right' is particularly misleading in this argument, because it does indeed suggest that I have achieved some insight that transcends me so as to be binding for other agents.) All I can say about others at this point is that their negative interference would be practically difficult for me and work against what I evaluate (for me). I would not like it if they disregarded my value; their behaviour would be at odds with what I cannot but have a practical pro-attitude towards. I certainly desire that they should not act in this way, but this is not a reason that entitles me simply to expand the 'ought' categorically so as to spell out a rationally justified demand.

This pivotal flaw can be demonstrated by looking at what would follow if the necessity of some value judgements were sufficient a justification for considering a value as objective. In this case, the same would be true for the more modest evaluation of my particular end when I act. Judgement (1), though severely limited in range and time, is equally 'necessary' as judgement (3) at the moment of my acting. But not even Gewirth argues that at the moment of acting I must see all my particular ends E as objectively good. Why should this be different for my freedom? That I evaluate it whenever I act will allow us to conclude that agents *always* evaluate their freedom *qua* being agents, but not more.

What Gewirth has shown is substantially weaker than (iv). The correct judgement resulting from (iii) therefore reads as follows:

(iv)* I must judge that F ought not to be restrained by me. (Further, if F were restrained by anyone else then this would be a hindrance to a successful realization of my practical pro-attitude towards it.)

Or, expressed in terms of judgement (6) above:

(6)* *I necessarily regard my freedom to act and my well-being as something which I ought not to restrain.*

It goes without saying that the illicit step towards other-regarding ought judgements affects the alleged claim-rights as well—and their subsequent universalization to the principle of generic consistency. I cannot judge that I have certain rights. This makes Gewirth's basis for his moral principle collapse. His argument, that everyone has to accept the claim-rights of all others, because everyone sees his own agency as a sufficient reason to claim them in his own case, will no longer work. When Gewirth argues that we can claim 'rights' because there is a 'justifying reason or ground . . . by virtue of which the right is had' (1981: 65), this is overestimating what sort of ground he has found.

From my necessary positive value judgement about my freedom to act there is only one logical universalization which I must make: that others will make positive value judgements of the same underdetermined kind about *their* freedom and well-being also. But this is a descriptive judgement without any prescriptive force for me, so long as I am not entitled to conclude that this value is objective. From what has been achieved, the moral principles would only follow if we presupposed a fundamental norm, such as the Sidgwickian 'principle of benevolence', which says that one ought in action to consider the interests of all beings in the universe.[21]

---

[21] Gewirth's argument would also work if we accepted the rights of others for prudential reasons, or in a contractualist fashion (see Narveson (1980))—but this is not what he promises, and surely not a rational justification of the kind moral realism demands.

4.5. THE 'OBJECTIVATION PRINCIPLE'

Both shortcomings of Gewirth's dialectically necessary method seem to have the same origin: he reads too much into implicit value judgements—more than he can do without begging the question. Gewirth's argument sheds light upon the relation which I necessarily have towards my freedom, but it neither tells me that freedom must be understood as a timeless ideal, nor that I must think everyone else should have the same relation to my freedom. As already said, Gewirth makes an assumption which is never clearly spelt out nor justified and which I will call the 'objectivation principle'. It can be stated as follows:

> My necessarily making a positive value judgement about some x is a sufficient reason for me to judge x as an objectively positive value. (OP)

Only then could I infer that my evaluations address other agents as much as me. If we take 'objective' to imply a time-independent reality, then the OP would also allow me to grant a timeless status to those values and thus cure the first problem of Gewirth's argument. It alone would make Gewirth's peculiar move transparent, according to which the *reasons* for the positive evaluation (and the subsequent obligation) are linked to me as a subject, while the *content* of this judgement can transcend this limitation by demanding a general pro-attitude.[22]

But the OP seems to be stipulated at exactly the point in the argument where the sceptic would enter. It cannot simply be presupposed, *not even for me*, that the justificatory force of 'my necessarily making a positive value judgement' is strong enough to include everyone. Admittedly, it remains a peculiar feature of the implicit value judgement to be uncircumventable for me. However, as said before, this peculiarity is silent with regard to the status of its content; it simply leaves it open. If one could show that values must be either subjective (in the sense of freely chosen) or objective (in the sense of universally binding), this would allow Gewirth's conclusion—since the judgements under discussion are not freely chosen, they would have to be objective. But we cannot be sure that this is the only alternative; it might be that while they are necessary

---

[22] The following comment from his introduction to *Morality and Reason* shows that Gewirth makes this very move from my necessity to evaluate something towards it having objective necessity: 'The dialectical necessities that derive from what every agent must say or think because of the nature of action reflect the necessities of the existing world, including the limits set by its own structure and potentialities' (1981: 45).

for me to make, they are yet values for me alone.[23] Consider devils and their 'values', as Mephistopheles spells them out: 'I am part of that force, which would | Do ever evil' (Goethe, *Faust*, trans. Walter Arndt (London, 1976)). Devils, if they exist, must evaluate wickedness and vice positively by virtue of what they are. But even if these negative values are necessary for them, we do not have to regard them as objective and thus universally binding.

There is another way to express this point. Gewirth presupposes, though he hardly ever puts it like this, that everyone regards his positive value judgement about his freedom as true in an objective sense on the basis of its necessity (for this criticism see also M. Stohs 1988). Thus, Gewirth seems to hold that if I must make a value judgement about something, then it is (objectively) true that this is a value (cf. e.g. Gewirth 1981: 153). As said before, this is a questionable point. The claim that I must evaluate x is not identical with the more substantial one that I must see it as true that x is a value (and hence binding for everyone).

This does not mean that Gewirth employs something like the 'verification principle' which Stroud sees at work in transcendental arguments; namely, that there is an illicit move from truth 'within' towards truth claims about some external reality.[24] I am not following MacIntyre's

---

[23] G. E. Moore assumes this exclusive alternative when he argues in the *Principia Ethica* (§ 59) that the position, which he calls 'anti-altruistic Egoism' (1903: 97–8), is inconsistent: 'There is no longer any meaning in attaching the "my" to our predicate, and saying: The possession of this *by me* is *my* good. Even if we interpret this by "My possession of this is what I think good", the same still holds: for *what* I think is that my possession of it is good *simply*; and if I think rightly, then the truth is that my posssession of it is good simply—not, in any sense, *my* good; and if I think wrongly, it is not good at all . . . The *good* of it can in no possible sense be "private" or belong to me; any more than a thing can *exist* privately or *for* one person only . . .'. But it seems questionable and in need of further justification why the egoist must automatically think that his well-being is 'simply good' in a full and objective sense and why there cannot be things which someone considers as good only for himself.

[24] It seems that Beyleveld (1991: 113–14) grants Stroud too much. In his defence of Gewirth against Stohs (1988)—whose objection has some resemblance to mine—Beyleveld argues that there is *no* 'transforming premise' like 'What logically must be accepted by every agent is right (true)' (see Stohs 1988: 62). According to Beyleveld, Gewirth only holds: 'What logically must be accepted by the agent must be regarded as true by the agent' (1991: 114). He adds that the judgements and the assertoric necessity are therefore not to be taken theoretically, but practically (ibid. 111). Beyleveld takes this 'practical' understanding to mean that the judgement's validity remains in some way limited to us as agents, something he calls 'relational validity' (ibid. 115). In this context, he quotes Gewirth's remark that the principle of generic consistency is only 'necessary and universal in the context of action' (1981: 158) and that the resulting principle is only 'relatively true' (ibid. 89). Beyleveld refers to a rather ambiguous passage by Gewirth (1982: 407) which seems to support his point: 'The truths attained by the

Stroudian critique of Gewirth, specifically that it is impossible in principle ever to come 'within' to judgements which can make claims to universal validity (1985: 67).[25] As already stated against Stroud, we are indeed entitled to do so *if* we cannot but judge 'within' that something must be objectively the case. There would be no room left for scepticism as to whether things really are the way we must judge them. Gewirth's shortcoming is different: he has simply not shown that we must see 'within' our freedom as an *objective* good. (A shortcoming, however, which can be found in different forms quite frequently: there are many philosophers who have straightforwardly argued that we always act under the assumption that the ends of our actions are objectively good. Most prominently Plato (*Gorgias* 466de) writes that even the tyrannical ruler does what he thinks to be the best[26].)

However, it must be stressed that Gewirth provides more than a mere contingent *ad hominem* argument. He is right to insist that the resulting positive value judgements are not only consequences of the fortuitous and contingent purposes the agent might happen to espouse; his argument is based upon transcendental investigations of what agency involves.[27] Gewirth's deficiency is that he shows with indisputable logic

---

Dialectically Necessary Method are relative to the conative standpoint of the agent ... [C]ertain value judgements and right-claims made by the agents are true when they are viewed from within the conative standpoint that agents must adopt ... [which] are not necessarily true outside this standpoint. But the truths in question are relational; they are propounded as relative to the agents' standpoint, not as true *tout court*'. Yet the transformation of this 'relational truth' into an objective one is not problematic—the crucial point is whether the 'relational truth' already includes the status of the value. (But NB: any talk about a 'relational truth' seems to be a rather suspect notion. If he wants to say that the truth under discussion employs at its heart practical consistency then this does not matter. Either it is still a *valid* argumentation to base some argument on practical consistency—as I think it is—in which case there is nothing 'relational' about it. Or the argument on this basis is not seen as valid; but then no truth at any level would follow.)

[25] MacIntyre (1985: 67) and other authors also argue that it is impossible to make any right-claims from 'within' independently of any agreed framework of rights (cf. B. Williams 1985). This would surely be true if Gewirth referred to *legal* rights, but not if one presupposes a notion of ideal, natural rights. The structure of Gewirth's shortcoming is not so simple.

[26] e.g. Aristotle (*Met.* 1072^{a}29–30) and Leibniz (1996: i. 276–7). In recent times J. Finnis (1977; 1998) has suggested a very interesting retorsive transcendental argument against scepticism about the goodness of truth. According to Finnis this scepticism is self-refuting since in order to argue at all the sceptic has to presuppose that truth is objectively good.

[27] Regis misreads Gewirth's result in this way: 'Within the Dialectically Necessary Method, a claim is backed not by evidence but by need, and what warrants claims is not reason but conation' (1981: 794), and continues: 'This epistemology is problematic because, in general, the truth of an assertion is not a function of the wishes or needs, even the agency

only that I *qua* agent must see freedom, etc. as values of kinds, and that every agent must do the same and evaluates his freedom. He has not demonstrated that the agent is threatened by inconsistency when he denies that or even leaves it open as to whether the more substantial judgements about a value *for everyone* are true. Even if it is psychologically uncomfortable for us to have to make certain judgements while not knowing anything about the range of their validity, this is no sufficient justification for granting them a universal status straight away.

Ultimately, Apel and Gewirth have a similar difficulty. When it comes down to *implicit* evaluations as performative conditions of agency or, as in Apel's case, reasoning, both read too much into them without proper justification. Apel claims that every act of reasoning implicitly aims at the approval of the discourse community, while Gewirth sees as the implication of its general condition 'freedom' being an objective good. They give in to the temptation to smuggle in implicit judgements—which are by their very nature not already clearly spelt out—of whatever kind they need for their argument to work. In both cases, although for different reasons, the step from a value 'for me' to an objective value, i.e. the rational step from the individual to the universal, remains questionable.

---

needs, of its utterer' (ibid.). Against Regis, there is one kind of 'need', which would provide a reason; namely, the rational need to avoid an inconsistency.

CHAPTER 5

The Argument from Normative Consistency and the Goodness of Truth and Freedom

5.1. AIM AND STRUCTURE

Transcendental arguments provide, as I have argued in Chapter 2, the most promising methodology for moral realism. With such tools we may be enabled to discover the solid rock of truth upon which we may set the foundation of the ambitious edifice of the three theses of moral realism. But neither the argument from discourse nor Gewirth's reasoning suffice as they stand.

In this chapter I suggest a transcendental argument which, if successful, can respond to this challenge. I wish to show that we must share a universal evaluation of every agent's freedom and of every agent's ability to make true judgements. These two fundamental values together constitute a normative ideal of human existence. Since the argument that I propose is of a rather complex structure, it might be useful to sketch the outline in advance. It starts from a basic presumption which the rational sceptic must accept; namely, that we necessarily make judgements that have truth-values. This (rather Apelian) starting-point will be secured with an initial retorsive transcendental argument. The second step is Gewirthian in spirit: since making judgements with truth-values is an activity, I will argue that any such judging implies the positive evaluation of its end; namely, the making of true judgements (in the following called 'truth-judging'). This result can also be expressed in the form of a self-imposed demand, and this is the third step: I must see myself as obliged to make true judgements whenever I make judgements that may be either true or false. It is important to see that this demand is still without force for anyone besides myself at this point in the investigation. The fourth step follows a very different route from the one Apel and Gewirth have chosen. I will argue that in normative matters a special criterion of truth seems to be defensible; namely, that a positive value judgement must be regarded as true if everyone must have a pro-attitude towards that which the judgement concerns. On this basis, I argue that the implicit evaluation of my making true judgements falls in the domain of this criterion and may therefore be either true or false. (The value judgement would be true if it were universally (hence for all agents) necessary to acknowledge the goodness of my truth-judging.) Then, as I will argue in the fifth step, the self-imposed demand to make true judgements applies also to this value judgement. Hence, and this is crucial, we ought to make a true judgement in the case of the necessary value judgement—for this is the only way to be consistent with our own implicit evaluations. This obligation constitutes what I will call a 'normative need' that our value judgements turn out to be true. And since all agents face the same normative need, this universal need itself justifies us in regarding truth-judging as truly good: The goodness of truth is something every agent must have a pro-attitude towards and the truth-criterion for this value judgement is thus fulfilled. This discussion will end with a short reflection on the structure and strength of the transcendental reasoning employed.

In the subsequent section (5.5), I will sketch an expansion of the argument by combining it with what Gewirth has successfully argued for; namely, that I place positive value in my freedom to act. The demand to make only true judgements can also be applied to this implicit and necessary value judgement about freedom that Gewirth has spelt out. Here, again, we find a state of affairs towards which everyone must have a pro-attitude. The suggested argument allows us to go further where Gewirth held back: to take the step from myself to all rational agents. A short sketch of how to bring the two necessary values, 'truth' and 'freedom', together will follow (5.6). They might be seen as two aspects of a normative ideal of rational agency and thus a basis for the notion of fundamental human dignity of a moral-realist kind. In a final remark I will argue that the suggested argument withstands the objections raised against Gewirth and Apel (5.7).

5.2. THE ARGUMENT FROM NORMATIVE CONSISTENCY

5.2.1. *Judgements with Truth-Values as a Starting-point (First Step)*

Since any transcendental argument has to start somewhere, I should be explicit about my starting-point. The 'argument from normative consistency', as I will call it, starts from us making intelligible judgements that are either true or false. The first task is to show that we do indeed make judgements of this kind, i.e. judgements that subscribe to the rules of logic—for example the principle of non-contradiction—that express a belief about some state of affairs in a meaningful way, and that have a truth-value, which we can attach to them. Examples of these judgements are: 'There is a world outside my mind'; 'The outer world consists mainly of Limburger cheese'; and 'There are judgements that may be true or false'.[1]

How solid is this starting-point? A short retorsive transcendental argument can demonstrate that even the sceptic is committed to accepting it; he cannot deny it consistently without self-defeat.[2] When the rational sceptic argues, he implicitly acknowledges that the topic under discussion allows us, at least in principle, to make judgements that may be true, since his judgement is designed to be true and the rejected one false. If a sceptic denied this minimal condition for all reasoning, he would be incapable of giving any intelligible account of his own position when he raised his sceptical objection. Only if there is a distinction between right (or 'true') and wrong judgements, or between 'better' and 'worse', and only if there is a means for us to make this distinction, does it make sense to argue at all. The rational sceptic must imply that his critical judgements are 'closer' to the truth than the judgements he rejects, or at least that they help him to come to judgements which are closer.[3] We have

---

[1] There might also be meaningful judgements with no truth-values, or with truth-values impossible to determine, and there are mere sentences such as Chomsky's 'Colourless green ideas sleep furiously'. But these are not relevant to the present argument; they fall outside the objective good of making true judgements that I will argue for.

[2] An even shorter argument would arrive at this result straightforwardly from the rationality of the sceptic (cf. pages 6–8). To begin with this rational type of scepticism is not dogmatic-axiomatic, but, as argued above, there is no rational way to consider irrational scepticism at all.

[3] There is an inconsistency in the minimal position of someone who discriminates only between making 'better' and 'worse' judgements while denying that we could ever *in princi-*

already looked at Apel's powerful arguments for the inconsistency of any such scepticism (1980: 265): it would be self-contradictory, since if the sceptic did not presuppose that his judgement itself were possibly true he would not raise any sceptical contribution which could be taken seriously. As Spinoza has put this point quite generally: otherwise 'they ought to remain silent, lest perchance they might suppose something which has the savour of truth' (1986: 241).[4] To give up any commitment to judgements with truth-values would make scepticism unintelligible even for the sceptic.

This does not imply that the sceptic is committed to assuming that he will come to the point of being certain about the truth of a particular judgement. He can still hold a weak tenet of human fallibilism—the thesis that we can never be absolutely sure that we have not made mistakes in our reasoning and have possibly reached wrong conclusions (Berlich (1982) has raised this point against Apel). The rational sceptic can defend this position consistently so long as he subscribes to the *possibility* of making true judgements. Thus, a moderate theory of fallibilism can be vindicated if it is seen only as a general warning for us to be careful with regard to the apparent truth of judgements. (There are, however, at least some judgements where it is very difficult to see at which point a mistake in our reasoning could possibly have occurred, such as the conclusion that some of the principles of logic are valid.)[5]

---

ple know the truth of any judgement. This is inconsistent because we can only make the distinction between degrees of truths in a meaningful way if there is a criterion for what it means to be closer to the truth and if we are able to use it. This entails that we must be capable of identifying the truth of judgements; at least the ones which spell out the criterion. Similarly, in the case of someone who thinks that we make judgements of mere probability, he must presuppose some fixed (hence true) framework within which these judgements are justified (cf. Hösle: 1990; 172).

[4] For a very potent argument for a general premiss about our capacity to make truth-assertible judgements and to distinguish between right and wrong judgements see R. Harrison (1974: 51–88).

[5] In contrast to this, to uphold the tenets of an extreme fallibilism (a '*malin génie* hypothesis', following Descartes, where *every* judgement which we make is wrong) is either inconsistent or no longer a meaningful argument. This is so because it leaves only two possibilities to the sceptic. If he made an exception for his own judgement about human fallibilism, then he would be inconsistent; if he included his judgement, then he would no longer want us to take his comment seriously, since he would state that what he says cannot be right. There would be no stable and interesting position left for a rational sceptic to occupy.

A similar inconsistency faces a defensive version of this extreme fallibilism, which states: 'There are true judgements in principle. But for each concrete judgement we cannot decide whether it is right or wrong.' This seems simply a confused and enigmatic notion of 'truth'—

The present argument has limitations. It shows that it cannot rationally be denied that we make judgements that have truth-values and it specifies one example in which we must presuppose their possibility. In particular, however, it should be noted that the present result does not tell us whether value judgements may be true or false. As the argument stands, a sceptic may still deny this possibility, as moral anti-realists have mostly done.

5.2.2. *The Positive Evaluation of Making True Judgements (Second Step)*

The starting-point was secured by means of Apel's retorsive transcendental argument. This section combines this first result with Gewirth's analysis of what it means to act.

There is a significant parallel between making judgements and engaging in actions. Both are free, intentional events; 'to judge' is a speech-act, since it means that someone becomes engaged in the activity of forming (and sometimes uttering) beliefs. The person who is engaged in this activity makes a particular judgement (the one which he believes to be true) rather than another or no judgement at all. Thus, he expresses in a practical way that he sees it as favourable, or good, to make this judgement *qua* being true rather than false. If someone makes a judgement about what a certain liquid before him is (for example: 'This is petrol'), he considers it good if the judgement matches reality; that is, if his judgement is true. This is implicit in his being engaged freely in the formation of this judgement, and independently of whether or not this judgement is mediated towards a further end he might have (such as knowing whether he can drink the said liquid).

The activity of making judgements with truth-values can thus be described as a favourable, positive appraisal of the end 'true judgement', and *qua* action a practical affirmation of this appraisal. It fulfils all requirements for an implicit value judgement of the kind Gewirth detects. It is important that this value judgement is independent of what he desires or values in other respects (e.g. whether he prefers the liquid

what could it mean that there are these inaccessible true judgements? Even if we do not reduce truth to the consensus of rational beings, we must yoke it to the possibility of its being grasped in our judgements. If, however, this objection is a criticism of any epistemological tool, then a debate like that in Chapters 1 and 2 would have to follow—and, of course, the question would have to be raised as to what the epistemological basis for this version of radical fallibilism might be.

to be Muscat). We can therefore conclude that an implicit value judgement about the goal of judging (namely, to come to a true belief about something) is necessarily given. This positive valuation of making a true judgement can also be expressed in a negative way: he considers it bad to make a false judgement.

There is no reason to limit the scope of this implicit judgement to any context or to publicly uttered judgements. In all areas where someone makes judgements that may be true, and where he forms them freely, his practical engagement shows that he is implicitly committed to regarding it as good to make the true judgement. Let us formulate the first result:

> *My making true judgements is good.* (NTJ)

(For the discussions to come, I wish to call this positive value judgement 'NTJ'; 'N' stands for normative, 'TJ' for making a true judgement.)

It is important to stress two points. First, there are as many different judgements NTJ as there are persons. Every agent 'x' makes the judgement 'NTJ(x)' about his truth-judging being good.

Secondly, an important *caveat* must be added: the positive evaluation NTJ is underdetermined with regard to the question of how *others* must see it; whether they also regard it as good that I make true judgements. The reasoning shows only that *I* must see *my* truth-judging as valuable, good, positive (whatever we want to call it) and other agents must think the same of theirs.[6] Although the judgement is necessarily implied by the individual person, it implies nothing about its scope, because the evaluation merely mirrors the fact that the agent places so much value in the end of his action that he performs it. Thus, I cannot conclude that I must see 'my making true judgements' as a good for everyone, a 'universal' good. At the moment, we have not found any reason why the structure of my agency should imply a commitment to a universal rather than a 'for me' type of goodness. Certainly, there may be other reasons why I have to regard truth as a universal good—I will suggest some such reason in my own argument—but it does not simply follow from me being implicitly committed to making NTJ. (To ignore a similar limitation is the flaw of Gewirth's argument, where he jumps too quickly from the implicit evaluation of freedom towards a 'right'.)

---

[6] I use expressions like 'regarding as good', or 'regarding as worthwhile', 'placing positive value in', 'making a (positive) value judgement about' or 'evaluating positively' (sometimes abbreviated as simply 'evaluating') as synonyms.

John Finnis has suggested an argument for the goodness of truth that is parallel to mine up to this point. It is exactly here that our ways diverge: he concludes straightforwardly that we are committed to the universal (as he says, 'intrinsic') goodness of truth. According to Finnis, the mere analysis of implicit commitments of any interlocutor is sufficient to come to this strong result: ' "I assert that p" entails "I believe that truth is [a good] worth [pursuing or] knowing" ' (1977: 259; the bracketed terms are introduced by him to give alternative formulations). And he expands this claim as follows:

'Truth is worth knowing' is to be understood as meaning that truth is a good to be pursued, and is good to attain in one's judgement; and ignorance and errors are to be avoided . . . 'Truth is worth knowing' is to be understood as affirming that truth is an intrinsic good. (Ibid. 262.)

Against what Finnis says, I do not think that there is a reason yet to detect an 'intrinsic good' at this point of our investigation—the analysis of the implicit commitments does not tell us what sort of goodness we are talking about. The reason for Finnis's unjustified jump seems to be an ambiguous use of the term 'objective'. He defines the term as follows: 'A judgement or belief is objective if it is correct; a proposition is objective if one is warranted in asserting it, whether because sufficient evidence is in, or because there are compelling grounds, or because . . . it is obvious or self-evident that in asserting it one asserts what is the case' (ibid. 264–5). On the basis of this understanding, Finnis concludes that we can say 'that truth is *objectively* a good'(ibid. 264)—because we are warranted in asserting its value. Obviously, I agree with Finnis that we must necessarily regard the end 'truth' as good, and that this necessity counts as a compelling ground. In this sense, it is 'objectively' true that I regard truth as good. But the objectivity is about the status of the judgement, *not about its content*. Let us make this more explicit. It can be objectively true that I regard X as a good for me alone—someone committed to a celibate life might well be so committed because of the positive value that this life has for him and for those around him, but at the same time *not* believe that *everyone* should be celibate. Similarly, it might be someone's merely subjective impression (hence, it is not objectively true) that y is an *objective* positive value—someone might hold that to abstain from killing animals is an objective universal imperative (motivated, perhaps, by his personal dislike of killing animals).

To argue as Finnis does would require an objectivation principle, according to which the necessity of my regarding some y as good provides sufficient reason to judge y as truly good in some objective sense. But this principle is not well founded since the value commitment is underdetermined. The sceptic will have a safe ground from which to raise his objections. *He* can consistently question the goodness of *my* truth-judging. And that's why he can also consistently question the objective, all-binding, character of my value judgement as much as of his own.

One might argue that a valid transcendental argument normally leads from the necessity to think something to the conclusion that something must objectively be the case. Why can we not conclude on these lines that we must see our true judgements as objectively good (i.e. a good for all which rightly demands respect from all)? We cannot because there is a significant difference. Judgements like 'There *is* truth' are from the start about something being the case independently of me. In stating that kind of factual matter, the 'I' and also any 'I–it relationship' seem always transcended, and a 'view from nowhere' is taken (to use Nagel's (1986) classic formulation). Due to the unique nature of evaluations, this is not automatically the case when we attribute goodness to something. The implicit value judgement is about a necessary relationship between myself and something else—*I must value it*—and does not transcend this evaluative perspective, for it is not entailed that *others* have to value it as well. Therefore, a transcendental argument about normative matters might well lead to the result that *I* am committed to having a pro-attitude to something, while *no one else* has a compelling ground to consider himself committed to it.

Let us illustrate this point by looking at another implicit commitment. If Alice helps herself to tea, she makes an implicit positive value judgement. At least at the moment of action, and within the context of options available to her, she is committed to a limited amount of practical approval of her drinking tea. Certainly, this value judgement is restricted by the situation and might change within a minute (the tea might be unpleasant in some way). But *even at the very moment* of it being performatively expressed by Alice, there is no reason to conclude that she is committed to any rich judgement such as 'tea-drinking is a universal good'. We can only conclude transcendentally that, at some point, Alice has regarded the object as being sufficiently good to merit her trying to attain it. Is there anything fundamentally different in the case of truth-judging that might justify a stronger conclusion than in Alice's case? I do not think so. It is true that, first, drinking tea is less frequently pursued than making judgements. But this is surely of no importance—we are looking for implicit commitments of types of actions and the number of instantiations of such actions is not part of the transcendental analysis. Secondly, with NTJ we have reached a judgement that everyone *must* make. But even this difference is not relevant. Everyone is necessarily committed to the goodness of his truth-judging, but this does not mean that he has to regard *everyone else's* truth-judging as a good. (Similarly, if for some reason Alice could not but place value in her drinking tea, if this were a crucial and inevitable aspect of her nature (as, possibly, of the Mad Hatter's nature), this would not lead to the conclusion that she would have to regard *everyone else* as likewise being committed to the value of *her* drinking tea.) In other words, I can claim consistently that I see my making true judgements necessarily as a good that I have to regard, but I do not know whether it is a good anyone else has to regard. The point where Finnis was led astray is right at the beginning. We must not be too vague about what *exactly* is affirmed in a performative way. To talk in too general terms about 'truth' being 'worth pursuing' is imprecise and smuggles too much into the evaluated good.

Still, as with Gewirth's analysis of freedom, the resulting value judgement about making true judgements is peculiar. It is surely not simply 'subjective', if we understand 'subjective' as indicating a direct dependence upon free decision or preferences. Although the making of a particular judgement with truth-values is always a free practical enterprise, the particular resulting value judgement is necessarily implied once we form judgements of this kind—while we might change our preference for tea or Muscat. In this sense, the judgement is uncircumventable for everyone *qua* rational agent, and thus subject-independent. But this is not the same as saying that it is 'objective' in the sense that we could demand that all rational agents should acknowledge and respect it. After all, it might only be a good that *I* must respect.

5.2.3. *Objections to and Supportive Arguments for the Result of the Second Step*

Does the making of judgements with truth-values necessarily imply a commitment to NTJ? Doubt about this cannot be expressed consistently by any sceptic, because his rejection—'I do not place value in making true judgements'—would (*qua* being a judgement) fulfil exactly the requirements for the implicit judgement which he denies. He must imply the claim that his denial is a right judgement (or at least that it is 'closer to the truth', which is sufficient) and he implicitly affirms that he sees making this judgement as worthwhile by his act of stating it. This is true also for the sceptic who does not believe his scepticism but constructs a straw man in order to test the strength of an objection (cf. p. 7): his actions still express the positive evaluation of his truth-judging, because his objection is ultimately raised in order to come to a secure basis for truth-judging. It thus transpires that no rational agent can consistently dispute the above result.

The suggested retorsive transcendental argument shows that the sceptic must regard it as good to make true judgements, at least in the case of his or her own judging. But this result seems to leave another, more modest, objection unchallenged. What about the claim that not *all* instances of making judgements with truth-values imply NTJ? There seem to be three possible exceptions: first, an intentionally made wrong judgement; secondly, a situation where the speaker does not care; and, thirdly, a dominant subconscious wish that something be true or false irrespective of whether it really is. Let us look at them in turn.

One example of the first case will surely spring to mind: the liar—i.e. someone who wants to form and utter wrong judgements. In this case, the deed is the wilful act of not expressing the truth though the judgement does have a truth-value. But let us look more carefully. For a start, it does not imply that the liar does not place value in *his* making the right judgement about the matter for himself. On the contrary, his first making the right judgement is the necessary condition for him being able to lie at all: the liar needs the truth in order to abuse it for his purpose. Hence the liar regards it as good to form true judgements and to disguise the truth subsequently before others, but he does not regard it as good to make wrong judgements himself. Furthermore, his public act of uttering a wrong judgement is not correctly to be understood as making a judgement at all, but as an *act of deception*. He simply uses an acoustic entity (a speech-act seeming to convey a judgement) as the most useful tool to achieve his end; and surely this tool works because people consider it to be something else; namely, a proper judgement with the implication of truth.

Let us consider the second group of examples of the instrumental use of judgements; that is, when we do not want to make wrong judgements, but when their truth-value is of no importance to us. Think, for example, of a password to enter a barracks ('We have no king but

Edward'), of an expression of flattery ('You speak as beautifully as Oscar Wilde writes') or simply of cases where one wants to pacify an interlocutor ('Yes, you are right'). But in all these cases we are not really dealing with people forming beliefs about how things are; it is again a strategic use of speech-acts which seem to convey judgements. In brief, the liar is similar to the person who does not care about the truth-value of a judgement he uses for some purpose. Neither one represents a counter example; in both instances what they utter does not reflect what the speaker actually judges to be the case. (And *prior* to their utterance they regard it as good to make a true judgement about what would be a suitable means to their end.) Thus, the only evaluation accompanying these 'judgements' is that they work successfully as tools—so this does not deny the conclusion that any formation of judgements, when they are about how things are, is accompanied by an implicit evaluation of the truth.[7]

Much more difficult is the case of self-deception. An example is someone who simply wants to believe something, irrespective of whether it really is true. Imagine, for instance, a woman who prefers to lead a life built on the *wrong* judgement that her husband has not been killed in the war and might yet return home. Or consider the case of Norman Bates in Alfred Hitchcock's film *Psycho*: he believes that his mother is still alive, even though he is daily confronted with the sight of her wizened and dead body. Can such cases disprove the result above? I do not think so, since unconscious self-deception is not an implicit positive valuation of the wrong judgements but of a different reality. The problem with self-

---

[7] Pragmatic theories about truth hold that all judgements with truth-values should be reconstructed in terms of practice: to call something true means that it is useful, e.g. the solution of a problem (as Dewey would argue). Then, of course, the above distinction seems questionable, since truth simply amounts to the quality of being a successful tool of some sort.

But the fact that certain distinctions can no longer be made is one of the reasons why the pure pragmatic theory is not very attractive: demonology is a system of allegedly true beliefs which proved very useful for the purposes of religious groups for many centuries. As it has been pointed out quite frequently, demonology cannot be distinguished structurally from, for example, a system of claims in natural sciences. If one wants to question the sense in which they were 'useful' or even whether they were *really* useful one would have to employ a different standard—obviously usefulness cannot be its own standard. To see natural science as 'more useful' in the sense that it ultimately covers a wider range of phenomena would lead us back to a traditional theory of truth: if we ask why some such set of beliefs has a greater pragmatic power, the *pragmatically* most useful answer (in the sense of covering all cases) is, that this is so because it gets things *right*—and because there is only one way in which we get things right. Thus, it seems that, for pragmatic reasons, the pragmatic theory of truth would have to accept a non-pragmatic interpretation of truth.

deceivers is that they have other and very powerful aims besides truth; most of all, that things should turn out to be other than they appear. This is the reason why they have to *deceive* themselves: although they aim at the truth and regard it as good to make true judgements, they are dominated by the wish that certain judgements rather than others be true. As a consequence, they form judgements that are not made to fit the world but rather to fit their hopes.

Of course, all this does not show that it is necessary that we make judgements that are true in the first place. We can be silent and remain in thoughtless passivity. There are surely good empirical reasons to assume that we could not live very successfully in this way, but this is a contingent matter. Transcendental reasoning only shows that it is necessary to place positive value in making true judgements *when* we make judgements that can be true or false. We have to accept NTJ as an a priori valid condition for all those beings who form judgements with truth-values.

5.2.4. *The Self-imposed Demand for True Judgements (Third Step)*

If I must see my truth-judging as good or a positive value and if a good or positive value is something towards which a practical pro-attitude is appropriate (cf. 79–81) then I must see a practical pro-attitude towards my own making of true judgements as appropriate. That means I must impose this pro-attitude upon myself. We might express it:

In judging, I ought to aim at making true judgements. (T!)

(In what follows, I use the abbreviation 'T!'; T stands for a true judgement and the exclamation mark symbolizes that I am talking about a demand. When I want to specify a person 'x' who imposes this demand upon himself I will call it 'T(x)!'.)

We may also state it more simply in all situations when we make judgements with truth-values: 'Make true judgements!' But we should be aware that, at this stage of the argument, the demand is addressed *only to ourselves*. This positive demand as much as the value judgement itself corresponds directly to a negative attitude to wrong judgements. In the same way in which I see my making true judgements as good, I must see my making false judgements as bad. Hence to make wrong judgements is a state towards which I should not have a pro-attitude whenever I make judgements with truth-values.

What is the authority of this demand? This demand is self-imposed only to the degree to which it is given with the appraisal which we implicitly make; to deny it would contradict the value judgement that we are committed to. The rejection of this demand leads therefore to an inconsistency between implicit and explicit judgements. And since it is rationally grounded in that consistency between the different judgements we make, to self-impose the demand is an uncircumventable aspect of rationality. That is all there is to it.

For reasons given in the first chapter, it is not possible to make the objection that consistency is smuggled in as a kind of secret value. Consistency is as indispensable to a rational person as anything *can* be, since it is constitutive for him. Further, if we regard true judgements as good, this entails that we regard consistency as good—for there cannot be any inconsistent truths. Thus, NTJ will cover the evaluation of consistency as being one of the most essential, constitutive aspects of truth. (See, for example, the laws of logic: once I have realized that I can only speak reasonably and reach the truth if I subscribe to some of them, I am rationally committed to respect these laws when I make judgements.)

What exactly a 'true' judgement is will depend on the *type* of judging we are dealing with. Judgements about matters of fact, for instance, are considered to be 'true' according to most theories of truth when they are subject-independent.[8] Everyone with the necessary knowledge, insight, and intellectual capacity would have to make the same judgement about matters of fact. Thus, in this case, the self-imposed demand T! could also be expressed as a prohibition on making any judgement with a claim to universal validity which is crucially based upon my subjective perspective, with its deceiving '*idola specus*', as Francis Bacon calls it. Nagel has put this condition of objectivity in a different context: 'What we want is to reach a position as independent as possible of who we are and where we started' (1986: 74). If, of course, I want merely to express my subjective feelings or how things seem to be to me, I am free to do so and not hindered by T!. It does not seem that much more detail can be teased out

---

[8] This is consistent with the coherence theory of truth as much as with the correspondence theory. It must be so with the former because, according to this theory, the ideal state of a universal convergence of beliefs is exactly what truth is. It must be so with the latter, because it follows from the correspondence theory that a belief is true on the basis of its correspondence with reality independently of the believer. Thus, a true belief about a matter of fact is the same for everyone and, in this sense, universal.

at this point; T! cannot be transformed into one easily fleshed-out epistemological code of behaviour.

What is the scope of this demand? I have no reason yet to assume or postulate that T! is directed towards anyone but me. Since it is only the corollary of the evaluation of truth-judging, it shares its indeterminate status with respect to objective validity. All we can say for the moment is that *I* am necessarily committed to the value judgement NTJ and therefore to T! with regard to my making judgements. The result does not commit us as to whether or not *others* have to place value in *my* making true judgements, or whether *I* must do so in the case of *others*. Certainly, I must acknowledge everyone's normative commitment to *his* making true judgements on the basis that he has exactly the same reason for so judging as I have; but that is a different judgement. I am not committed by other people's commitment. (Thus, it is not possible to express the value judgement in terms of any 'right'-claims about other people, as Gewirth assumes too abruptly in his argument about freedom.)

There is an important point with regard to the kind of normativity we are dealing with. The argument as it stands does not determine whether the self-imposed demand is a moral one or not. According to the understanding of a 'moral value' which I have introduced above (p. 80 f.), something can only be classified as 'moral' if it is a value *for everyone*. Another point should be added. To realize that my implicit evaluation demands some self-imposed obligation is not the same as my being already sufficiently motivated to obey it. The awareness of the demand does, of course, provide some motive, but not necessarily that which overrides all others. Robert Nozick's remark (1981: 407) has already been quoted in the first chapter:

The motivational force of the argument . . . can be no stronger than the motivation to avoid the particular inconsistency specified by the argument.

Of course, in a particular case there can also be further and different motivations for aiming at true judgements besides avoiding inconsistency. Someone might, for instance, see it as sinful to lie; he might be afraid of being punished for doing so; or, as in the case of the golden-brown liquid mentioned above, might also be motivated by a prudential reason to get things right. But these are quite different and independent motives for trying to form true judgements; these motives are not our concern in the present investigation.

The present result has some relation to Aristotle's point in the

Nicomachean Ethics: every practical pursuit seems to involve striving for excellence in this activity; the harp player, for example, aims at being a good harp player. In this sense we could say: everyone who is engaged in forming judgements that may be true must implicitly aim at making true ones. However, the basis for this demand is substantially different. While Aristotle can only tell us what he observes as a matter of fact and what most people would agree upon, the self-imposed demand T! is not based upon any empirical fact or general agreement (and independent of any possible additional motive or desire). The suggested argument has not looked for any inconsistency between the negation of T! and some contingent belief, desire, or purpose one might happen to have. Our obligation to make true judgements has a much stronger foundation: it results from the performative conditions for making judgements and is hence uncircumventable for any rational being inasmuch as he makes judgements of this type at all.

5.2.5. A Criterion for the Truth of Value Judgements, and its Application (Fourth Step)

The result as it stands does not provide any Archimedean point for morality. It has neither been shown that NTJ nor that the connected demand T! concerns a universal, and hence moral, good. In order to expand the present result, an important observation will have to be added; namely that *NTJ itself is a judgement that has a truth-value*.

Most moral anti-realists will reject the mere possibility of any judgement of the type 'x is good' having a truth-value. But why should we? There is no obvious reason to reject this possibility *tout court*; and the fact that value judgements are different from descriptive judgements is, by itself, no reason to assume that they cannot be true. If the objection is merely a stipulative restriction of usage of the term 'true', then it does not have weight at all.

However, the claim that value judgements can be true requires further reasoning. I will do this by, first, arguing that there is a plausible truth criterion that we might employ. Secondly, I will apply the criterion to NTJ, showing what would have to be the case for the criterion to be fulfilled and hence for NTJ to be true.

The criterion for the truth of a value judgement that I suggest reads as follows:

If there were some state of affairs which everyone had to regard as a positive value (as good), and if this evaluation were consistent with all other rational judgements that we must make[9], then this state would rightly be regarded as a positive value.

This criterion is based on the crucial feature of moral judgements; namely, their imperative nature. They are not neutral in relation to us; or, rather, in our relation to them. A positive 'value' is a relational term which expresses a positive attitude towards something as being appropriate, and is therefore a judgement about how we should be *motivated*. Thus, by stating that there is a universal, necessary appraisal of (or pro-attitude to) some state of affairs, we have affirmed the truth of this state being a positive value. Of course, if the appraisal were merely contingent, then it would not be a basis for the truth of a value judgement even if *everyone* shared it. This is so because positive attitudes that are held for contingent reasons have often all sorts of origins, even if they happen to be shared by everyone—most of the objections against the consensus theory of truth would be applicable in this case (cf. Sect. 3.5.1). The universal appraisal must be *necessary*, thus transcendentally required, for the criterion to be sufficient. For, the criterion is spelling out what it would mean to have a retorsive transcendental argument for a normative state of affairs. That is why it has the same anti-sceptical force: if the criterion is fulfilled, then there is no space left for a sceptic to occupy when he wants consistently to question its goodness. It must be shown transcendentally that even he must be committed to regarding it as good.[10]

We cannot raise a further objection as to whether it is 'really' (objectively) good; as if we could imagine that there might be a necessary universal pro-attitude towards something where there *should* not be (in a

---

[9] The second point, consistency with other rational value judgements, is not really a further criterion, but follows from rational compulsion to accept a judgement: there can never be good *reasons* to accept something if it is inconsistent with other things we must rationally assume to be true.

[10] This criterion is independent of, and compatible with, common truth theories. It is obviously in accordance with the coherence theory of truth (where truth is a coherence of judgements—and the criterion is suggesting some such general coherence) and also with pragmatic theories of truth (since if we are rationally compelled to make a certain judgement then this seems to be the most *useful* judgement to make in order to respond to this challenge). Depending on their presupposed ontology and on their interpretations of the correspondence, proponents of the correspondence theory of truth might also accept the criterion. If everyone has to regard something as good, then this might result from it being in fact good. (In this interpretation, necessities of thought are the consequence of a reality that is itself in some way rational.)

moral sense).¹¹ There is no space for this scepticism, since either something must be seen as having this demanding character for everyone (including the sceptic), or not. (This response is similar to the one given to Stroud above; see p. 60–2.) Nothing can be necessary for everyone, and hence have full authority, *and* be wrong in some further sense at the same time. We simply could not make intelligible what this 'further sense' would mean. It is therefore quite understandable that the most elaborated account of this meaningless 'possibility' is not to be found in philosophy but in literature. As already mentioned in Chapter 1, some of Kafka's novels present us with a world of values (or moral laws) which are radically opaque. We are, he writes in *The Trial*, in front of the locked doors of the law room and there is no hope of ever entering it. Kafka's normative realm is so frightening because it pretends to be well organized and have full authority—but cannot be dealt with rationally by us at all. Thus, to be a (Stroudian) sceptic about the goodness of something which is necessarily and universally seen as a good is to place us in a Kafkaesque world and simply to misunderstand what a value is.

Can this criterion for the truth of a positive value judgement ever be applied? Of course, according to the suggested criterion, we can attach truth-values to every value judgement, if it is about something being good that requires a practical pro-attitude. (The criterion will not work for aesthetic value judgements because beauty does not seem to demand the same support as goodness). Still, we have not yet found a positive value judgement that fulfils the criterion by being *necessarily made* by everyone. However, in the case of regarding one's own truth-judging as good, at least a *part* of it is already fulfilled. Judgement NTJ stands out from many other normative judgements, since we know that in each case NTJ (x) one person must make it; namely, x. But we do not have a reason to assume that the criterion is fully satisfied. This would be the case if everyone had to regard the truth-judging of some x as good. If, for example, everyone were committed to 'Illies's truth-judging is good', then we would have to see it as true that my truth-judging is a positive value that everyone has to respect.

At present, this is all we can say: The judgement 'NTJ(x)' has a truth-value, the criterion for it being true is fulfilled to a minimal extent by

---

¹¹ The only way to ask this question would be to assume that a voluntarist god might have different values from the ones that we, qua being rational, must have. But this assumption is irrational. And, as said before, we cannot rationally take irrational sceptics—or gods, we might add—seriously.

some x, yet no argument has been brought forward that shows why anyone should make this judgement besides x.

5.2.6. The Application of the Demand T! on the Value Judgement NTJ (Fifth Step)

The next step of the argument is important. The reflection in the fourth step shows us why we cannot, more exactly why we *should* not, be satisfied with the *necessity* of making NTJ. This is so because NTJ has a truth-value and we are under the self-imposed demand T! to make true judgements whenever they can be true. Consequently, we should make NTJ *only if it is true* and not if it is false. And the required 'truth' must be the kind of truth that is appropriate for the present situation. Since we have a clear criterion for what truth means with regard to positive value judgements, the demand T!, applied to NTJ, is not satisfied by mere opinions about what is good.

But how do we know whether NTJ is true in the appropriate sense? We are in an awkward situation. There is a judgement that we *must* make, namely the particular judgement NTJ, but which is indeterminate with regard to its truth (we do not know whether it is true or not), and there is also an obligation telling us what we *should* do; namely, make only true judgements. Structurally, this is a tension between two necessary implications of our making judgements with truth-values. If NTJ turned out to be false, then this would lead to a collision between an 'is not' and a 'should be'; I will call the threatened collision a 'normative inconsistency'. It is noteworthy that this is not the same as the inconsistency or self-defeat that we find in the above-discussed examples of retorsive transcendental arguments: there we had an inconsistency between an explicit 'is not' and an implicit 'is' (like that between an explicit denial of truth being possible and the implicit acknowledgement of the possibility of truth *qua* making a rational judgement).[12] That is why the retorsive transcendental arguments above allow us to conclude the truth of some judgement—to judge the opposite turns out to be logically inconsistent—where the present argument does not. Normative inconsistency is not impossible in the same way as logical inconsistency, and thus not a sufficient reason for the (indirect) inference of some judgement that

---

[12] However, Apel and Kuhlmann try to show that this is also a normative claim. But the relevant inconsistency is between the two descriptive aspects of the judgements, not between what ought to be and what is.

avoids the inconsistency in question. Nor can we infer the truth of NTJ directly from our commitment to regarding NTJ as good, as I have argued above.

What is the appropriate response to this threat? It is impossible to disregard one for the sake of the other, since the 'must' and the 'should' are both uncircumventable and have therefore identical authority; they are but two aspects of the same commitment. For the same reason it is impossible to disregard both—we are not free to assert or not to assert NTJ or T!; the positive value judgement *and* the self-imposed demand are necessarily implied whenever we make judgements. The only possibility of escaping this commitment to them seems to arise when we abstain from making judgements with truth-values altogether. But this is no real 'solution' of the tension; at least, it cannot be expressed as such consistently, for any such attempt would involve making judgements with a claim to be true.

Obviously, the best and only solution to this normative problem would arise if NTJ turned out to be true. We should therefore hope that NTJ is true, or, as we might express it, *we have a necessary pro-attitude towards NTJ being true*. This pro-attitude originates in the normative inconsistency that we face otherwise. Its force is exactly the same as the original demand T!, since the pro-attitude is the consequence of imposing the demand on ourselves—as we are committed to do. It is therefore not a contingent attitude, but another necessary implication of making judgements with truth-values.

Unfortunately, at the moment there is still no evidence for NTJ actually being true. But before continuing this line of argument we should look more carefully at what it would mean for NTJ to be true.

5.2.7. Possible Interpretations of 'It is True that Truth-judging is a Good'

Since NTJ is underdetermined not only with regard to its truth but also with regard to the range of the evaluation, 'NTJ is true' can be interpreted in three different ways. The three possible interpretations of 'NTJ is true' are:

(1) It is true that my truth-judging is a good for me—but not for anyone else (no one but me must respect it).[13]

---

[13] NB: to be 'a good for me' does not mean 'good for me' in the sense of something being merely useful or convenient. The implication of my making judgements is that I have a pro-

(2) It is true that my truth-judging is a good for everyone (everyone, including me, must respect it).

(3) It is true that my truth-judging as much as everyone else's truth-judging is a good for everyone (everyone, including me, must respect everyone's truth-judging).

(3) is a universalization of (2). (1), on the other hand, is compatible neither with (2) nor with (3) because of the exclusiveness of its notion of good. (But, of course, if (2) or (3) is correct then truth-judging is *also* a good for me.)

However, for two reason we can ignore (2) in what follows. First, the truth of (2) is based upon the objectivation principle that has already been criticized in this and the previous chapter as a stipulation. The mere fact that I must regard my truth-judging as a good is simply not a sufficient basis to conclude that it is binding for everyone. And, secondly, if the objectivation principle turned out to be valid after all, then (2) would turn into (3). Why should this be? If I were entitled to regard my truth-judging as a good for everyone on the basis of my necessarily making the value judgement, then I would have to regard everyone else as *likewise* entitled to regard his or her own truth-judging as a good for everyone on the basis of their implicit commitment. Everyone's situation *qua* reasoner is the same. Hence I would have to acknowledge the goodness of their truth-judging in the same way in which I would expect them to subscribe to the goodness of my truth-judging. We would have reached a universal positive value judgement about truth in general; namely, (3).

So we are left with (1) and (3). Do we have any reason to assume that one of the two might be correct? Let us look at them in turn.

5.2.8. Why it is Not True that my Truth-judging is a Good Exclusively for Me (Sixth Step)

One might want to reject the possibility of something being a good exclusively for me by a simple argument: Is it not a very strange (or 'queer') assumption that the realm of normativity would truly contain goods of this kind? Is the accusation of strangeness, though, a serious

---

attitude to truth-judging, that I regard it as having some positive value—and that is different from seeing it as useful, since I am free to do or say things that I consider to be against my own interests (e.g. to tell the truth in court). But even then I must have a pro-attitude to doing so—hence I must regard the end of my acting as sufficiently valuable to make the action worth performing.

objection? There is lot of strangeness in the world, so why not here? Why should the world not contain elements which are necessarily good only for, and in the eyes of, one agent, while absolutely neutral or even despicable in the eyes of all others? Kierkegaard seems to have this type of morality in mind when he talks about the religious stage of being. According to him, there can be very specific obligations for individuals at this level, such as the demand to sacrifice one's son in the Abraham story—though it is by no means a general good to sacrifice one's children. Certainly, in this case there is a second person who seems to consider the sacrifice valuable—God. And it is not clear whether we can make any sense of Kierkegaard's conviction that these normative judgements are 'subjectively true'. Let us therefore look at another, though rather melodramatic, example—Lucifer, the prince of devils, who needs the surrender of human souls for his existence. He cannot but place value in this because otherwise he would contradict what he is. Thus, *for him* the surrender of a human soul is an essential good. Yet, as Christopher Marlowe amongst others has reminded us, we have no reason to satisfy his appetite by offering him our soul. It is simply not a good for us. He is, after all, the devil; that is, he is by definition bad.

Let us therefore assume that the normative realm might contain some 'goods' that are only good for and in the eyes of certain individuals. Can the truth of my value judgement be based upon this interpretation of its range—would, in other words, (1) satisfy the demand T!? I do not think so. There are two powerful objections against this, that explain why (1) can neither be regarded as valid nor as a solution to the threatened inconsistency. The first objection is that we have simply no reason to assume the validity of (1). To claim its truth would amount to a mere stipulation. Secondly, to presuppose (1) gives way to an infinite regress; the original normative trouble would not be solved but merely 'postponed' in an endless iteration.

Let us turn to the first objection. Why should the necessity to regard something as a good provide a sufficient ground for considering it as *true* that it is a good for me? For it to do so would require a variation of the objectivation principle, according to which it is 'true' that some y is a good exclusively for me whenever I must regard y as a good. But this variation of the principle is not well founded at all. The only 'reason' for the principle one might conjecture is that I *must* regard y (i.e. truth-judging) as good—but, as argued above, it would be begging the question simply to conclude its truth from this necessity. We need an argument for this being a criterion of truth and not simply an affirmation. Any sceptic, including the agent in question, could easily question it—everyone can consistently reject (1) by arguing that his truth-judging might turn out to be a good for everyone. Why should (1) with its exclusive reference to me be true? To think so boils down to a dogmatic solution of the normative trouble we wish to avoid.

Let us turn to the second objection to (1). For this, we should look more carefully at what it would mean if (1) were true. If something is a value for me but for no one else then this can be expressed as follows: There is an epistemological (or normative) system which allows value judgements about components of a system in relation to each other. Within the system 'hell', for example, we can state that the surrender of a human soul is a good for Lucifer, who is an essential part of this system. And this seems to leave it open as to how we judge the entire system. Whatever we think about hell's goodness or badness in general, once we start from the framework 'hell', the judgement 'the surrender of souls is a value *for Lucifer*' would follow.

But things are not so easy with judgement (1). In the case of the value of truth we face the problem of how to express this response to the demand T!. Whenever I talk about the system and its components I have already *transcended* 'my' framework and entered a normative meta-level, because I make a claim about this first normative system as a whole. If I say 'y is truly a good exclusively for me', I am speaking about the relation between components in the system from outside the system; otherwise the claim to truth would be vague and pointless. The judgement contains two subordinated ones. But, since the same evaluation of truth is also implied by this meta-level judgement (and by any further meta-meta-level judgement), T! raises its head again and again. Yet what are the truth-conditions of *this* meta-level evaluation? If we say that, again, it is only true that it is a good *for me* that this meta-level judgement is true, then we face an infinite regress of meta-systems. The account of the evaluation as expressing merely a relation between some entities (judgements with truth-values and rational agents) could never be completed, and the demand T! thus never really be satisfied. And there is no theoretical level at which the regress might stop—any judgement with truth-values itself implies a positive value judgement and is thus potentially the source of a new normative problem.

Marlowe seems to have been aware of this. Lucifer, or rather Mephistopheles (Lucifer's 'companion-prince in hell' (1909: 138)), is not

The Argument from Normative Consistency · 151

willing to make any meta-judgements about the infernal system of thoughts or evaluations. When Faustus asks Mephistopheles, 'Tell me who made the world?', the response is: 'Move me not, for I will not tell thee.'

FAUSTUS Villain, have I not bound thee to tell me anything?
MEPH. Ay, that is not against our kingdom; but this is. Think thou on hell, Faustus, for thou art damned. (Ibid. 137.)

To see his own system of thought from a meta-level outside hell and the evaluative relations which are valid there would, Marlowe suggests, reveal exactly this: namely, that infernal evaluations cannot be expressed consistently as being true. Marlowe's language is poetic and epic (he had no analytic training), but we can use it to express the important objection: we cannot follow T! by limiting ourselves to a notion of exclusive goodness, because we are then damned to the 'hell' of normative inconsistency.

5.2.9. Why it is true that Everyone's Truth-judging is a Good that Everyone must Respect (Seventh Step)

If we have no reason to accept (1) in order to follow the demand T! (and thus to be normatively consistent) then (3) seems to be the only possibility left. But even then we are not entitled simply to declare that it is the case; such a stipulation is not adequate to resolve the threatened normative inconsistency. And, from what has been said before, we cannot conclude (3) *directly*, since this would require the validity of the objectivation principle. In brief, we still face the threat that there might be no way for us to find out whether NTJ is true, yet we are nonetheless committed to making this value judgement.

Still, there is something more that we can say: Since we have argued that NTJ in the interpretation of (1) cannot be regarded as true, and since I have a pro-attitude towards NTJ being true, I must have a pro-attitude towards the truth of NTJ in the interpretation of (3). At least, as long as it has not been shown that (3) is not correct either, it is the only possible way left in which NTJ might be true, and thus the only way for me to avoid my normative inconsistency. But we can specify further what this entails. If we have a pro-attitude towards it being true that some y is a positive value, then this implies that we have a pro-attitude towards y actually being a positive value (because this amounts to the same thing).

Thus, by having a pro-attitude towards (3) we have also such an attitude towards what (3) is about; namely, everyone's truth-judging. Therefore, we can state quite generally: By being a rational agent and by being under the demand for consistency, I am committed to having a pro-attitude to truth being a positive universal value. But, taken by itself, this does not seem to grant the correctness of (3).

Now, let us look at the other rational agents and their pro-attitudes. Since *all of them* are under the obligation T!, and since all of them have no way of avoiding the normative inconsistency other than through (3), it follows that *everyone* must have a pro-attitude towards truth being a universal positive value. Two things must be stressed. First, no one is in a privileged position and everyone faces the same danger of being normatively inconsistent—everyone is committed to having this pro-attitude. Of course, there will be many people who do not feel moved by self-imposed demands at all, and who, consequently, would not acknowledge their pro-attitude towards the truth of NTJ. But this does not have any importance for our argument, because even they *should* have the pro-attitude under discussion. Secondly, everyone's pro-attitude has exactly the same state of affairs as its object; 'everyone's truth-judging' is the same, independently of whether I or you or someone else has a pro-attitude towards it. It abstracts from any particular person.

This result is good news. It means that we have discerned something towards which everyone should have a pro-attitude. And this is exactly what the criterion for a true value judgement requires—as argued above, something can be truly considered to be a positive value if everyone must have a pro-attitude towards this state of affairs. Everyone's truth-judging has exactly these characteristics. But then I (and everyone else) have more than a mere pro-attitude towards (3)—we have a *reason* for regarding it as correct. The reason is exactly this: namely, everyone's commitment to NTJ and everyone's subsequent pro-attitude towards the only interpretation of NTJ that could be true. On this basis, we can conclude that NTJ—interpreted in this way—*is* true and that truth-judging is justified as a universal value.

One might wonder whether the result really does show that we have a reason to assume the truth of this value judgement about truth; or does it merely supply a psychological placebo? No, because we do not have a mere subjective feeling but a positive evaluation—a universal pro-attitude—*that we are necessarily committed to*. And this provides exactly the basis needed for the value judgement to be true. Of course, we do not know independently of the suggested argument whether truth-judging is a good—but this lack of further evidence can be found to be the case with other retorsive transcendental arguments as well. It does not diminish the strength of the conclusion.

What is the difference between the present argument and Gewirth's (as I argued, unjustified) conclusion on the basis of what is implied in agency? The necessary value judgement that I make implicitly is not straightforwardly about a positive value or 'right' that I consider myself to have towards everyone else (or about an intrinsic good, as Finnis argues). In the first place, the suggested analysis arrives at a more limited result; it is merely that I must regard something as a good, without knowing whether it truly is a (universal) good. The argument then takes two steps. First, I realize that to obey my self-imposed demand would require it to be true that truth-judging is a universal good. I have therefore a pro-attitude towards this being the case. (What Gewirth concluded directly remains a conditional at this point: *if* truth were a universal value, *then* I could follow the self-imposed demand. However, I do not know why I should be entitled to follow the demand.) Secondly, I understand that everyone else should have the same pro-attitude. But *thereby* the criterion *is* fulfilled and my pro-attitude can turn into a justified value judgement. I have found something to which everyone should have a pro-attitude—a universal good. The 'argument from normative consistency', as I will call it, has come to an end.

5.2.10. *A Brief Discussion of Two Objections*

There are some objections I wish to examine, according to which the result of the above argument is crucially limited.

First, one might suspect that the 'should' which results from the normative need is not sufficiently strong to fulfil the criterion. But it is; at least we regard it normally as sufficient. Any reasoning requires some such normative need as its basis. Reasons always tell us only why something *should* be the case. Reasons never force us in the way the physical world can; even if we have good reasons to deduce some conclusion from a premiss, in less controversial spheres, as for example mathematics, reasons do not conclude by 'themselves' but, to put it metaphorically, they need us to follow them. To give a 'reason' is simply to state that there is only one right way to move from some insight to the next—yet rational beings have to make the move. We are never compelled to make this move, we must compel ourselves in order to avoid inconsistency. Hence there is nothing odd about normative needs. *Any* rational inconsistency ultimately involves a normative inconsistency, because it involves an agent having ignored the demands of what he should have done. If 'normal' reasons say that some x is the consequence of some y, then it is itself a (transcendental) obligation, and not a further logical conclusion, that one should conclude x given y. To be rational (and conclude x) is always a kind of rule or norm; not to do so is therefore a normative inconsistency.[14] That is why any scepticism about the force of 'normative needs' does not lead very far: in order to be a rational sceptic the sceptic has to subscribe to the binding force of reasons. If he objects that a demand, which necessarily springs from the avoidance of an inconsistency, has no binding force, then no reason whatsoever can convince him to accept anything. (That even the laws of logic require a form of practical commitment has been convincingly argued for by several authors[15].)

A second, and closely related, objection runs as follows. Some agent might not take the self-imposed demand seriously in the first place. He simply might not care—and might argue that he simply lacks the pro-attitude under discussion. And he does not see why everyone should take T! seriously, and therefore fails to see evidence for the criterion being fulfilled. But this agent does not raise a real difficulty. Although the pro-attitude is indeed an inner directedness that shares some features with a *motive* (I will say more about this in the next chapter), it is not dependent on me taking the demand seriously. It is implied by my making judgements with truth-values—via being committed to NTJ, and via being committed to T! and its application to all possible cases (including NTJ)—thus I and everyone should have the pro-attitude. That is all the argument requires. The acknowledgement of my pro-attitude is surely

---

[14] The difference between a 'normal' inconsistency (which says that we should not conclude contradictory things) and the 'normative' inconsistency (which tells us not to deny TVT) could be put thus: the former situation refers to reasons at two levels—namely, to normal ones but also, ultimately, to the normative one of accepting these reasons as binding—while the latter situation refers more straightforwardly to normative reasons alone.

[15] e.g. Smith (1987/8) and Walker (1982; 1993).

In an interesting paper Gewirth (1970) argues in a way which is supportive of the thesis that 'reason' must always entail a certain commitment. He writes that a person who did not use the concept of a self-directed, prudential 'ought' would not be aware of *any* requirements or constraints set by himself for his own conduct for any reason whatsoever. Here I agree with Gewirth, but do not think that he has shown that the 'ought' already refers to others in the way he requires it to do.

the epistemological condition for my understanding the argument from normative consistency—but it is not the condition of its validity. The crucial criterion is fulfilled if everyone *should* have a pro-attitude towards some state of affairs, independently of whether everyone actually *does* have it.

5.3. TRUTH AS A MORAL VALUE

In what follows, I will use 'TUG' to designate the judgement that results from the argument from normative consistency; namely, 'truth is a universal good'.

There is an important but obvious point which we have not yet looked at. The judgement TUG is a universal and therefore *moral* value. This follows immediately from the suggested understanding of 'moral value', which involves universal validity in a twofold sense; it must be a good *in the eyes of* everyone and *for* everyone (cf. p. 80 f.). Both criteria are fulfilled by the value of everyone's truth-judging. It is a value any rational being must acknowledge as being justified, and, furthermore, the value is a universal good, which means that it refers to everyone's judgements with respect to truth-values.

But once TUG has been identified as being a moral good, something interesting follows. In the light of TUG we can see that the self-imposed demand T! must be moral as well. If the making of true judgements must be seen as a *moral* obligation in general, then T! is a moral imperative. This implies that a person who accepts the authority of his self-imposed obligation and follows it already *acts morally*. He does what he is morally obliged to do; hence to acknowledge the truth of the value judgement on the basis of the normative reason *itself* can be interpreted as the actual imposition of a moral demand. This leads to the unique consequence that the acceptance of a certain kind of argument requires one already to be moral, at least to a minimal extent.

The aim of this book has been to develop a 'meta-ethical argument' in order to justify some fundamental normative judgements. Yet the project, if successful, turns out to have a misleading label: to ground substantial ethical claims is *itself* part of ethics, so not a 'meta'-level above and outside the normative realm. The present attempt to argue for material norms is already in the domain of a basic norm which governs our rational behaviour.

There is, however, a possible confusion here which is worth mentioning. On the one hand, the argument requires that if one were to acknowledge the justification, then this fact would show that one *was* (for whatever reasons) *already motivated* to act morally. On the other hand, the justification also shows that the agent *should be motivated* to support the universal good 'truth' further. Obviously, the two motivations are not identical; an agent might be motivated to a minimal extent to obey T! in one case—and he should be to the fullest extent. But he might fail to do so. His original willingness to acknowledge the authority of T! will not necessarily last long enough, or be sufficiently strong, to serve also as a motivation for further situations. Weakness of the will remains possible.

It is not as strange as it might appear that the present justification will convince only someone who is already moral to a minimal extent. It allows us to explain a common intuition, which can be found in much moral philosophy. Aristotle observes in the *Nicomachean Ethics* that 'the Supreme Good only appears good to the good man; vice perverts the mind and causes it to hold false views about the first principles of conduct' ($1144^a 10$). A similar idea has been advanced, based on Augustine and Luther, within a theological framework: since the Fall, it is argued, mankind is so much entangled in original sin that reason can no longer guide him—he needs God's grace in order to distinguish the good from the bad ('the depravity of man'). If we recall that Adam and Eve's fall is described as human unwillingness to subscribe to the authority of a demand, then this story can be used to illustrate the present point. The serpent can finally be identified as lying: to disobey the fundamental demands which reason imposes does not itself open the eyes for the discovery of good and evil, but rather closes reason's capacity to discover it. Darkness follows when reason stops taking itself and its self-imposed demands seriously.

5.4. STRUCTURE AND STRENGTH OF THE ARGUMENT FROM NORMATIVE CONSISTENCY

As much as the arguments from Apel and Gewirth, the suggested transcendental argument from normative consistency contains several steps which make use of different epistemological methods. It begins with a retorsive transcendental argument in order to secure its starting-point; namely, that we make judgements with truth-values. This Apelian result is expanded by performing a Gewirthian analysis. I argue that making such judgements implies a positive evaluation, hence that this evaluation is analytically given with the judgement-formation. The transformation of this value judgement into a self-imposed demand is similarly analytic.

The self-application of the demand T! is mere deductive reasoning. We have a practical syllogism with the self-imposed demand T! as the first premiss and the value judgement NTJ as the second premiss. Since NTJ can be true, it falls under the class of entities spelt out in the demand, and we can therefore deduce that T! is valid for NTJ. This in turn spells out a normative need to regard NTJ as true. This leads to a retorsive transcendental argument of a special type: *not* to acknowledge truth-judging as a universal value would be *normatively inconsistent*—and we have therefore a pro-attitude to it. Two subordinated arguments are employed to go further. First, my pro-attitude is generalized on logical grounds alone— everyone is in the same situation as I am and should therefore have the same pro-attitude towards the truth of the same state of affairs. Secondly, it is concluded that *therefore* truth is a universal good. This follows from the introduced criterion of truth for value judgements.

The argument from normative consistency avoids the naturalistic fallacy for reasons similar to those raised in connection with Gewirth's argument. Normativity is not something which enters the stage suddenly; the reasoning is supposed to reveal that we must acknowledge that we already presuppose it—that normativity is at the very heart of the way we must understand our rational activity. We are always acting in a way (forming judgements) which necessarily implies some evaluations and demands; these are therefore uncircumventable for us and any rational being. The argument only makes evident that these evaluations and demands have to be seen—for reasons of consistency—as universally valid and thus moral.

At this point we might raise the question of whether a justification of a moral value could be different. Any argument for morality which tries to start from a necessary matter of fact would have to find a 'place' where moral values are necessarily realized. But where would this be? And how, if we came across it, could we ever hope to identify the normative nature of this necessary matter of fact? It seems that this state of affairs could always be mistaken for a mere (possibly metaphysical) fact.[16]

---

[16] See, e.g. K-H. Ilting's critique of Kant's normative notion of freedom (1972/4).

158 · *The Grounds of Ethical Judgement*

Any 'given' will have difficulties in answering Moore's famous open question; it is not clear how we could ever find a powerful reason to attach positive value to anything of this kind. We might find external reasons, but this will not suffice for the fundamental values. It is therefore more plausible to hope for a retorsive transcendental argument of the suggested type, exactly because it does not focus on the ideal directly, but on the pro-attitude that we are committed to having. An 'ideal' feature will appear as a demand in our imperfect world; that is, an obligation to move in a certain direction, to act in a certain way and not in another. Can this be called an Archimedean point? The 'point' which this retorsive transcendental argument provides is itself a universal (moral) demand—and we have (and are entitled) to respond to it by accepting TUG. If I refused to do so, I would have no reason of the kind that could justify my position. Thus, I think that we should replace the metaphor (and expectation) of an Archimedean point for moral philosophy with a different metaphor: reason is the firm, since uncircumventable, starting-point for us, and it finds in itself the rational leverage of an 'Archimedean demand' which allows us to lift ourselves, and the world, into the normative, ideal realm of truth.[17]

5.5. FREEDOM AS A MORAL VALUE

As it stands, the argument establishes a kind of epistemological virtue—to see a moral good in everyone's making true judgements (whenever they make judgements with truth-values) has implications for our intellectual behaviour. But the value 'truth' seems too limited to provide a basis for the general concern of morality, at least for most cases of interaction with people. Why should we help someone in need if that does not enable him, or us, to make any true judgements? There are many

---

[17] Kant might be interpreted as making a similar point when he argues that the moral law must be self-imposed. We are, he writes, the 'author of the authority of the law, but not . . . the author of the law' (*KGS* VI. 227). Or, as he says on another occasion: morality is ultimately built upon a 'self-commitment through the idea of a law alone' (ibid. 380). In a similar spirit, the argument from normative consistency shows that we are not free to create any arbitrary 'moral' values ad lib—we are not the 'origin of the laws'—we only self-impose the moral law's authority. But we do not self-impose the moral law for arbitrary purposes, from whim or caprice, or simply because we feel that we should act in that way. We have a good *reason* why we *should* accept the authority of the moral principles and impose them on our behaviour.

The Argument from Normative Consistency · 159

aspects of life to which the established value seems of no relevance. I will accordingly sketch a strategy to expand the present result and to look for further value judgements that can be true besides judgement NTJ.[18]

There is indeed a promising candidate which we came across in the previous chapter. Gewirth has shown—and rightly, as I argued above—that I must make a positive value judgement about my freedom to perform actions in general. I will call this normative judgement about freedom 'NF' and express it in a fashion similar to NTJ:

My freedom to act is good. (NF)

Although I argued against Gewirth's hidden assumption that the value judgement NF is 'true' simply because it is necessary for me to make it, I do think that the truth of NF can be concluded using an argument parallel to the one above.

First, we can rightly conclude that NF has a truth-value in the same way judgement NTJ has. Any agent x must make judgement NF about his freedom to act, and we can ask whether judgement NF(x) must be made by everyone. As in the case of judgement NTJ, this already partly fulfils the truth criterion for judgement NF—and if *everyone* were committed to make the same NF then its truth would be justified.

Secondly, since TUG is valid and since we are under the moral obligation T! to make a true judgement whenever a judgement can be true, we have a normative need to make NF only if it *is* true. Again, we cannot escape from the threatened normative inconsistency by not making NF at all; this is not a viable alternative for us as agents. Thus, we have a pro-attitude towards NF being true and should look for an interpretation of NF that could be true—that could be the object of everyone's pro-attitude. To regard freedom as a good exclusively for me would not find any support, for the same reason that I find no justification for the claim (1) above (namely that truth is a good exclusively for me). It does not fulfil the criterion for a true value judgement and gives us therefore no reason

---

[18] It might be possible to explore the present result in an Apelian manner. For this, we would have to show that 'true' judgements can only be achieved in a discursive community, and that such a community must necessarily be governed by certain rules (such as mutual respect, tolerance, etc.). I wish to leave it open whether this strategy might ultimately prove possible, even though I consider it extremely unlikely. The moral value TVT does not seem wide enough in its scope for the far-reaching ambitions of Apel's argument. As argued above, there are many situations which are morally relevant but fall outside the domain of the making of true judgements. This value would allow us to exclude any agent who was not capable of ever forming a true judgement.

why we should accept it. The only circumstance in which NF is true is that in which we regard everyone's freedom as a good for everyone, because then, as in (3) above, the criterion is fulfilled: everyone has the same pro-attitude towards this evaluation because it is the only possible way for them to escape from normative inconsistency. In parallel to our conclusions concerning TUG, we reach the result that it is true that *everyone's freedom to act is a good for everyone*—thus a *universal* good. The only difference between the reasoning leading to judgement TUG and the present argument is that the reasoning for TUG was based upon a self-application of T! to judgement NTJ—while that for the demand T! is now applied to a different judgement; namely, NF.

This result, that everyone's freedom to act is a universal good, must be further qualified. For reasons of consistency, it cannot be that *all* freedom to act is held to be a positive value. The positive value can only refer to that freedom to act whose realization is compatible with the freedom of all other agents to act—what we might call a 'non-curtailing freedom'. This results from its being a universal value. Everyone's 'freedom to act' could not be a consistent true value if this included the freedom to curtail the freedom of others. To value 'curtailing freedom' positively would simply be contradictory to the *general* evaluation of freedom.[19] If my freedom to act is a positive value, then it is good to support it, to exercise it, etc. But to use it to limit another's freedom could not be an expression of a pro-attitude toward this *universal* value. In this case, the valuation of a 'curtailing freedom' would be a pro-attitude towards freedom being a good and also a rejection of freedom being a good at the same time. Thus, the implied evaluation of freedom would be at least indirectly inconsistent. True value judgement can only be about a qualified freedom, which does not curtail other agents' freedom. The problem of tolerance towards the intolerant, which is notorious in many ethical systems which are based upon some concept of individual freedom, would therefore not occur were the positive value resulting from the present argument employed. It can only justify individual freedom as long as it is not directed against other people's freedom. We may there-

---

[19] Freedom is a term used for (at least) two different things: it can mark both a capacity and the realization of a capacity. If we speak only about the capacity in abstract terms, then no contradiction will follow. My mere capacity to kill someone does not limit his capacity to act, as long as I do not realize it. But the freedom relevant to the present argument is the one which finds expression in actions; it is therefore the realization of a capacity—and the realization of a freedom which curtails other agents' freedom *does* limit their freedom.

fore rephrase the established value judgement more accurately (for obvious reasons I will call it 'FUG'):

> *Everyone's freedom to act (so long as it does not curtail other agents' freedom) is an objective good.* (FUG)

Is this convincing? One might question whether this objective valuation of a qualified form of freedom is what T! demands from me when I make the judgement NF. The freedom in NF seems to be unqualified. After all, NF, which is implied by *all* actions I perform, appears to include also those cases of exercising freedom which *do* curtail the freedom of other agents. Hence one might object that the judgement FUG, with a notion of non-curtailing freedom at its heart, is not the judgement which would make my necessary evaluation NF (which is about unqualified freedom) true. Obviously, there are actions that are practical expressions of an underlying freedom to act in the non-qualified way. And someone who acts in this way does implicitly place positive value in freedom quite generally, including this 'curtailing freedom'. But this possibility simply marks the case where the value judgement becomes important for our actions. If there are actions that express a curtailing freedom, then there is only one possible way for me to obey the moral demand T!: not to perform these actions. This is the only way for me to stop myself making this implicit value judgement about curtailing freedom which cannot consistently be true. This response is possible because individual actions (and thus their implied positive value judgement) are *not necessary*. Although, *qua* human beings, we *must act* and therefore must always make the implicit positive value judgement about freedom in general, we need not (and as we know now, we should not) act in those particular ways which imply an immoral (since not possibly true) positive value judgement about freedom; that is, in a way which curtails other people's free agency. We can conclude that there is only one 'true' and therefore moral way to act freely; namely, to act in such a way that it expresses mutual respect and support of the universal positive value 'non-curtailing freedom'.

This can be spelt out as a moral demand which comes close to Kant's categorical imperative (I will call it 'F!'):

> *Never act in such a way that your action violates the universal good of the freedom to act!* (F!)[20]

---

[20] This could also be expressed as follows: We must act in such a way that the value judge-

5.6. TRUTH, FREEDOM, AND THE DIGNITY OF THE RATIONAL FREE AGENT

These two universal goods, freedom and truth, demand that I, and every other rational agent, should have a certain pro-attitude towards them. We have just spelt out what this means in the case of freedom. With regard to truth it means, most of all, that we should not lie; neither to others nor to ourselves. The moral good 'truth', and the associated required pro-attitude towards it, requires further that we should make it easier for us, as much as for others, to come to true judgements.

To see 'truth' as a primary moral value is of course not uncommon in the tradition of ethics. Kant, for example, emphasizes that original sin is accounted for in the Bible as an act of *dishonesty*, and not as the murder of one's brother. It is, according to Kant, the lie 'through which evil has come into the world' (*KGS* VI. 431).[21] This even accords with Montaigne's maxim that lying is the greatest of all vices: 'Truly, to lie is a mortal sin. We are only human beings and we only regard others as such through the truth' (*Essais* bk i. ch. ix).

Yet any such value must withstand absurdity. In a way similar to Phillips-Griffiths's objection to discursive ethics (cf. 1957/8: 116), one might wonder if the suggested principle of morality would entitle an agent to 'beat his fellows mercilessly' if they were 'less enthusiastic about finding out the truth about something'. There are two reasons why such an appearance does not lead to the relentless sacrifice of all other positive values to the search for truth. First, truth is not the only moral good; the argument has shown that freedom can make an equal claim to being a moral value. That is, for example, why the only absolutely safe refuge from falsity, namely the abstinence from *all judgements* (if necessary through suicide), is not required—and even immoral. It would be strongly against the moral *value* of free agency. Secondly, T! says that we should make true judgements *'whenever we make judgements with truth-*

---

ment implied by our action is universalizable. If we define 'maxims' as the value judgements that are implied by a type of action, we gain a surprising and unusual account of what the universalizability in the test of the categorical imperative might amount to: universalizable maxims are the ones which refer to those actions which *imply a true value judgement*.

[21] This finds strong textual support elsewhere; there are numerous places where Kant emphasizes the absolute demand for truth. See, for instance, the paper about the murderer at the door (*KGS* VIII. 273 ff.), several obligations of the *Rechtslehre* and *Tugendlehre* (e.g. *KGS* VI. 303, 441, 446), and the second example of the *Grundlegung*.

values'. It is not an absolute command to make judgements with truth-values whenever possible. There is, for example, a woman who wanders through the streets of Milan and stops when she sees someone with a big nose in order to tell him or her how huge and ugly their nose is. She should not be praised according to this argument. (Probably, she needs a psychiatrist more urgently than a tutorial in moral philosophy.) If I do not speak about certain things, then I am not obliged to tell the truth about them. If, however, my silence is seen as a contribution (someone might misread it as an affirmation), then this very silence can become a lie.

It is important to observe that the two moral values 'truth-judging' and 'non-curtailing freedom' must be compatible with each other if both are rationally founded.[22] Moreover, there seems to be a deep connection between the two. Let us look briefly at two aspects that might make this clearer. On the one hand, we could not act in a meaningful, intentional way if we did not make some true judgements about how things are *prior* to any action. True descriptive and normative knowledge is required for any realization or support of qualified, true freedom to act. There is an important analysis by G. Taylor (1994: 149–52), who shows that fundamental vices are crucially based upon a wrong judgement concerning the self and its positive value. If we act upon a wrong judgement concerning ourselves—or, as Taylor says, a 'misguided self-creation' (ibid. 151)—we will not be able ever to exercise true freedom. On the other hand, we can interpret the making of true judgements itself as a moral *free action*. It is a moral realization of non-curtailing freedom since the action 'making true judgements' does not interfere in principle with the freedom of others to act—it might even help them to be freer in a true sense (since, as argued above, truth is required for qualified freedom).

Of course, there will surely be empirical situations in which a conflict between the two values might arise. Kant's notorious example of the murderer at the door will spring to mind (*KGS* VIII. 273 ff.); this is a situation where truth seems to lead to a permanent inhibition of the (potential) victim's freedom. But examples of this kind show only that there will be conflicts once we reach the level of applying moral demands to particular situations, since the demands are norms about ideal states of affairs for a defective world. Many situations will show imperfections in

---

[22] Hence the universal validity of moral values can also serve as a criterion of rational identification of further ones (if there are any): if some candidate value contradicts a rationally justified value, then it cannot be classified as a value (or the prior justification was wrong).

different ways, and we cannot respond to all of them at once. How to deal with these challenges is a difficult issue that cannot be discussed here, but it is important to stress that these possible conflicts at the level of application do not reveal any 'structural' inconsistency between the two moral values. (Such a *structural* inconsistency would arise, for instance, between the value of making true judgements and, *ex hypothesi*, a value of ignoring reasons as the basis of one's judgements.) According to the suggested argument, both values are equally fundamental and thus there seems no absolute hierarchical relation between them.[23]

The deep connection between the two moral values could also be expressed in a different way: they are two aspects of one ideal of human agency and existence. Let me sketch a way in which this thesis might be argued. Both—everyone's making true judgements as much as everyone's freedom to act—refer to human activities or, since there is no reason to restrict them to humans, to the capacities of any being that is capable of making judgements with truth-values and of free agency.[24] They are values of, and with respect to, *all rational free beings*. We might also put it thus: the two judgements TUG and FUG tell us that there is something valuable in rational free beings behaving or acting in a certain way. Reason gives us a notion of moral good, in our own case as much as in the case of others. These capacities are, however, not simply some feature which man might have, but instead crucial characteristics. They are commonly used to define man. If we are entitled to see these notions as at the heart of what we are, then we could regard them as aspects of one larger value; we can see them as two subsumed aspects of the value *of* all free and rational beings; that is, all beings which have the capacity

---

[23] The order of rational justification would surely be that truth comes before freedom; as I argued above, we have to acknowledge the moral value of truth *before* we can hope to discover any other moral values. It alone provides us with the (moral) epistemological tool which allows us to expand the result. But the order of discovery, even if it is a necessary one, is not automatically a mirror of the hierarchy of values. After all, one needs drills to mine diamonds out of a mountain. Yet in modern times we use diamond-headed drill bits to work the mines even more thoroughly. The same seems true for truth and freedom: truth is the tool for the discovery of further values, but to grasp this tool, as much as to discover it, is itself already a free act. (Truth seems the ratio cognoscendi of the value of freedom, but freedom the ratio essendi of the act of discovering truth.)

[24] Nothing in this justification would allow us to restrict the established true judgement to any particular species of beings. This would be exactly the kind of restricted truth which we had to exclude as insufficient to guarantee the truth of the necessary judgement NF or NTJ.

to act freely and to make true judgements. When we value free and rational beings in these capacities, we value them in their full personality. To express it in more traditional language: these two moral goods are essentially about (and aspects of) the 'dignity' of human beings.

And since we grant agents a moral status with respect not to any *end* to which they might be subordinated but to what they *are*, or what capacities they have, this larger moral value can be seen as intrinsic. From what has been said above, it follows that we should never treat other people as means, because this deprives them of their freedom to act and to set their own goals, and is therefore a violation of their fundamental intrinsic value. To lie to someone is depriving him of the ability to make true judgements and hence a violation of his intrinsic value with respect to TUG. Further, the value judgements do not demand an instrumentalization at a second level—we must not respect others only instrumentally, as a means for, or instrument of, free action or the making of true judgements. Kant writes at one point that to lie is an instrumentalization (of oneself) for a further end, as if one were a mere 'talking machine' (KGS VI. 430)—using this expression we can say that it would be absurd to see others as 'truth-machines' or 'act-machines' when we respect their truth-judging or freedom.

We might put the resulting demand in terms of a general moral principle (MP). It reads as follows:

In your deeds and words, always respect the dignity of everyone, i.e. support your and their capacity to come to the truth and to be truly free!
(MP)

Everyone, whether he is moral or immoral, whether he is mature, a child, or even a 'marginal' agent, deserves this respect in his mere (even minimal) capacity to make true judgements or to act freely.[25] And it should be added that the demanded respect is *not* due to other people simply 'as they are' but for what they can or might be. That does not make the value less intrinsic, but it gives it a clear direction: *the aim is not to respect everyone else with all his wishes and desires, but to support him towards the realization of his own moral capacities.*[26]

---

[25] Just as Kant sees autonomy (as a notion which includes freedom and a rational capacity) as the reason why we must respect the intrinsic value of others (KGS IV. 428/9), in the same way the intrinsic value of man is found in my argument to be based upon the two capacities. No one is excluded, even if he does not yet exercise the capacities himself.

[26] This promises also to be a substantial basis for universal human rights. There are differ-

5.7. FINAL REMARKS

Let me end by pointing out why the argument from normative consistency withstands the pivotal objections that have been raised against the transcendental arguments in the last two chapters.

If it works, the present argument avoids the main problem of the argument from agency by not being based upon an objectivation principle. The step from what I must evaluate to the judgement about an objective positive value is argued for transcendentally and not simply presupposed. Similarly, the fragmentation of the positive value over time, which lurked behind Gewirth's reasoning, is avoided. In affirming the truth of the evaluation, it is acknowledged that truth-judging is always a positive value. While present actions do not imply directly future evaluations, my acknowledgement of the full truth of this evaluation does so by virtue of its being true. To be directed towards the future and to care for one's future agency become moral demands, simply because free agency—other people's as much as one's own—has to be regarded as valuable, now and in the future. Hence I *should not* regard myself as a bundle of mini-subjects of short duration, and should act with consistent, long-term (good) purposes.

The argument from normative consistency also allows us to escape the difficulties Apel and Kuhlmann face. It demands respect for each individual equally, irrespective of whether or not he is likely to contribute towards rational discourse. Certainly, we still value in him the capacity to form true judgements and to act freely, but this is no longer instrumentally linked to any outcome. Mentally handicapped people deserve this moral respect as much as any fully autonomous agents—it seems enough that someone has the most minimal capacity to form judgements or to act. Even in those critical cases the moral demands remain applicable. Agents are not respected because of their contribution to something else (such as rational discourse), nor do they have to express

ent ways to make such a universal evaluation of rights. Utilitarianism, for example, grants equal respect to the extent that everyone contributes to the overall value of happiness: individual rights, etc. have to be obtained indirectly. The tradition of social contracts treats equality as a direct good. Everyone has equal rights and must be treated and respected in the same way. Although the result of the argument from normative consistency comes close to this position, it is not identical with it. Most importantly, the content of the rights is not dependent on people's claims, it is established independently from subjective preferences. Everyone has a right to act freely in accordance with the freedom of others, and to be capable of forming true judgements.

their interests directly. Anyone who merely implies some value judgement through thinking or acting is an addressee of TUG and FUG. Most importantly, the present argument provides the justification for that crucial step which remained unexplained in Apel's and Gewirth's argument: the very first moral step—which is that which takes me from me, as an individual, to the universal world of agents.

CHAPTER 6

Truth and Beyond

6.1. THE APPARENT TYRANNY OF TRUTH, AND THE FAILURE OF ETHICAL FOUNDATIONALISM

That ethical foundationalism is dangerous is an objection more prominent in philosophical than in ordinary discourse. But that ethical foundationalism is utterly doomed to fail is the common view of many philosophers and non-philosophers alike. Let us look briefly at these two criticisms: the first in general terms, the second in the version of Alasdair MacIntyre.

What is the danger of foundationalism? There is a common suspicion of any 'ultimate justifications' or of any claims to a strong notion of truth (or 'absolute truth'), especially in practical philosophy. Philosophers such as Popper and Habermas see this high aspiration as a moral swamp whence flow all too rapidly the dark waters of intolerance and totalitarianism. Anyone, they claim, who considers himself to know the truth about how we should behave or think is more than likely to dismiss people with different opinions and will be tempted to force others to accept his view. And, ultimately, he will feel justified in sacrificing others for his ideas, or, more exactly, for his ideology—in brief, any such claim to knowledge is the cradle of inhumanity. Only someone who is more modest about the status of his insights will be tolerant and open to others. 'If it is always possible', so the non-foundationalist seems to say, 'that I am wrong and another person is right, then I will have neither inclination nor reason to force my views upon him. Of course, I wish to argue with him, so that I (or he) may correct my (or his) wrong views, but this discussion will always be friendly and respectful. Such respect is, after all, the most promising way to learn from another.' Is ethical foundationalism, like the suggested attempt to ground some values transcendentally, capable of any such tolerant openness?

The second criticism is that foundationalism itself is a futile philosophical endeavour. Several arguments against its possibility in general, and against transcendental arguments as a suitable methodology in particular, have already been discussed and rejected in the course of this book. They will not be repeated here. It is, however, interesting to look at MacIntyre's accusation in *After Virtue*. Here he writes that ethical foundationalism of the enlightenment type—and the argument from normative consistency belongs in this tradition—is doomed to fail if it is not based upon a strong ontological commitment to a teleological structure of human nature. He criticizes philosophers as various as Diderot, Hume, Kant, and Adam Smith.[1] All of them, MacIntyre says, share a flawed type of argumentation.[2] They

> share in the project of constructing valid arguments which will move from premises concerning human nature as they understand it to be to conclusions about the authority of moral rules and precepts. I want to argue that any project of this form was bound to fail because of an ineradicable discrepancy between their shared conception of moral rules and precepts on the one hand and what was shared—despite much larger divergences—in their conception of human nature on the other. (Ibid. 52)

---

[1] For peculiar reasons—since he does not even attempt to justify moral norms or principles—MacIntyre even includes Kierkegaard in this list. According to MacIntyre, Kierkegaard's approach has 'precisely the same structure' (1985: 52) as the others. It is not clear why this should be the case.

[2] In addition, MacIntyre argues that they share a highly specific historical background (namely, a particular Protestant form of Christianity—Diderot's Catholicism was sufficiently Jansenist to belong to this background). It should go without saying that this fact itself (even if true) cannot serve as an argument against (or for) them. It says nothing about the validity of their contribution, just as the quality of MacIntyre's arguments itself does not depend on his twentieth-century Irish Catholic background. MacIntyre would heavily disagree: 'Moral philosophies are, before they are anything else, the explicit articulations of the claims of particular moralities to rational allegiance' (1985: 268). He tries to defend his historicist view against the crucial attack that even he needs some non-historical standards for judging the different moralities with a pragmatic argument. We don't aspire to a 'perfect theory, one necessarily to be assented to by any rational being ... but rather the best theory to emerge so far in the history of this class of theories' (ibid. 270). However, it remains difficult to see how MacIntyre will avoid Rorty's relativism and still decide what the 'best theories' are without some timeless standard in respect of which they are 'better'. If the standard for a 'better theory' is that it replaces prior theories (as he suggests on p. 270), then Nietzsche's theory (according to MacIntyre, 'the moral philosopher of the present age' (ibid. 114)) must be regarded as much better than Aristotle's or MacIntyre's own—after all, there are many more philosophers following Nietzsche's rejection of truth in moral matters than philosophers who look to the Aristotelian tradition for the *telos* of man.

The discrepancy which MacIntyre detects results from an altered framework of ethical enquiry. Most notably, Aristotle's *Nicomachean Ethics* had for centuries given the paradigm of a teleological ontology: man was seen in two ways, 'man-as-he-happens-to-be' and 'man-as-he-could-be-if-he-realised-his-essential-nature' (MacIntyre 1985: 52). In this scheme, ethics was supposed to spell out rules and precepts which tell man how to realize his essence. Thereby the function of reason was twofold: it 'instructs us both as to what our true end is, and as to how to reach it' (ibid. 53). This view changed dramatically during the rise of modernity. Reason was no longer seen as capable of discovering essences and ends, but reduced to a mere calculative faculty, which assesses only the 'truths of fact and mathematical relations' (ibid. 54; that MacIntyre names Kant amongst philosophers who are characterized by this understanding of reason is rather surprising). MacIntyre argues that they all share an a-teleological ontology: 'all reject any teleological view of human nature, any view of man as having an essence which defines his true end' (ibid.). Without the notion of a human *telos*—and this is MacIntyre's central point—the idea of moral rules and precepts becomes vain, and they lose their direction. Without this ideal, the continued search for rules shows the 'impossible and quixotic character of their self-appointed task' (ibid. 55). In other words, if all we have is the plain, quasi-mechanical notion of man that is detached from any concept of his essential function and potential goodness, then no meaningful rules can be deduced. According to MacIntyre, human nature understood in a non-Aristotelian way is not only an infertile soil for morality; even worse, it nurtures nihilism. Nietzsche most clearly understood this consequence and was willing to draw the radical conclusions. He comprehends, to use MacIntyre's words, that 'what purported to be appeals to objectivity were in fact expressions of subjective will' (ibid. 113) and turns this insight into the only honest form of 'morality' that is left for non-Aristotelians. He proclaims unrestricted powerful subjective willing, exemplified in the *Übermensch*, as the source of all values. Here the ultimate failure of the moral project of the Enlightenment is finally obvious. It is not surprising that the only possible remedy for a world without moral orientation is, according to MacIntyre, the surrender of the foundationalist project and a return, *mutatis mutandis*, to Aristotle.

The present foundationalist enquiry makes claims to justify true judgements and it is placed exactly in what MacIntyre would call the failed Enlightenment tradition.[3] Does the argument from normative consistency, which starts from reflections on our individual rational agency, avoid the failure named by MacIntyre?

In what follows, I will reject these two criticisms by placing them in a wider discussion. For this, I will return to the three theses of moral realism that were introduced in the first chapter—namely, the truth thesis, the motivational thesis and the moral-fact thesis. I will give an outline—admittedly a very rough one—of how the three theses can find support from the argument from normative consistency. Thereby I hope to show that the two criticisms are not decisive.

6.2. THE TRUTH THESIS OF MORAL REALISM

6.2.1. Does the Argument from Normative Consistency Lead to True First Principles?

The truth thesis of moral realism says that we can make moral judgements with truth-values we are able to determine. And the argument from normative consistency aspires to provide exactly this; namely, the justification for the truth of some fundamental value judgements. The resulting truth might be called 'absolute' (although this term makes many philosophers shudder) or we can use a plainer expression and simply say 'true first principles'. (If there are true first principles, then there can be, by definition, no way of 'getting behind' them. In this sense, they are rightly called 'absolute'.)

Let me add another remark on terminology at this point. The central project of this book is to show that judgements of the type 'x is good' or 'x is a moral value' have truth-values, and that some of them are true. To talk about the 'truth' of judgements of this type is in accordance with a common tradition of cognitivist moral philosophy. But in connection

---

[3] The argument from normative consistency is placed, though, more or less exclusively in the part of this tradition which began with Kant and was continued by German Idealism. MacIntyre's analysis of the enlightenment tradition fails to recognize that there are very different approaches in Great Britain, France, and Germany. In particular, there are two main tenets of Kant and his successors firmly established in the German Idealist tradition, and to these MacIntyre does not pay sufficient attention: first, transcendental reasoning with reason as its starting-point (which is not a mere contingent fact), and, secondly, an attempt to bridge the gap between the plain factual world and norms—as, for example, in Kant's *Critique of Judgement* and in Hegel's elaborate system (see esp. Hösle 1988).

with norms the term 'right' is used more commonly (see, for example, Sidgwick 1901: 2 ff.). In what follows, I will accept this distinction as a mere manner of speech, but not as a way to reduce covertly the validity of judgements about norms.

However, we should specify what is—and what is not—meant when speaking about the truth of first principles. There are two caveats to keep in mind. First, to justify first principles (and thus to claim 'absolute' knowledge) is not the same as being absolutely sure or certain. The former is an epistemological enterprise, the latter a psychological state. They are logically independent of each other: some people are 'absolutely' sure about something, even about first principles, without providing any justification at all. Sometimes their claim is merely based upon some feeling, intuition, or authority (common in religious fundamentalism). Other people might provide a valid justification for some thesis but are nonetheless doubtful about its truth (as argued in Chapter 2, retorsive transcendental arguments in particular have a tendency not to satisfy the psychological desire for direct insight). A second caveat follows immediately: a justification of first principles is—like any other type of reasoning—possibly wrong. To talk about 'true first principles' is not to suggest that our search for it is immune to error. And we can err in many ways with regard to the choice of a methodology or with regard to the conclusions we draw on the basis of a methodology. However, if someone wants to object in a particular case that a justification is invalid, he must show that some applied standard, some premiss, or the inference is unintelligible, wrong, or insufficiently justified. (Of course, any such criticism will have to reflect upon its own standards and will have to demonstrate why they are appropriate and superior. If someone merely claims that the choice of methodologies is beyond rational criticism, then this claim would have to be justified.) Simply to be suspicious is not a 'reason' proper to reject the foundationalist project.[4]

---

[4] This seems to be the rather odd thesis of radical fallibilism; namely, that knowledge of first principles is straightforwardly impossible. If it is meant to be more than a general warning—and some authors clearly see their tenet as being stronger—then this objection itself must be regarded as a (dogmatic) first principle. It would therefore require a justification of exactly the type it claims is unattainable. In this sense, Hösle (1990: 168–75) replies cogently to H. Albert's radical-fallibilist criticism (1975) of Apel's project. Hösle shows that it does not help if the radical fallibilist sees his central thesis itself as being radically fallible (Albert 1975: 123). In this case, the radical fallibilist would have to see his own thesis as simply one (more or less aesthetic) view among others. All of them could make equal claims to validity—they are all likewise fallible. But then the fallibilist can no longer use his principle in any rational way to

We should explore in some more detail the question of whether the argument leads to 'truth' in the rich, literal sense that is required by the truth thesis. Although it seems pointless to question whether a judgement can be called 'true' if it finds support from sufficient, and sufficiently strong, reasons—what else could 'true' mean?—we can surely question whether the reasons that are employed in the argument from normative consistency are sufficiently strong. The methodology of retorsive transcendental arguments in general, and their relevant truth-conditions, namely that the impossibility of denying a statement consistently is an adequate reason to accept it if there is no further alternative, has been argued for at great length above (Ch. 2). I do not want to repeat the discussion here.

Let us, rather, look at the suggested criterion for the truth of value judgements, since on this the entire argument depends. The criterion reads: 'If there were some state of affairs which everyone had to regard as a positive value (as good), and if this evaluation were consistent with all other rational judgements that we must make, then this state would rightly be regarded as a positive value.' Essentially, this criterion is based upon a certain understanding of what objective moral values are; namely, some state of affairs towards which everyone should have a pro-attitude. (And the suggested argument detects this universal 'should' in the normative need to bring a self-imposed demand into accord with a value judgement that we make.) Once this account of moral values is accepted, the criterion follows analytically.

At this point, one could raise the following objection: Is the criterion not making the allegedly 'objective truth' of a judgement dependent on our attitudes and thus relative to agents? Thomas Nagel has stressed that 'truth' needs independence from a merely subjective perspective. Something can only rightly be called 'objective' if it must be seen as such from the 'view from nowhere' or, more exactly, 'the point of view of detached self-observation' (1997: 112). He calls this the demand for generality of reasons (ibid. 119). A reason is something one person could rightly claim to have if everyone else had it as well, were he in the appropriate circumstances. Thus, to achieve objective knowledge in ethics (as in any other area) we need this kind of 'agent-neutral reasons' (1986:

'criticize' the high aspiration of transcendentalists. Further, this fallibilism can become dogmatic: if the fallibilist does not take any criticism seriously (because he sees all first-principle reasoning as flawed), then his position makes itself immune to rational objections (Hösle 1990: 171).

152–3; 1997: 120), not 'agent-relative, essentially egoistic' ones (1997: 120). Does the suggested criterion for the truth of value judgements fall into of this agent-relativity? No, it does not—although the normative need to respond to the self-imposed demand T! is indeed not agent-neutral (it is always the discrepancy between my self-imposed demand and the judgement that I must make). But my demand is not reason enough to accept the value judgement (*pace* Gewirth). The reason is that everyone is committed to an agent-dependent demand and has therefore a pro-attitude towards some end, and that there is only one possibility of understanding this end in a way that fulfils the demand consistently. It is here that the subjective point of view must be transcended. The fact that everyone must transcend the agent-dependent point of view provides an agent-independent reason to acknowledge the truth of the value judgement.

Let us look at a further requirement for a meaningful truth criterion. In order to be substantial, it must account for a distinction between true and false judgements. The fulfilment and a non-fulfilment of this criterion must be sharply separated and this must be done in a way which is not itself obscure but transparent (failure in this was one of the main objections against intuitionism, cf. p. 22 f.). This, again, is granted by the suggested criterion. The main tool in this task is the difference between necessary and contingent pro-attitudes. The criterion is only satisfied, and a value judgement true, if everyone must have a pro-attitude to the state of affairs expressed in the judgement. If there are no pro-attitudes, or if these attitudes are only contingently held, then no truth follows. Of course, I do not claim that it is an easy task to determine the exact character of pro-attitudes in particular cases and to find out whether they are necessary. There is always 'a great danger of our defending transcendental arguments that express the conceptual idiosyncrasies of twentieth-century Europeans', as Wilkerson says quite rightly (1976: 205). But this is a practical difficulty that we have to be aware of—and not a refutation of the criterion.[5]

There is a further requirement for a true, i.e. rationally justified, value judgement. At the outset (pp. 14–17.) a rational justification was distin-

---

[5] To argue from a fashionable perspective that there are no universal rational features but, once again, that all we have are the rational idiosyncrasies of Europeans is either literally irrational or self-refuting. I will therefore not discuss this objection any further. It would be in vain anyway—I cannot but argue within the framework of this allegedly contingent conception of reason, and I assume that any opponent of this type of reason will not have accepted any of the argument stated thus far.

guished from an explanation by the stipulation that it can 'survive reflection' (Korsgaard 1996: 49). That means the resulting value must retain the normative force even if we know everything about it. And, indeed, reflection does not seem to threaten the authority of the value judgement about truth and freedom. On the contrary, I have argued that to realize that the criterion is fulfilled is only possible if I take prescriptive performative conditions of reasoning seriously. Within the argument from normative consistency, the point of the reflection is to become aware of implied evaluations, and to realize that we are consistent only if we acknowledge their authority. It is the opposite of reducing the true value to any descriptive matter of fact.

6.2.2. A Typology of True (or Right) Moral Judgements: Levels of Generality

I have called the content of the fundamental normative judgements rather vaguely (following Korsgaard) the 'source of normativity'. In the course of the above investigation we were able to specify 'values', which, however, can also be expressed as fundamental norms. For us, moral values and norms appear to be but two sides of the one coin. I have argued that the demanded universal pro-attitude is identical to the granting of the status 'positive value'. Still, it seems in some way that the values are logically prior, to the extent that the demands are dependent on them. Norms are about our maintaining a pro-attitude towards the state of affairs which is expressed in the value.

The argument from normative consistency has been employed to ground the truth of two fundamental moral values, and of the human dignity which seems to be constituted by these two values. I have argued that these values—and the corresponding demands—are universally binding. Since they result from our rational nature, we must see them also as invariant. It is not possible to think about a radical change in the constituent features of reason. As argued above, we cannot think rationally about any essentially different conceptual schemes if they are untranslatable into schemes with which we are familiar. The same conditions make it impossible to think about an altered notion of reason. This does not mean that we could not imagine our rational capacities increasing, or imagine some aspects of our understanding being modified (for example, in an evolutionary process). But we cannot understand what it would mean to call a type of activity 'rational' which would imply that the most basic features of our reason (such as *modus ponens* and the positive evaluation of truth) would no longer be 'rational'. Even an increased level of reason could not make things irrational which we regard as rational. It would be irrational to suppose it could.

Although the universal validity of the fundamental positive values cannot be questioned rationally, these values or, more exactly, the accompanying fundamental demands or norms are surely not universally applicable. There are many situations where they are simply not relevant. If, for example, an artist is painting an imaginary portrait of an alchemist, the demand to make true judgements about alchemy or its practitioners does not seem of much importance for her painting. Besides, these norms will not always present themselves in the same way to us; they need to be adjusted to the particular situation. Both TUG, for example (truth is a universal good) and T! (the accompanying categorical imperative) are at the highest level of generality. They can be spelt out very differently in different contexts; for example, when Peter is asked by the maid: 'Are you not also one of this man's disciples?' (John 18: 17); or when, in Joseph Conrad's 'Heart of Darkness', Marlow is asked by Mr Kurtz's fiancée what the last words of the late 'remarkable man' were.

Given these considerations, it seems useful to separate two levels of values or norms:

(1) The first and most fundamental level of morality is the one which is the main subject of this book. The truth of judgements about positive values at this level is a priori, and the accompanying demands must be regarded as categorical because there is no rational alternative to them. We might call them 'first-order norms'. Two values of the fundamental kind were introduced in the previous chapter (truth and freedom[6]), and three first-order norms accompany them (T!, F!, and MP). It has not, however, been shown that there are not possibly more positive values or norms at this level.

(2) At the second, subordinated level we have to specify norms for particular situations. We can call them 'second-order norms'. It is here, to put it metaphorically, that the abstract norms are translated into the everyday language of our world. This task is a continuous, dynamic process. Structurally, this 'translation' can be expressed in the form of a mixed syllogism. The first premiss is the statement of an a priori moral

---

[6] One might also call human dignity, the summary formulation of truth and freedom, a fundamental 'positive value'. This is merely a question of convenience.

value or norm (from the first level), the second premiss spells out some empirical facts about our world which are relevant to the maximum realization of this value.[7] In order to be a valid deduction, it must be true in all cases that in a sufficiently similar situation every agent would do the same. The 'translation' of the first-order norms should be invariant with respect to the individual agent or recipient.

If, for example, we start from FUG (or F!), then we must ask for the particular conditions of life which foster or inhibit the freedom of people. Chains, for example, obviously inhibit people, but not chains only—and not all limitations of freedom must always be seen as bad ('Being your slave, what should I do but tend | Upon the hours and times of your desire?' (Shakespeare, Sonnet 57)). These are insights that we gain through experience, and that are therefore expressed as synthetic judgements a posteriori. The conclusion of this mixed syllogism is the specified second-order norm for particular situations, such as 'Do not chain people up!' (And there might also arise situations where we see it as appropriate and even morally demanded to chain people up.)

We might also find values at this second level. In some cases the first-order values could be used to deduce some (indirect) second-order values. Examples could be respect for the environment (which respect helps people to live and thus to realize their freedom), or generosity (which will help people to be free from oppressing needs, and might help them also to acquire some manner of education which will afford them greater insight). Friendship might be the most profound way to respect the dignity of another person. But all those second-order values would be only indirectly good, their status depending on the service they (and their accompanying norms) provide for the fundamental moral values.[8]

---

[7] When Aristotle differentiates between the eternal, invariable ends and the ways one might bring them into existence, he seems to make the same distinction (although it should be noted that this reading has recently been regarded as contentious). The practical wise man must know both, first, what is good or valuable (e.g. contemplation) and, secondly, through the mental operation of deliberation, what the best means of achieving it might be (NE 1140^{a}1141).

[8] This is, however, not entirely satisfying. Is friendship good only because it liberates people in the right way and makes them come to true insights? Is it wrong to torture an animal only because it might make us more likely to be violent to human beings? At least intuitively, it seems appealing to grant, for example, animals or ecological systems an intrinsic value. It must, however, be noted that our intuitions about further intrinsic values might be wrong: 'The claim that morality is cognitive and that we have some moral knowledge is not the claim that all our moral convictions as they now stand are true or justifiable' (Schneewind 1970: 260).

At the second level we find many difficulties which can only be mentioned briefly here. What will we do in cases when the inhibition of an agent's freedom is the only way to support the freedom of someone else? It seems that to arrest a notorious murderer is a minor inhibition of his freedom compared with the limitation of his (potential) victim's freedom. But how do we measure, and how do we compare the realizations of moral values? And what do we do if there is a conflict between two different values (Shall I tell the murderer at the door where his victim is?). Can we strike a balance between their realization—and if we do so by a type of consequentialist reasoning, how do we link this with the transcendental methodology employed in justifying the two moral values in the first place?

There are many riddles that I cannot answer here. Yet these problems do not provide a reason to resort to anti-realism, let alone nihilism, since the justification of the first-order values remains valid and is not affected by problems of application (*pace* B. Williams (1966)).

We should note that second-order norms can be at different levels of generality, depending on the generality of the empirical premiss. We can ask what to do when a type of situation turns up, but also look for the very specific action we should take at some particular moment. Thereby, the most general kind of second-order norms might seem to blur the sharp distinction between the first and second order. Basic human rights, for example freedom of speech or the right to live, seem to be very close to the first-order norms F! and T!. The mountain of moral realism has no sharp cliffs but, rather, gentle slopes.

Still, it is important not to confuse the different kinds of justification available. First-order norms are justified a priori, while even the most general second-order norms take some empirical limitations or conditions within our world into account. These second-order norms are moral because they are placed within a well-defined normative framework, but they are substantial because they are located within an empirical context. To adopt Kant's famous expression: norms are empty without empirical knowledge—and empirical knowledge is blind without guidance through norms.[9] If, for example, we do not know anything about freedom and its limitations, we could not put the demand to foster

---

[9] The exception being the self-application of T!. Here, the first-order norm is not empty but gives a concrete imperative for all rational beings beyond and before any empirical knowledge of the world. In general, however, first-order norms need this translation.

freedom into practice. Hence Moore is right to emphasize that our practical task always requires twofold knowledge:

> Whenever, therefore, we ask 'What ought we to do?' or 'What ought we try to get?' we are asking questions which involve a correct answer to two others, completely different in kind from one another. We must know *both* what degree of intrinsic value different things have, *and* how these different things may be obtained. (1903: 26)

With regard to 'truth' or 'rightness', there is an important difference between the two orders. There is a priori truth (or rightness) to be found at the first level, and weaker, since partly empirical, truth at the second. This is due to the second premisses and to the changing conditions of our world. This leads to two difficulties.

First, exploring and comparing empirical situations:

> Hence we can never be entitled to more than a *generalisation*—to a proposition of the form 'This result generally follows this kind of action'; and even this generalisation will only be true, if the circumstances under which the action occurs are generally the same. (Moore 1903: 23)

Secondly, there are the difficulties of anticipating the future:

> It is, indeed, obvious that our view can never reach far enough for us to be certain that any action will produce the best possible effects. (Ibid.)

Accordingly, the second-order norms are only contingently right.[10]

6.2.3. Truth and Intersubjectivity

Gewirth's step towards universal community by mere analogy, as I have argued above, is unsatisfying. But the immediate connection between transcendental arguments and intersubjectivity, as proposed by Apel, is

---

[10] Following Apel's account, we might add a third category of norms: those that result from an actual consensus. Yet in order for them to be 'moral' norms they must be based upon a moral second-order norm which demands consensus about a particular matter. Furthermore, the procedure of reaching the consensus must be governed by second-order norms like fairness, freedom of speech, mutual respect. That is why we could call them 'collateral moral norms'. Conventions about how to behave towards each other (like the rules of friendliness) might be an example; to break them is then not only rude but also, to a certain extent, immoral. (It is obvious that there can also be a consensus about 'norms' which are not moral. Remember Joseph's brothers: 'Come now therefore, and let us slay him, and cast him into some pit, and we will say, Some evil beast hath devoured him' (Genesis 37: 20).) With regard to truth, these collateral moral norms can only be indirectly right; their rightness depends entirely on the rightness of the appropriate second-order norms.

too tight. As stated above, in contrast to the view of Apel (and also Kuhlmann, Habermas and other proponents of the consensus theory of truth), the validity of norms or value judgements is not constituted by any real or anticipated consensus. I have argued at great length that the truth of a normative judgement requires different epistemological tools, i.e. transcendental arguments, which can be used by any individual reasoner. If the argument from normative consistency is valid, then the truth resulting from it would be independent of the agreement of other people. Its basis is merely that everyone has a good reason—which he can find through reflection—why he should agree. This marks an important departure from Apel.

One might object, however, that consensus plays a central role in the argument from normative consistency: the criterion of the truth of value judgements (that everyone is committed to having a pro-attitude) reads prima facie like a reference to some ideal consensus. But this is not the case. The argument states that it is a feature of every rational being to have this commitment, whether or not there is any consensus about it. Here truth comes before the consensus and is independent of it.

Still, there is something more we can say about intersubjectivity. Even if general consensus and cooperation are not the ultimate methodological requirements, some such consensus can be morally required. I would argue that the moral principle (MP) demands the quest for an intersubjective agreement in some areas. The first area is the very common situation where people disagree about a matter of fact. Since truth leads ideally to consensus (if something is true, then every rational being should agree), disagreement is a sign and indicator of (at least one) false belief. Because it is a moral imperative to seek to arrive at true judgements (and to assist others in doing so) the disagreeing rational agents are, by virtue of the value 'truth', obliged to aim at agreement. MP implies, amongst other things, that it is my duty to help others avoid wrong beliefs. Yet this agreement is not an intrinsic value ranking over and above truth—if someone knows that he is right, in the face of a widespread disbelief, he should not sacrifice his conviction merely for the sake of an agreement. And there is an important caveat to bear in mind. As finite beings, it is more than likely that we err. A general disagreement with others should be a warning, and should make us think twice (if not more) about our beliefs. On the whole, critical cooperation with others is more likely to help us approach the truth. (Thus, to a certain extent, there is a methodological reason for setting consensus as a goal, but this is not the same as in the argument from discourse—it does not constitute truth, it merely helps practically to overcome errors.) There is another area where we should strive for a consensus; namely, moral values. The demand for consensus here follows from the fact that each agent has an obligation to act on the values 'truth' and 'freedom' more consistently than he actually does, and that he is obliged to support this end in his own case as much as in the case of other agents. However, knowledge of these values seems indispensable for their full realization. Therefore, we should support everyone's insight into what is truly valuable, and thus seek general agreement on the issue.

The ideal of the argument from normative consistency is therefore not the solitude of an individual thinker who contemplates the highest truth for truth's sake, and for his own sake, as seems to be suggested by Plato, Aristotle, and many philosophers in the wake of Descartes. The argument from normative consistency synthesizes two elements of the two previous transcendental arguments: as in the argument from agency, the actual transcendental justification is grounded in the individual subject independently of all others. This result is combined with the insight of Apel that the reflection of the single subject does not suffice. In contrast, however, to the latter, the anticipated intersubjectivity is not regarded as the condition of successful individual reflection, but as its normative completion.[11]

6.2.4. Truth and Tyranny: A Short Remark

From what has been said in this section it follows that the suggested 'absolute' values are not likely to become the means of moral tyranny. On the contrary, there are good reasons why no moral oppression should find legitimization on this basis. First, it is performatively inconsistent to force others to accept the two fundamental moral values—because this would disregard their dignity and thus violate exactly the values that are so important. Besides truth, everyone's freedom is a fundamental moral value and it is simply unclear what it would mean to force someone to

---

[11] The problem of strict solipsism remains, and is not dispelled by the argument from normative consistency. But the argument is not entirely silent on the subject. It demands that I should make the step from respecting myself to respecting others—even if the solipsist thinks that he is not certain of their existence, the moment he claims to others not to be certain he contradicts himself. He would be obliged not to disrespect them. At least, so long as he acts *as if* other people exist, normative consistency demands this behaviour (even if they prove a mere phantom of his mind).

be free. Secondly, to force or manipulate others so that they accept the proposed values would not be any (morally required) aid to their making true judgements. This can only be the consequence of a rational process. If I am forced to repeat some words without fully understanding them, this is not an act of judgement-formation. Thirdly, the demand for truth is merely conditional upon making judgements in some area. So the argument entitles people to correct others in a rational way when they err in words or deeds (i.e. when they disrespect others). But the argument retains a sharp distinction between, on the one hand, arguing for a judgement and criticizing wrong tenets (i.e. making reasons available to people) and, on the other hand, manipulating them in ways which have nothing to do with rationality. Fourthly, the high value 'truth' is not to be identified with subjective opinion. Rather, the argument from normative consistency can criticize, for example, all forms of arbitrary subjective stance in ethics on the grounds that they make unjustified claims to validity (they are not judgements everyone must make). In particular, the argument allows one to criticize the subordination of truth or freedom under other (not justified) values such as my power, my pleasure, or my advantage.

Let us look at the issue from a different and less defensive perspective. The suggested fundamental values are not only useless for a tyranny of moral absolutism, they are the best protection against it. What could be a better philosophical safeguard against any oppression and abuse of power than to state that the dignity of human beings is to be respected universally? In the argument from normative consistency respect for my intrinsic value is interwoven with respect for the value of others, and I can only respect my own dignity (my freedom and the value of my making true judgements) to the degree that I respect and value the same in others. And what other, better basis could we hope for than an argument to the end that it is literally true that truth and freedom are moral values and that they are therefore categorically demanded? Of course, we are dealing with thoughts and arguments—and they cannot necessarily stop the immoral use of power. To keep that in check, more is needed: a whole armoury of persuasive techniques, ranging from appeals to feelings and intuitions up to direct force. But this does not mean that philosophical reasoning is a mere intellectual game without any cash value. With the argument from normative consistency and its results we have a practical compass in our hand with which we may navigate to moral ends by clearly legitimized means.

6.3. THE MOTIVATIONAL THESIS

6.3.1. Reasons, Motives and Hume's Challenge

There is a much-discussed ambiguity when we speak of 'reasons for actions'. The term 'reason' can have two quite different meanings, both of which are used to make actions intelligible. On the one hand, a reason for acting explains why an action occurred, on the other hand, reasons are used to determine whether an action is justified.

In the first sense, i.e. when explanatory reasons for actions are at stake, we also talk about the 'motives' of an agent. They describe what we might call very generally 'psychological states . . . that play a certain explanatory role in producing actions' (M. Smith 1994: 96). This is independent of what exactly these states might be (e.g. feelings, passions, desires, beliefs, mere neurophysiological conditions) and of how they actually operate (e.g. causally through some neurotransmitter). We can say quite generally that a motive is best accounted for in terms of the agent's pursuit of an end or goal.

This is to be distinguished from 'reason' in the second sense, where a *justification* for the rightness of actions is called for. This is the stricter understanding of reason, and I will call it (and have done so throughout this book) simply 'reason' or 'justifying reason'. Justifying reasons normally operate within a normative framework; they show whether or not an action, or its end, is in accordance with some general normative principle. In this sense, reasons are dependent on, and relative to, the normative framework the agent applies. However, reasons can also be employed to justify the normative framework itself—the task of this book's transcendental reasoning. Thus, there are two distinct tasks that justifying reasons can perform: in their transcendental function, they found a normative framework (I will call this the 'first' level of enquiry); in their deductive function, justifying reasons allow us to judge the rightness of particular actions or ends within the parameters set by this framework (the 'deductive' or 'second' level).

Hume's challenge is a thesis about the interaction of justifying reason and motives, or, more precisely, his denial of a direct influence of justifying reasons upon motives. All motives are, according to Hume, essentially based upon passions, and 'reason alone can never be a motive to any action of the will' (1978: 413). He argues for this thesis by looking at the achievements of reason: it 'judges from demonstration or probability; as it regards the abstract relations of our ideas, or those relations of objects, of which experience only gives us information' (ibid.). Thus, neither of these operations is apt to give us ends or goals. In the first case reason looks for abstract relations in the 'world of ideas' (here Hume thinks mainly of mathematics), and is apt for mechanical calculations or for 'fixing the proportion of numbers' (ibid. 414). In the second case reason leads to empirical knowledge about the causal connection between things in the world. Knowledge of things, and of the relations between them, is itself mute with regard to what our goals are. According to Hume, only passions can provide goals—'when we have the prospect of pain or pleasure from any object, we feel a consequent emotion of aversion or propensity, and are carry'd to avoid or embrace what will give us this uneasiness or satisfaction' (ibid.). These two fundamental passions are not dependent on anything else, they are 'certain instincts originally implanted in our nature' (ibid. 417), and an 'original existence' (ibid. 415). In particular, it is obvious to Hume that reason can never give birth to passions. Reason's sole function is to tell us how to achieve desired goals; that is, what means we should choose in order to achieve our ends. Thus, reason's contribution to motives is merely indirect, it remains the 'slave of passion' (ibid.): 'And these emotions extend themselves to the causes and effects of that object, as they are pointed out to us by reason and experience' (ibid. 414).

One could object that Hume's argument is simply based upon his definition of reason. If reason is accounted for in a merely instrumental way, then it seems a truism that it will never provide goals or ends (for this see Korsgaard 1986a). If we replaced this understanding of reason with a richer one that included the capacity of setting ends and goals (like Kant's concept of *Vernunft*), then reason would have a motivating force. Many moral realists follow this path when they argue that the Humean picture of reason and our psychology is simply false (for example, Nagel (1978), McDowell (1978), and Platts (1979)). Here, however, Humeans try to shore up Hume's thesis with further arguments (see e.g. B. Williams 1979) and sense some dogmatism on the part of the anti-Humeans. They ask, correctly, for evidence as to why reason should be more than a means-detecting faculty and how, in particular, its motivating force is meant to work. In this Hume/anti-Hume debate each side seems to suggest that the other has to do the proving: it is hard to tell in whose court the ball lies.

One of the problems of the ongoing debate over Hume's challenge is that it is rather difficult to fasten upon the appropriate criterion or method for the solution of the puzzle. We do not even have a clear common-sense view on the matter. On the one hand, it seems simply a common fact about us that an alteration in our behaviour follows quite regularly in the wake of a change in moral belief or judgement. There is thus a certain appeal in the view that one cannot sincerely accept any ethical judgement without an accompanying (at least prima facie) motivation for acting in accordance with it. On the other hand, we can never exclude the possibility that some desire was (possibly covertly) at work and was the real basis for action. Empirical research seems not very promising as a channel of enquiry, so long as we know so little about what exactly is going on in the brain. And, even if we did know much more, neurophysiological facts need an interpretation; that is, we have to decipher impulses as specific desires or beliefs. This is particularly difficult because we have no clear phenomenology of desires. Schopenhauer, for example, and, most famously, Freud have taught us that desires can operate at a subconscious level, which makes it impossible to use the mere lack of a desire phenomenon (where introspection does not find anything) as a clear indicator of the absence of a desire. This has been used by some Humeans—and already by Hume (consider his 'calm passions' (1978: 417))—to make their theory withstand objections from a phenomenological perspective. But it has also led to the accusation that the Humean position boils down to a self-immunizing dogmatism. (As Popper has reminded us, a sound theory must tell us the criteria for its possible falsification.) That is why some authors have seen the puzzle as insoluble, and the diverse answers as merely expressions of different attitudes (cf. Richard Galvin 1991).

6.3.2. Why Moral Realism Should Not Give Up the Motivational Thesis

Is Hume's (and the neo-Humean) thesis that reasons themselves cannot serve as a motive merely a subtle point of philosophical psychology without much relevance to ethics? No, it is of central importance, especially for any cognitivist moral realist, to refute Hume. If the realist gives up the claim that moral judgements have motivational force by themselves, then the way people behave will ultimately rest on a psychological contingency; namely, on the desires they happen to have. In this case no reason could move them to have different aims or goals, and this would deprive any attempt to argue for certain ends or goals of practical importance. People who do not happen to have the right desires could not possibly pay any heed to the imperatives which might adjust their goals and actions, because this would be contrary to the way the motivational apparatus functions.[12] Consequently, if people were never moved by reasons, it would be literally irrational to demand obedience to any rational categorical imperative—since these imperatives are justifying reasons or judgements about what sort of ends we should have. Yet moral demands are only meaningful (and thus rational) if they can be obeyed. Hence if Hume were right, the authority of moral demands would be heavily restricted. *Ultra posse nemo obligatur*. In this picture, at most, cognitivist moral philosophy could clarify the details of the moral law for those who happen to be passionate about it—but it would lose its prescriptive character for all others. In other words, if Hume were right, we would have to abandon the strict claim to moral objectivity. As Kant says with his legendary Königsberg wit, it would be the 'euthanasia (the soft death) of all morality' (*KGS* VI. 378).

That is why moral realists are well advised to hold the motivational thesis; namely to presuppose that there is a correspondence between moral judgements and a person's motives.[13] It is not necessary to defend an extreme motivational thesis, according to which *all* motives have to be built essentially upon beliefs or reasons. All that the moral realist has to hold is that if someone sincerely judges y to be better than not-y, i.e. if he knows a justification reason, then he has a *ceteris-paribus* motive to do or support y. It does not, of course, mean that after having realized the

---

[12] Hume's own view on this was clouded by talking about 'original existences', which he saw as an appropriate basis for a general ethics of benevolence. But it seems empirically wrong to assume that everyone has the same (or some same) passions. Further, it would require a proof as to why this should be the case. But what would such a proof look like? If it were the rational demonstration that everyone must have something as his or her goal, then—given that my account of the truth of value judgements is right—the Humean position would undermine itself and would give way to a type of moral realism.

[13] A kind of moral realism without the motivational thesis is defended by David Brink (1986). See also, for the problems of this position, M. Smith (1994: 60–91), who raises a further argument in favour of the motivational thesis. According to Smith, Brink's position would give an unconvincing account of moral action: people would need some prior general desire 'to do the good' and would aim at concrete good ends only in a derivative, indirect way (moral realism would tell them what the good consists of). Yet this would not capture what we mean when we say that someone is a good person. The common-sense understanding is exactly that he cares non-derivatively about other people (1994: 75). He would instrumentalize his concern for others, as a means for the end 'goodness'. Smith's argument is surely not without force, but, since it is based only on common sense, I will not explore it further.

demands of reason people will always follow them; it is sufficient to show that they can in principle be motivated by a rational imperative and can act accordingly. This means that the moral realist can happily agree that in the case of many, probably the majority of, morally neutral actions, our motives are based on impulses, desires, or habits, and that the motives are often mixed. He can even accept as an empirical matter of fact that this is normally the case when we act morally. As Aristotle reminds us, it is perhaps a good thing that we learn to act in the right way without explicitly and laboriously reasoning towards such right action in each case. (We might even argue that it is morally demanded not to reason all the time since it increases our freedom if we do not have to reflect upon everything we do over and over again. It may be a demand of ethical economy. This is particularly important when people are not naturally inclined to do good.)

It should be added that many cognitivist moral realists consider the motivational thesis to be an analytic truth about moral judgements. Otherwise, a further factor would be required to explain why this correspondence must take place. But what could this further factor be? Surely not further reasons, since reason's influence is the very *explanandum*. Only passion then (or a third yet unknown category) seems to remain. The same old problems enter the stage.[14]

It is exactly this motivational thesis that has made several authors argue that moral realism tries to achieve the impossible. Philippa Foot, for example, rejects the possibility of objective truth in ethics for this very reason (1978: 154):

> there is no such thing as an objectively good state of affairs. Such constructions as 'a good state of affairs', 'a good thing that p' are used subjectively, to mark what fits in with the aims and interests of a particular individual or group.

Is Foot right, or can there be objectively good states of affairs (for example, truth and individual freedom) that are linked to the individual aims of people? Or, in other words, can moral beliefs provide goals? It seems that, having developed a long argument for moral realism, I cannot simply leave Hume's challenge open and undecided. Let me therefore sketch a response.

---

[14] Obviously, the motivational thesis can also be linked with non-cognitivist ethics such as emotivism. If moral judgements are merely expressions of what people happen to desire (this position is therefore also called 'expressionism'), then it is analytically true that the judgements correspond to motives.

6.3.3. How Moral Beliefs can Motivate

Let us first look at a rather refined version of Hume's (rather crude) picture that has been suggested by several philosophers during the last few decades (e.g. M. Smith 1987/8; 1994). It is argued that having a belief is different from having a goal and that is why beliefs are structurally unsuitable ever to be a motive for an agent. This argument is based upon a distinction according to which desires and beliefs are mental states which have a very different 'direction of fit'. M. Platts sees Anscombe's *Intentions* (1957) as the *locus classicus* of this distinction, which he formulates as follows (though he is himself quite critical about it):

> Beliefs aim at the true, and their being true is their fitting the world; falsity is a decisive failing in a belief, and false beliefs should be discarded; beliefs should be changed to fit with the world, not vice versa. Desires aim at realization, and their realization is the world fitting with them; the fact that the indicative content of a desire is not realized in the world is not yet a failing in the desire, and not yet any reason to discard the desire; the world, crudely, should be changed to fit with our desires, not vice versa. (1979: 256–7)

The neo-Humeans, who base their argument upon this analysis, draw the following conclusions. If motives are about the pursuit of ends, then desires are the only acceptable bases for them. Beliefs' direction of fit seems simply incapable of doing this job. Their business is to mirror the world, and mirrors do not show people where to go. They are neither windows nor doors. Hence no belief in any state of affairs could possibly by itself explain why this state should be seen as good or ideal and why everyone who shares this belief has thereby accepted a certain goal. Beliefs and desires are completely separate states, and it would be wrong to assume that anyone could have a desire simply because he has a certain belief. As a consequence, there can be no rational insights into (i.e. beliefs about) certain special 'facts' which have the capacity to determine people's desires (as moral realism claims). Such moral 'facts' would be but red herrings.

The argument from normative consistency is based upon a close connection between value judgements (rational insights into the good) and pro-attitudes, as necessary performative conditions for any reasoning. This provides a setting that allows us to overcome the strict dichotomy between desires and beliefs—because the argument is about having the right goals, and it spells out what they are. It does so not by pointing to external goals in a motive-neutral way (which, again, would leave the question open as to why we should accept those goals). The argument detects, rather, some internal directedness which every agent necessarily has *qua* agent (i.e. the performative conditions of his being a rational agent). The crucial contribution of the argument is to show what the consistent, that is ideal, form of these internal goals is. The resulting moral judgements appear to be a third category: they have some of the features which the Humeans attribute to desires, and some features that they grant to beliefs.[15] On the one hand, the judgements about truth and freedom are like desires because they are about goals people have (expressed in the form of pro-attitudes). In contrast to normal desires or passions, these reasons are not about contingent or merely factual preferences or goals, not even about goals people always have for psychological reasons (like kleptomania, or like the fear of death) or physiological ones (like the desire to breathe and eat). They are, as argued above, performatively necessary pro-attitudes everyone must have *qua* rational being. Since they are implied in all acting or reasoning, it is impossible not to have and, therefore, not to accept them. It is no objection to this 'desire aspect' of transcendental reasons that they have a propositional content (like NTJ), for many desires have such a content (like 'my goal is x'). On the other hand, these value judgements are like beliefs in that they are about the truth of these positive values. To be sure, they are not about neutral matters of fact, and that is exactly the reason why they are not mere 'Humean beliefs' but something more— judgements with a motivational force.

To put the third category in terms of the 'direction of fit', we might say that this mode of reasoning is supposed to fit an ideal world or state of affairs. Falsity is a failure to mirror this ideal state correctly, and false beliefs will have to be changed. At the same time, by being about an ideal state, these beliefs aim at realization, and therefore demand a practical pro-attitude. Thus, correct beliefs about ideal states are not given up in the face of a recalcitrant world—the world, crudely, should be changed to conform to these ideal states.

There is a fundamental objection to the possibility of any such third category. Smith argues that we can be in any 'belief like state' without being in some 'desire like state' at the same time; that is, we can always have a moral belief without being motivated to act in accordance with it:

[15] J. E. J. Altham (1986) also suggests regarding normative judgements as a kind of third category, which he calls 'besires'. A similar point is made by McDowell in his defence of cognitivist ethics.

190 · *The Grounds of Ethical Judgement*

It is a commonplace, a fact of ordinary moral experience, that when agents suffer from weakness of the will, they may stare the facts that used to move them square in the face, appreciate them in all their glory, and yet still not be moved by them. (1994: 122–3)

Let us rephrase Smith's objection so that it is directed against the argument from normative consistency. Is it possible that someone could follow the argument, appreciate it 'in all its glory'—and remain still unmoved by it with regard to his actions? Certainly, this is possible. But it does not show what Smith wants it to; namely, that there are always clear-cut cases of mere beliefs and mere desires that are 'totally remov'd from each other' (Hume 1978: 413). The Humean armoury itself provides us with a response to Smith's objection: the person will be moved, but insufficiently strongly to become decisive or even self-conscious. And this is in accordance with the motivational thesis, which claims neither that the motive which comes from transcendental reasoning must be strong enough to lead to action, nor that it must be conscious for the agent. Weakness of the will is, and can be, granted by any sensible moral realism.

One might suspect that this would deprive the motivational thesis of its cash value and make it, according to Popper's standards, highly questionable. But this is not the case. The argument from normative consistency states that there are necessary pro-attitudes (i.e. goal-directed states) which every rational being must upon self-reflection admit to having—for example, a pro-attitude to the forming of exclusively true judgements. Reason's job is to 'enlighten' the agent about his own goals and about the possibility of being consistent. This happens in three steps: first, the reasoner realizes his ultimate, necessary pro-attitudes or goals (such as NTJ). Secondly, he reflects upon the only consistent way to understand them (by expanding the goal 'truth' so as to include everybody). And, thirdly, he acts upon this, or he fails to do so because he falls prey to other ends or goals he happens to have. And there are, contrary to Popperian suspicion, clear criteria for testing whether there is a motive given with a certain transcendental reasoning: the argument from normative consistency aims at the discovery of necessary motives (pro-attitudes) and is designed to make us aware of what they include. And the test for the presence of a motive is to ask whether we rightly judge some pro-attitude to be constitutive of a rational being.

From the start, the argument sees reasoning and pro-attitudes as inseparably connected; pro-attitudes are the performative conditions for all reasoning. And it is the very same pro-attitude at the beginning of the argument that explains why the reasoner who has fully understood the reasoning will have a motive to be moral. It is the only consistent realization of exactly this original goal. There is no further goal that he needs in addition to his necessary pro-attitudes.

One might raise a further objection to this conclusion. The pursuit of consistency might require a *desire to pursue*, prior to any reasoning. But this does not work: the pursuit of consistency is a necessary performative condition of being a rational agent at all. As argued above, we cannot simply withdraw from being rational agents and from constitutive performative aspects of so being.[16] What would it be like for there to be an agent without the original pro-attitude towards consistency? About what *agent* could we say: He does not happen to have a desire to be consistent?[17]

To sum up: the argument from normative consistency can withstand Hume's challenge. To acknowledge first-level norms like MP can rightly be regarded as providing a prima-facie motive for acting upon them, because it merely brings to light a goal which has always been there. And the motive is neither arbitrary nor contingently given with the human condition, but constitutive of us. Its rightness as much as its authority show therefore a unanimous non-rejectability by all rational beings.

---

[16] I twice quoted Nozick's remark that the motivational force of an argument cannot be stronger than the desire to avoid the inconsistency which is spelt out in this argument. The argument from normative consistency points to an inconsistency which cuts to the very heart of rational agency; so the price of rejecting it is to be at odds with one's own 'nature'. Certainly, one can be willing to pay the price and will not literally fall apart, but one would be fundamentally irrational to do so. More can never be shown by an argument.

[17] Hence the present argument is immune to Bond's attack on Gewirth: 'I need not desire, let alone value, this state of affairs itself, i.e. being an agent. And therefore I need not desire or value, per se, the generic properties (essential conditions) thereof' (1980^a: 45). The pro-attitude towards consistency is more fundamental than any desire to be an agent could possibly be—it is constitutive of any possible desire-bearing entity. This can also explain why there is a profound connection between happiness and morality. As Kierkegaard has reminded us in *Either-Or*: to be truly happy requires an inner continuity and consistency. Otherwise, there is simply no one there who could experience this happiness. The aesthete strives, according to Kierkegaard, for the impossible: he dismisses precisely this overall consistency in his life and will therefore never find real satisfaction. His life is an endless and ultimately tragic striving for more, new, and different amusements.

6.4. THE MORAL-FACT THESIS

6.4.1. Can We Escape the Ontological Question?

Moral realism has been introduced as the view that there are moral facts which exist independently of our evidence for them. In the main part of this book I have tried to develop a rational justification for judgements about some such moral facts. The main evidence for accepting them was a retorsive transcendental reasoning: we cannot deny consistently that they are valid. But what are they exactly? It has been argued that any transcendental reasoning must be connected with an appropriate ontology (cf. Quine 1964). And we should add that even if moral values are not deduced from metaphysics, an unintelligible metaphysics will block our understanding and practical appreciation of them. Where shall we place ideal goals in such a metaphysics, given that we understand this world normally in non-teleological terms (and that this is a very successful way, as we learn from modern sciences)? Do we populate reality with mysterious extra entities that do not fit into the picture of the world that we have?

At this point, it might be tempting for moral realists, using transcendental arguments, to accept a version of Stroud's objection and to argue that values or first normative principles would simply be entailments of our conceptual scheme, some facts about our thinking—and nothing more. This would dispense with metaphysical worries about the ontology of moral facts and might be a comfortable way of avoiding all unnecessary entities. But, as already argued above, Stroud's sceptic aims at the impossible. He cannot step back rationally and question his beliefs as being 'mere' beliefs. Stroud's obstinate sceptic is unable to raise a meaningful, rational objection and can therefore not deliver us from the ontological problem. A valid transcendental argument does not make claims about our beliefs as such, but about what some normative first principles must be like, in themselves and independently of us. In this sense, I have argued that Stine is right to see in transcendental arguments a verification (see p. 62), if this means that we must take certain things truly to be the way that we consider them to be, independently of us.

Some transcendental philosophers have dismissed the ontological problem on the basis of a coherence theory of truth, claiming that any enquiry about correspondence is illegitimate. Kuhlmann, in his powerful defence of transcendental arguments, says that we can simply disregard correspondence, since there is no position outside our conceptual scheme from which we could compare this scheme with the world as it is in itself. But we should not conflate an epistemological problem with an ontological one: our purpose is not to look in some way at the 'world in itself' in order to justify our beliefs about it. Kuhlmann is correct in his claim that this cannot be done. The intense philosophical debate around the correspondence theory of truth has taught us that we do not have direct access to some facts which could 'exert some leverage in the investigation of truth' (McDowell 1997: 222). Yet there is still the challenge of explaining the possibility of harmonizing the picture of a mind-independent world with our beliefs—beliefs obtained through a justification that is independent of any correspondence. Transcendental arguments share with the correspondence theory at least this: that they insist on the truth of some independent facts—but without using this as a criterion. They share with the coherence theory this: that the truth is to be found in some internal manner (although not on the basis of the ideally coherent system of beliefs, but through transcendental reflection). That is why I think we must raise the question: what kind of things are these ideal states of affairs or moral values? And how do they fit into the picture of the world we normally have?

6.4.2. *The Teleological Structure of Rational Agency*

The main challenge to the resulting ontology is that there exist (if the proposed argument works) teleological elements; namely, rational agents. These agents are parts of the world which are structurally directed towards some states of affairs. We are not simply like other neutral things, but, as I have argued, by being rational free agents, we are necessarily directed in a prescriptive manner towards being morally free beings. And this is not a contingent fact about our world, but spelt out by transcendental argument as a fundamental truth about a whole class of entities. Whenever there are free rational agents we must acknowledge that they have this normative structure or moral directedness. Thus, at the heart of the ontological view of the world which results from our proposed moral realism a teleological anthropology (inclusive, however, of all free rational agents, even the non-human) must find its place. We are beings with an intrinsic value which lies in our capacity to enjoy free agency and the rational capacity of making true judgements about the world. These are our normative structures which mark out what we are and what we shall be. To use MacIntyre's expression, we might say that the rational agent finds through transcendental reflections 'man-as-he-happens-to-be' *and* 'man-as-he-could-be-if-he-realised-his-essential-nature'. The argument from normative consistency has stated that we must see this agency as something which is, on the one hand, given (we cannot opt not to be rational agents) and, on the other, essentially goal-directed (we cannot deny these values). Yet both aspects are linked through a categorical imperative. MacIntyre is right in thinking that ethics is supposed to spell out rules and precepts which tell man how to realize his essence. But, against MacIntyre's suspicion, these insights into the 'essence', as much as into the rules, are the result of exactly the type of reasoning which was at the heart of the project of the Enlightenment, at least in the tradition of Kant and his successors. (Its roots, however, are much older.)

Can we say more about the 'essence' which the old subject should realize? Essentially, man is a rational being who is goal-directed. This goal can be seen as a transcendence of the limited self-understanding of the subject, in that there is a prohibition on all those actions (and on, e.g., mendacity, since that belongs with those actions) which mark out an exclusive orientation towards oneself. The crucial goal of morality is this transcendence of our solipsistic egoism. That itself, however, is of course not new—it has often been pointed out that the step away from the (old) self is the first and crucial moral action. Most prominently, it can be found in Leviticus 19: 18: 'Thou shalt love thy neighbour as thyself'. Our teleological structure tells us the direction of this move: the orientation of the moral subject must be towards an intersubjective realization of the goals which are structurally given with universal agency, and thus towards universal freedom and the universal capacity to discern truth. The subject is morally obliged to transcend his subjectivity for the sake of this good, whether or not it will ever be achieved.

This account of a crucial element in the metaphysical architecture of the world might seem to some extent Platonic. However, it does not employ a realm of value-objects existing independently of the self-understanding of agents (though I doubt that this is a correct reading of Plato), but emphasizes the moment of 'methexis'. The teleological structure is not entirely removed from the external empirical reality (as some interpretations of Plato suggest): we as rational agents are at the same time elements of this world. But the structure points towards an ideal realization which is not simply given but transcends the present state. (The most interesting departure from the world of Plato's forms might be that these normative principles, discovered by transcendental argumentation, are in a peculiar way self-referring, that is, reflexive. In us as rational beings, reason and hence these principles can become aware of themselves.)

There is also a certain relation to the Aristotelian/Thomist tradition of moral philosophy. Albeit the gap between 'is' and 'ought' is taken very seriously, and surely much more than in virtue ethics, the argument from normative consistency detects rational agency as a point where the two spheres meet. If we understand rightly what agency involves, according to the transcendental argument, we will see that there is some good already presupposed in the way we live and act. The epistemology involved in discovering this *telos* of our existence is surely different from that suggested by neo-Aristotelians; but the results show some likeness. Truth and freedom, being constitutive ideals of our agency, can also be used to illuminate our conception of human flourishing: if we must, for transcendental reasons, see ourselves in the light of these values, then we cannot but regard them as what our agency is all about. We cannot reasonably expect a satisfied or fulfilled life as agents if we disregard the most fundamental direction given by our agency.

Wiggins (1988) has rightly argued for a close relation between moral realism and the meaning of life, his point being that we cannot see any true meaning in some end if we do not regard it as objectively good. The very notion of meaning implies more than merely subjective ends which depend on us; it needs the regulative ideal of something transcending our subjectivity. This outcome easily relates to the argument from normative consistency. If what I have argued for throughout is correct, then there are indeed ideals which transcend the individual agent and show him what he should strive for. At the same time, however, such ideals are apt to unite all rational agency in mutual regard and respect. To fulfil the end of my agency is fundamentally linked with my respect for the dignity of all agents. The meaning of my life, in other words, cannot be found without granting full importance to the realization of the agency of everyone else.

6.4.3. *Some General Metaphysical Reflections*

These teleological entities raise many questions about the unity of the world. After all, teleological structures seem to be very different from ordinary 'things', like Lake Titicaca and grandfather clocks—but all are part of the very same world. So how are they united? And how is it possible for us to know about them through transcendental reflection? Let me first add some very general metaphysical reflection here.

An empiricist approach cannot explain the unity: it fails to grasp the teleological structures of rational agency, and is thus not able to locate them within the empirically known world. Yet we cannot, and shall not, simply give up the insights of transcendental reasoning in the face of empiricism, since we know those transcendentally given insights with *greater* reliability. I have argued that they are known a priori (since not rationally deniable), while all empirical knowledge is merely inductive.

Of course, if we accounted for the world in a Berkeleian spirit of idealism the troublesome problem of explaining the unity of the world and our capacity to understand the world might be solved—everything would be made out of the same kind of (teleological) material; namely, our thoughts. But what a metaphysical price we would have to pay! Our individual reasoning seems overburdened with this task: there are too many things in the world which seem quite independent of our thinking; we can only discover them through experience and not through introspection, and we cannot influence them through thinking at all. And how do we account for other subjects? Are they our thoughts too? Do they happen to think (into existence) the same world? Are we their thoughts? Further, and more importantly, this kind of idealism does not seem compatible with some results of transcendental arguments. These arguments attempt to show that we can know a priori that there is something which exists independently of what is felt or thought about it, and which is therefore not a product or projection of our minds. In brief, to equate everything which exists with the fruit of subjective thoughts does not really make the matter clearer.

It seems that a third way, between empiricism and idealism, could be more promising; namely, if we see a priority neither in the objective world nor in our reasoning, but look to an underlying common and foundational structure of both. In other words, the same principles may well structure reason itself, and be keyed into the way the world is. On the one hand, it could explain why the use of reason can give us true insight into the world. If the world is structured by principles which are related to those underlying reason, then this would account for our ability to grasp rationally the things which are independent of our thinking. It would allow reason (in the sense of our individual use of it) to find in itself the resources to discover a priori through reflection some fundamental truths.[18] In this case, our reasoning would not be a mere contingent act, but the realization of a much more general structure. On the other hand, this structure might be the unifying bond between a-teleological and teleological elements in the world.

I do not claim, by any means, that this metaphysical picture of the world could easily be made plausible. We must surely avoid the Charybdis of explaining the obscure by the more obscure as much as the Scylla of a *deus ex machina* ('the most absurd argument one could choose', as Kant rightly remarks in a letter to Herz of 21 February 1771). Therefore, much more would have to be said about this issue—all I wish to say at this point is that it might be worthwhile, from a moral-realist position, to look in this direction towards a possible ontological interpretation of the results of transcendental argumentation.

6.5. A FINAL REMARK

The main task of this book has been to explore the possibility of grounding our notions of right and wrong by the use of transcendental argumentation. I have argued that 'truth' and 'freedom' are amongst these fundamental values and that we must regard them as justified and objectively valid because otherwise we are (normatively) inconsistent. This approach has been critical to the extent that is based on the argument that some candidate positive value cannot be denied consistently. It should be enriched by a topical approach; that is, by a search for further candidate positive values which can be tested and justified transcendentally. This will require further and deeper philosophical investigation; possibly new and different methods; and moral imagination and creativity. But the moral goal of truth should motivate us never to stop striving towards this significant and highest end of philosophy: the quest for the knowledge of the good.

---

[18] This would, however, imply that we also have some a priori insights into the world (for this see e.g. D. Wandschneider 1982; D. Koch 2002). Since the only fundamental principles which are demonstrated by reason are those which transcendental argumentation aims to disclose, and since—as we learn from Stroud's unsuccessful objection—we cannot argue that they are merely relative to our reasoning, we must assume that they are also true of the underlying common structure.

References

ADORNO, THEODOR W. (1966). *Negative Dialektik*, Frankfurt.
—— and HORKHEIMER, MAX (1998). *Dialektik der Aufklärung. Philosophische Fragmente*, Darmstadt.
ALBERT, HANS (1975). *Transzendentale Träumereien*, Hamburg.
—— (1980). *Traktat über kritische Vernunft*, Tübingen.
ALTHAM, J. E. J. (1986). 'The Legacy of Emotivism', in G. Macdonald and C. Wright (eds.), *Science and Morality: Essays on A. J. Ayer's Language, Truth and Logic*, Oxford, 275–88.
AMERIKS, KARL (1982). *Kant's Theory of Mind: An Analysis of the Paralogism of Pure Reason*, Oxford.
—— (1999). 'Kant's Deduction of Freedom and Morality', in H. F. Klemme and M. Kuehn (eds.), *Immanual Kant* (International Library of Critical Essays of Philosophy, ii), Ashgate, 163–89.
ANNAS, JULIA, and BARNES, JONATHAN (1985). *The Modes of Skepticism: Ancient Texts and Modern Interpretations*, Cambridge.
ANSCOMBE, G. E. M. (1957). *Intention*, Oxford.
APEL, KARL-OTTO (1965). 'Die Entfaltung der "sprachanalytischen" Philosophie und das Problem der Geisteswissenschaften', now in 1976a: ii. 28–95.
—— (1972a). 'Noam Chomskys Sprachtheorie und die Philosophie der Gegenwart', now in 1976a: ii. 264–310.
—— (1972b) 'Sprache als Thema und Medium der transzendentalen Reflexion', now in 1976a: ii. 311–57.
—— (1975). *Der Denkweg von Charles S. Peirce*, Frankfurt (M.).
—— (1976a). *Transformation der Philosophie*, 2 vols., Frankfurt (M.).
—— (1976b). 'Das Problem der philosophischen Letztbegründung im Lichte einer transzendentalen Sprachpragmatik', in B. Kanitschneider (ed.), *Sprache und Erkenntnis. Festschrift für G. Frey*, Innsbruck, 55–82.
—— (1979). *Die Erklären-Verstehen-Kontroverse in transzendentalpragmatischer Sicht*, Frankfurt (M.).
—— (1980). 'The *A Priori* of the Communication Community and the Foundation of Ethics: The Problem of a Rational Foundation of Ethics in the Scientific Age', in *Towards a Transformation of Philosophy*, ed. and trans. G. Adey and D. Frisby, London, 225–308.
—— (1987). 'Fallibismus, Konsenstheorie der Wahrheit und Letztbegründung', in Forum für Philosophie, Bad Homburg (ed.), *Philosophie und Begründung*, Frankfurt (M.), 116–211.

References

APEL, KARL-OTTO (1988). *Diskurs und Verantwortung. Das Problem des Übergangs zur postkonventionellen Moral*, Frankfurt (M.).

—— (1989). 'The Compatibility of the "Linguistic Turn" and the "Pragmatic Turn" of Meaning-Theory within the Framework of a Transcendental Semiotics', in G. Deledalle (ed.), 19–70.

—— (1998). *Auseinandersetzungen in Erprobung des transzendentalpragmatischen Ansatzes*, Frankfurt (M.).

—— (ed.) (1982).*Sprachpragmatik und Philosophie*, Frankfurt (M.).

—— and BÖHLER, D. (eds.) (1981). *Funkkolleg: Praktische Philosophie/Ethik*, Studienbegleitbrief, iv, Weinheim/Basel.

AQUINAS, THOMAS (1932). *Summa Theologica*, Taurini.

—— (1950). *In duodecim libros metaphysicorum Aristotelis expositio*, Taurini.

ARISTOTLE. *The Categories. On Interpretation. Prior Analytics*, ed. and trans. H. P. Cooke (Loeb Classical Library), Cambridge, Mass./London, 1938.

—— *The Metaphysics* [*Met.*], i–ix, trans. H. Tredennick (Loeb Classical Library), Cambridge, Mass./London, 1933.

—— *Nikomachean Ethics* [*NE*], trans. H. Rackham (Loeb Classical Library), Cambridge Mass./London, 1934.

ASCHENBERG, REINHOLD (1978). 'Über transzendentale Argumente. Orientierung in einer Diskussion zu Kant und Strawson', *Philosophisches Jahrbuch*, 85: 332–58.

—— (1982). *Sprachanalyse und Transzendentalphilosophie*, Stuttgart.

AYER, A. J. (1936). *Language, Truth, and Logic*, Oxford.

BAIER, KURT (1958). *The Moral Point of View: A Rational Basis of Ethics*, Ithaca, NY.

BAUM, MANFRED (1986). *Deduktion und Beweis in Kants Transzendentalphilosophie*, Königstein (Taunus).

BECK, L. W. (1956). 'Kant's Theory of Definition', *Philosophical Review*, 65: 179–91.

—— (1960). *A Commentary on Kant's Critique of Practical Reason*, Chicago, Ill.

BECKERMANN, A. (1977). *Gründe und Ursachen*, Kronberg.

BENHABIB, SEYLA (1990). 'Communicative Ethics and Current Controversies in Practical Philosophy', in S. Benhabib and F. Dallmayr (eds.), *The Communicative Ethics Controversy*, London, 330–69.

BENN, S. I., and PETERS, R. S. (1959). *Social Principles and the Democratic State*, London.

BENNETT, JONATHAN (1966). *Kant's Analytic*, Cambridge.

—— (1979). 'Analytic Transcendental Arguments', in P. Bieri, Rolf P. Horstmann, and L. Krüger (eds.), *Transcendental Arguments and Science*, Dordrecht/Boston/London, 45–64.

BEN-ZEEV, AARON (1982). 'Who is a Rational Agent?', *Canadian Journal of Philosophy*, 1/2: 56–72.

BERLICH, ALFRED (1982). 'Elenktik des Diskurses. Karl-Otto Apels Ansatz einer transzendentalpragmatischen Letztbegründung', in W. Kuhlmann and D. Böhler (eds.), 251–87.

BEYLEVELD, DERYCK (1991). *The Dialectical Necessity of Morality: An Analysis and Defense of Alan Gewirth's Argument to the Principle of Generic Consistency*, Chicago, Ill.

BLACKBURN, SIMON (1984). *Spreading the Word*, New York/Oxford.

—— (1993). *Essays in Quasi-Realism*, Oxford.

BLASCHE, S., KÖHLER, W., KUHLMANN, W., and ROHS, P. (eds.) (1988). *Kants transzendentale Deduktion und die Möglichkeit von Transzendentalphilosophie*, Frankfurt (M.).

BOND, E. J. (1980a). 'Gewirth on Reason and Morality', *Metaphilosophy*, 11: 36–53.

—— (1980b). 'Reply to Gewirth', *Metaphilosophy*, 11: 70–5.

BOYD, RICHARD (1988). 'How to be a Moral Realist', in G. Sayre-McCord (ed.), 181–228.

BRINK, DAVID O. (1986). 'Externalist Moral Realism', *Southern Journal of Philosophy*, supplement, 23–42.

—— (1989). *Moral Realism and the Foundations of Ethics*, Cambridge.

BROOKS, RICHARD (1981). 'The Future of Ethical Humanism, the Re-introduction of Ethics into the Legal World: Alan Gewirth's Reason and Morality', *Journal of Legal Education*, 31: 287–305.

BURNYEAT, M. F. (1980). 'Can the Skeptic Live his Skepticism?', in J. Barnes *et al.* (eds.), *Doubt and Dogmatism*, Oxford, 20–53.

CARNAP, RUDOLF (1972). 'Empirismus, Semantik und Ontologie', in *Bedeutung und Notwendigkeit*, Wien/New York, 257–78.

CHISHOLM, RODERICK (1957). *Perceiving*, Ithaca, NY.

—— (1978). 'What is a Transcendental Argument?', *Neue Hefte für Philosophie*, 14: 19–22.

DARWALL, STEPHEN, GIBBARD, ALLAN, and RAILTON, PETER (1992). 'Towards Fin de Siècle Ethics: Some Trends', *Philosophical Review*, 101: 115–89.

DAVIDSON, DONALD (1973). 'On the Very Idea of a Conceptual Scheme', *Proceedings and Addresses of the American Philosophical Association*, 46: 5–20.

DAVIS, FELMON JOHN (1994). 'Discourse Ethics and Ethical Realism: A Realist Realignment of Discourse Ethics', *European Journal of Philosophy*, 2/2: 125–42.

DAWKINS, RICHARD (1976). *The Selfish Gene*, Oxford.

DELEDALLE, G. (ed.) (1989). *Semiotics and Pragmatics*, Amsterdam/Phila.

DESCARTES, RENÉ (1985). 'Discourse on the Method of Rightly Conducting One's Reason and Seeking the Truth in the Sciences', in *Philosophical Writings of Descartes*, i, ed. and trans. John Cottingham, Robert Stoothof, and Dugald Murdoch, Cambridge.

EDWARDS, PAUL (ed.) (1967). *The Encyclopedia of Philosophy*, London.

FICHTE, JOHANN GOTTLIEB (1971). *Fichtes Werke* (reprint of the 1845/6 edn.), ed. I. H. Fichte, Berlin.

FINNIS, JOHN (1977). 'Skepticism, Self-Refutation, and the Good of Truth', in P. M. S. Hacker and J. Raz (eds.), *Law, Morality, and Society: Essays in Honour of H. L. A. Hart*, Oxford, 247–67.

FINNIS, JOHN (1983). *Fundamentals of Ethics*, Georgetown, Wash.
—— (1998). *Aquinas: Moral, Political, and Legal Theory*, Oxford.
FOOT, PHILIPPA (1958). 'Moral Arguments', *Mind*, 67: 502–13.
—— (1958–9). 'Moral Beliefs', *Proceedings of the Aristotelian Society*, 58: 83–104.
—— (1961). 'Goodness and Choice, Part I' (Part II: A. Montefiore), *The Aristotelian Society*, suppl. vol. 35: 45–60.
—— (1970). 'Morality and Art', *Proceedings of the British Academy*, 56, London.
—— (1978). *Virtues and Vices and Other Essays in Moral Philosophy*, Berkeley, Calif.
FREGE, GOTTLOB (1961). *Die Grundlagen der Arithmetik*, Darmstadt.
GALVIN, RICHARD (1991). 'Does Kant's Psychology of Morality Need Basic Revision?', *Mind*, 91/2: 221–36.
GETHMANN, C. F., and HEGSELMANN, R. (1977). 'Das Problem der Begründung zwischen Dezisionismus und Fundamentalismus', *Zeitschrift für allgemeine Wissenschaftstheorie*, 8: 342–68.
GEUSS, RAYMOND (1983). 'Bemerkungen zu Rüdiger Bubners Beitrag', in E. Schaper and W. Vossenkuhl (eds.), 88–90.
GEWIRTH, ALAN (1970). 'Must One Play the Moral Language Game?', *American Philosophical Quarterly*, 7/2: 107–18.
—— (1981). *Reason and Morality*, Chicago, Ill.
—— (1982).'Why Agents Must Claim Rights: A Reply', *Journal of Philosophy*, 79: 403–410.
—— (1984). 'Replies to my Critics', in E. Regis jun. (ed.), 192–257.
—— (1993). 'The Constitutive Metaphysics of Ethics', *Revue de Métaphysique et de Morale*, 93/4, 489–504.
GIBBARD, ALLAIN (1990). *Wise Choices, Apt Feelings: A Theory of Normative Judgment*, Cambridge, Mass.
GOODMAN, NELSON (1965). *Fact, Fiction and Forecast*, Indianapolis, Ind./New York.
GRAM, MOLTKE S. (1971). 'Transcendental Arguments', *Noûs*, 5: 15–26.
—— (1973). 'Categories and Transcendental Arguments', *Man and World*, 6: 252–69.
—— (1974). 'Must Transcendental Arguments be Spurious?', *Kant-Studien*, 65: 304–17.
—— (1978). 'Do Transcendental Arguments Have a Future?', *Neue Hefte für Philosophie*, 14: 23–56.
GRANT, C. K. (1958). 'Pragmatic Implications', *Philosophy*, 33: 303–24.
GRUNDMANN, THOMAS (1993). *Analytische Transzendentalphilosophie. Eine Kritik*, Paderborn/Munich/Vienna/Zurich.
HABERMAS, JÜRGEN (1973a). *Kultur und Kritik. Verstreute Aufsätze*, Frankfurt (M.).
—— (1973b). 'Wahrheitstheorien', in H. Fahrenbach (ed.), *Wirklichkeit und Reflexion*, Pfullingen, 211–65.
—— (1982). 'Was heisst Universalpragmatik?', in K.-O. Apel (ed.), 174–272.
—— (1996). *Die Einbeziehung des Anderen*, Frankfurt (M.).

HARE, RICHARD M. (1952). *The Language of Morals*, Oxford.
—— (1963). *Freedom and Reason*, Oxford.
HARMAN, GILBERT (1977). *The Nature of Morality*, Oxford.
—— and THOMSON, JUDITH (1996). *Moral Relativism and Moral Objectivity*, Oxford.
HARRISON, JONATHAN (1967). 'Ethical Objectivism', in P. Edwards (ed.), 71–5.
HARRISON, ROSS (1974). *On What There Must Be*, Oxford.
—— (1989). 'Atemporal Necessities of Thought: Or, How Not to Bury Philosophy by History', in E. Schaper and W. Vossenkuhl (eds.), 43–54.
HENRICH, DIETER (1989). 'Kant's Notion of a Deduction and the Methodological Background of the First Critique', in E. Förster (ed.), *Kant's Transcendental Deduction*, Stanford, Calif. 29–46.
HESLEP, ROBERT D. (1986). 'Gewirth and the Voluntary Agent's Esteem of Purpose', *Philosophical Research Archives*, 11: 379–91.
HINTIKKA, JAAKKO (1972). 'Transcendental Arguments: Genuine and Spurious', *Noûs* 6/3: 274–81.
—— (1974). 'Practical and Theoretical Reason—An Ambiguous Legacy', in S. Körner (ed.), 82–112.
HÖFFE, OTTFRIED (1979). *Ethik und Politik*, Frankfurt (M.).
—— (1981). *Sittlich-politische Diskurse*, Frankfurt (M.).
—— (1982). 'Kantische Skepsis gegen die transzendentale Kommunikationsethik', in W. Kuhlmann and D. Böhler (eds.), 518–39.
HOGREBE, WOLFRAM (1974). *Kant und das Problem einer transzendentalen Semantik*, Freiburg/Munich.
HONDERICH, TED (1985). *Morality and Objectivity*, London.
HÖSLE, VITTORIO (1986). 'Die Transzendentalpragmatik als Fichteanismus des Intersubjektivismus', *Zeitschrift für philosophische Forschung*, 40: 235–52.
—— (1988). *Hegels System*, Hamburg.
—— (1990). *Die Krise der Gegenwart und die Verantwortung der Philosophie*, Munich.
—— (1991). *Philosophie der Ökologischen Krise. Moskauer Vorträge*, Munich.
—— (1992a). *Praktische Philosophie in der modernen Welt*, Munich.
—— (1992b). 'Größe und Grenzen von Kants praktischer Philosophie', in (1992a), 15–46.
HOSSENFELDER, MALTE (1988). 'Überlegungen zu einer transzendentalen Deduktion des Kategorischen Imperativs', in S. Blasche, W. Köhler, W. Kuhlmann, and P. Rohs (eds.), 280–302.
HUDSON, W. D. (1967). *Ethical Intuitionism*, London.
—— (1984). 'The "Is-Ought" Problem Resolved?', in E. Regis jun. (ed.), 108–27.
HUME, DAVID (1978).—*A Treatise of Human Nature* [1739/40], ed. L. A. Selby-Bigge, Oxford.
ILLIES, C. (1999). 'Blind vor Gott. Zu einem zentralen Problem der Ausnahmeexistenz im Rahmen von Kierkegaards theonomen ethischen Realismus', *Theologie und Philosophie*, 74/1: 48–69.

ILTING, KARL-HEINZ (1972). 'Anerkennung. Zur Rechtfertigung praktischer Sätze', in G. G. Grau (ed.), *Probleme der Ethik*, Freiburg (Breisgau)/Munich.

—— (1972/4) 'Der naturalistische Fehlschluß bei Kant', in Riedel (ed.), 1972/4, i. 113–30.

—— (1976). 'Geltung als Konsens', *Neue Hefte für Philosophie*, 10: 20–50.

—— (1994). *Grundfragen der praktischen Philosophie*, Frankfurt (M.).

ISAYE, GASTON (1952). *La Logique scholastique devant ses récents adversaires*, Bijdragen Uitg. door de filosofische en theologische faculteiten der Noord-en-Zuid-Nederlandse Jesuiten, xiii: 1–30.

—— (1953). 'La Finalité de l'intelligence et l'objection kantienne', *Revue philosophique de Louvain*, 51: 42–100.

—— (1954). 'La justification critique par rétorsion', *Revue philosophique de Louvain*, 52: 205–33.

JONAS, HANS (1979). *Das Prinzip Verantwortung*, Frankfurt (M.).

KANT, IMMANUEL. Unless otherwise noted, all page references are to *Kants Gesammelte Schriften* [KGS], edited under the auspices of the *Königlich Preussische Akademie der Wissenschaften in Berlin* (Walter de Gruyter, 1902–); the translations are mine.

KGS ii: *The One Possible Basis for a Demonstration of the Existence of God* (1763)
KGS iv: *Groundwork of the Metaphysic of Morals* (1785) [Groundwork]
KGS v: *Critique of Practical Reason* (1788) [CoPR]
KGS v: *Critique of Judgment* (1790)
KGS vi: *The Religion within the Limits of Pure Reason* (1793)
KGS vi: *The Metaphysics of Morals* (1797)
KGS vii: *Anthropology*
Quotations from the *Critique of Pure Reason* [CPuR] give the pagination of the first (A) and second (B) editions.

KEUTH, H. (1983). 'Fallibilismus versus transzendentalpragmatische Letztbegründung', *Zeitschrift für allgemeine Wissenschaftstheorie*, 14: 320–37.

KOCH, DIETRICH (2002). 'Das Gesetz für die Offenheit der Zukunft. Was können wir in der Physik *a priori* wissen?', in H-W. Ingensiep and A. Ensterschulte (eds.), *Philosophie der natürlichen Mitwelt*, Würzburg, 181–92.

KÖRNER, STEPHAN (1967). 'The Impossibility of Transcendental Deductions', *Monist*, 51: 317–31.

—— (ed.) (1974) *Practical Reason*, Oxford.

KORSGAARD, CHRISTINE M. (1986a) 'Skepticism about Practical Reasons', *Journal of Philosophy*, 83: 5–25.

—— (1986b). 'Aristotle and Kant on the Source of Value', *Ethics*, 96: 486–505.

—— (1996). *The Sources of Normativity*, Cambridge.

KUHLMANN, WOLFGANG (1975). *Reflexion und kommunikative Erfahrung. Untersuchungen zur Stellung philosophischer Reflexion zwischen Theorie und Kritik*, Frankfurt (M.).

—— (1985) *Reflexive Letztbegründung*, Freiburg/Munich.
—— and BÖHLER, D. (eds.) (1982). *Kommunikation und Reflexion*, Frankfurt (M.).
KUTSCHERA, FRANZ VON (1994). 'Moralischer Realismus.', *Logos*, NS I: 241–58.
—— (1999). *Grundlagen der Ethik* (2nd edn.), Berlin/New York.
LANE, MELISSA (1992). 'God for Orienteering? A Critical Study of Taylor's Sources of the Self', *Ratio*, NS 5: 46–56.
LANGE, H. (1988). *Kants modus ponens*, Würzburg.
LEIBNIZ, GOTTFRIED WILHELM (1996). Essais de Théodicée. Sur la bonté de Dieu, la liberté de l'homme et l'origine du mal', in *Philosophische Schriften*, ii, Frankfurt (M.).
LYCAN, W. GREGORY (1969). 'Hare, Singer, and Gewirth on Universalizability', *Philosophical Quarterly*, 19: 135–44.
MCDOWELL, JOHN (1978). 'Are Moral Requirements Hypothetical Imperatives?', *Proceedings of the Aristotelian Society*, suppl. vol. 52: 12–29.
—— (1996). *Mind and World*, Cambridge, Mass.
—— (1997). 'Projection and Truth in Ethics: The Lindley Lecture', in S. Darwall, A. Gibbard, P. Railton (eds.), *Moral Discourse and Practice: Some Philosophical Approaches*, Oxford, 215–25.
MACINTYRE, ALASDAIR (1985). *After Virtue*, Notre Dame.
MACKIE, J.L. (1964). 'Self-Refutation—A Formal Analysis', *Philosophical Quarterly*, 14: 193–203.
—— (1977). *Ethics*, Harmondsworth.
—— (1985). 'Anti-Realism', in *Logic and Knowledge*, Oxford, 225–45.
MAHOWALD, MARY B. (1980). Review of Alan Gewirth, *Reason and Morality*, *Philosophy and Phenomenological Research*, 40: 446–7.
MARLOWE, CHRISTOPHER (1909). *Plays*, London.
MILL, JOHN STUART (1962). *Utilitarianism*, ed. M. Warnock, London/Glasgow.
MITCHELL, D. (1964). *An Introduction to Logic*, London.
MONTAIGNE, MICHEL DE (1958). *Essais*, Paris.
MONTEFIORE, ALAN (1961). 'Goodness and Choice, Part II' (Part I: P.Foot), *The Aristotelian Society* suppl. vol. 35: 61–80.
MOORE, G.E. (1903). *Principia Ethica*, Cambridge.
—— (1977). 'A Defense of Common Sense', in *Philosophical Papers*, London, 32–59.
NAGEL, THOMAS (1978). *The Possibility of Altruism*, Princeton, NJ.
—— (1986). *The View from Nowhere*, Oxford.
—— (1991). *Equality and Partiality*, Oxford.
NAGEL, THOMAS (1997). *The Last Word*, Oxford.
NARVESON, J. (1980). 'Gewirth's Reason and Morality—A Study in the Hazards of Universalizability in Ethics', *Dialogue*, 19: 651–74.
NIELSEN, KAI (1984). 'Against Ethical Rationalism', in E. Regis, jun. (ed.), 59–83.
NIETZSCHE, FRIEDRICH (1988). *Kritische Studienausgabe*, ed. G. Colli and M. Montinari, Munich.

NIQUET, MARCEL (1991). *Transzendentale Argumente. Kant, Strawson und die sinnkritische Aporetik der Detranszendentalisierung*, Frankfurt (M.).

NOZICK, ROBERT (1981). *Philosophical Explanations*, Oxford.

O'NEILL, ONORA (1989). *Constructions of Reason: Explorations of Kant's Practical Philosophy*, Cambridge.

PASSMORE, JOHN A. (1961). *Philosophical Reasoning*, New York.

PEIRCE, CHARLES SANDERS (1931–58). *Collected Papers:* i–vi ed. C. Hartshorne and P. Weiss, vii–viii ed. A. W. Burks, Cambridge, Mass.

PETERS, R. S. (1966). *Ethics and Education*, London.

PHILLIPS-GRIFFITHS, A. (1957–8). 'Justifying Moral Principles', *Proceedings of the Aristotelian Society*, NS, 58: 103–24.

—— (1967). 'Ultimate Moral Principles: Their Justification', in P. Edwards (ed.), *The Encyclopedia of Philosophy*, viii, London, 177–82.

PLATON, *Opera*, ed. I. Burnet, Oxford, 1900–7.

PLATTS, MARK DE BRETTON (1979). *Ways of Meaning*, London.

POPPER, K.R. (1958). *Die offene Gesellschaft und ihre Feinde*, Bern.

—— (1979). *Die beiden Grundprobleme der Erkenntnistheorie*, Tübingen.

—— (1983). *Realism and the Aim of Science (from the Postscript to the Logic of Scientific Discovery)*, London.

—— (1984). *Objective Erkenntnis. Ein evolutionärer Entwurf*, Hamburg.

—— and MARCUSE, H. (1971). *Revolution oder Reform?*, ed. F. Stark, Munich.

POTHAST, ULRICH (1987). *Die Unzulänglichkeit der Freiheitsbeweise*, Frankfurt (M.).

PUOLIMATKA, TAPIO (1989). *Moral Realism and Justification*, Helsinki.

QUINE, W. V. O. (1951). 'Two Dogmas of Empiricism', *Philosophical Review*, 60: 20–43.

—— (1964). *From a Logical Point of View: Logico-Philosophical Essays* (2nd edn.), Cambridge, Mass.

RAILTON, PETER (1986). 'Moral Realism', *Philosophical Review*, 95: 163–207.

RASPE, R. E., (ed.) (2001). *The Surprising Adventures of Baron Munchhausen* (1st pub. 1785), London.

RAWLS, JOHN (1972). *A Theory of Justice*, Cambridge.

REGIS, EDWARD, JUN. (1981). 'Gewirth on Rights', *Journal of Philosophy*, 78: 786–94.

—— (ed.) (1984). *Gewirth's Ethical Rationalism: Critical Essays with a Reply by Alan Gewirth*, Chicago, Ill.

RICOEUR, PAUL (1965). *De l'Interpretation: Essai sur Freud*, Paris.

RIEDEL, MANFRED (1979). 'Normative oder kommunikative Ethik', in *Norm und Werturteil*, Stuttgart, 67–90.

—— (ed.) (1972/4). *Rehabilitierung der praktischen Philosophie* (vol. i. 1972, vol. ii. 1974), Freiburg.

RÖD, WOLFGANG (1977). 'Transzendentalphilosophie und deskriptive Philosophie als wissenschaftliche Theorien', in G. Schmidt and G. Wolandt (eds.), *Die Aktualität der Transzendentalphilosophie. FS Hans Wagner*, Bonn, 77–92.

RORTY, RICHARD (1972). 'The World Well Lost', *Journal of Philosophy*, 69/19: 649–65.
ROSENBERG, JAY F. (1975). 'Transcendental Arguments Revisited', *Journal of Philosophy*, 72/18: 611–24.
ROYCE, J. (1969). *Basic Writings*, ed. J. J. McDermont, Chicago, Ill.
SAYRE-MCCORD, GEOFFREY (ed.) (1988). *Essays on Moral Realism*, Ithaca, NY/London.
SCHAPER, EVA (1972). 'Arguing Transcendentally', *Kant-Studien*, 63: 101–16.
—— and VOSSENKUHL, W. (eds.) (1983). *Transzendentalphilosophie: Bedingungen der Möglichkeit*, Stuttgart.
—— (1989). *Reading Kant: New Perspectives on Transcendental Arguments and Critical Philosophy*, Oxford/New York.
SCHLICK, MORITZ (1925). *Allgemeine Erkenntnislehre* (2nd edn., repr. 1979), Frankfurt (M.).
SCHNÄDELBACH, HERBERT (1977). *Reflexion und Diskurs. Fragen einer Logik der Philosophie*, Frankfurt (M.).
SCHNEEWIND, J. B. (1970). 'Moral Knowledge and Moral Principles', in *Knowledge and Necessity: Royal Institute of Philosophical Lectures*, iii (1968/9), Glasgow, 249–62.
SCHÖNRICH, GERHARD (1994). *Bei Gelegenheit Diskurs. Von den Grenzen der Diskursethik und der Preis der Letztbegründung*, Frankfurt (M.).
SEARLE, JOHN R. (1983). *Intentionality*, Cambridge.
SEXTUS EMPIRICUS (1933). *Opera*, ed. and trans. R. G. Bury, Cambridge, Mass/London.
SHOEMAKER, SYDNEY (1963). *Self-Knowledge and Self-Identity*, Ithaca, NY.
SIDGWICK, HENRY (1901). *The Methods of Ethics* (6th edn.), New York.
SMITH, MICHAEL (1987/8). 'Reason and Desire', *The Aristotelian Society*, 88: 243–88.
—— (1994). *The Moral Problem*, Oxford.
SPECTOR, HORACIO (1992). *Analytische und postanalytische Ethik. Untersuchungen zur Theorie moralischer Urteile*, Freiburg.
SPINOZA, BARUCH DE (1986). 'Tractatus de intellectus emendatione', in *Spinoza's Ethics and Treatise on the Correction of the Understanding*, London, 227–63.
STEGMÜLLER, WOLFGANG (1969). *Metaphysik, Skepsis, Wissenschaft* (2nd edn.), Berlin/Heidelberg/New York.
STEIGLEDER, KLAUS (1992a). *Die Begründung des moralischen Sollens. Studien zur Möglichkeit einer normativen Ethik*, Tübingen.
—— (1992b). 'Die Begründung der normativen Ethik', in J.-P. Wils and D. Mieth (eds.), *Grundbegriffe der theologischen Ethik*, Paderborn, 84–109.
STERN, ROBERT (1999a). 'Introduction', in Stern (ed.), 1–11.
—— (1999b). 'On Kant's Response to Hume: The Second Analogy as Transcendental Argument', in Stern (ed.), 47–66.
—— (ed.) (1999). *Transcendental Arguments*, Oxford.

STEVENSON, C. L. (1968). *Ethics and Language*, New Haven, Conn.
STEVENSON, LESLIE (1982). *The Metaphysics of Experience*, Oxford.
STINE, WILLIAM D. (1972). 'Transcendental Arguments', *Metaphilosophy*, 3: 43–52.
STOHS, MARK D. (1988). 'Gewirth's Dialectically Necessary Method', *Journal of Value Inquiry*, 22: 53–65.
STRAWSON, PETER F. (1952). *Introduction to Logical Theory*, London.
—— (1959). *Individuals*, London.
—— (1966). *The Bounds of Sense: An Essay on Kant's 'Critique of Pure Reason'*, London.
STROUD, BARRY (1968). 'Transcendental Arguments', *Journal of Philosophy*, 65/9: 241–56.
—— (1994). 'Kantian Argument, Conceptual Capacities, and Invulnerability', in Paolo Parrini (ed.), *Kant and Contemporary Epistemology*, Dordrecht, 231–51.
STURGEON, NICHOLAS (1985). 'Moral Explanations', in D. Copp and D. Zimmerman (eds.), *Morality, Reason and Truth*, Totowa, NJ, 49–78.
SULLIVAN, ROGER J. (1989). *Immanual Kant's Moral Theory*, Cambridge.
TAYLOR, CHARLES (1985). 'What is Human Agency?', in *Human Agency and Language: Philosophical Papers*, i, Cambridge, 15–24.
—— (1989). *Sources of the Self: The Making of Modern Identity*, Oxford.
TAYLOR, GABRIELE (1985). *Pride, Shame and Guilt*, Oxford.
—— (1994). 'Deadly Vices', lecture to the Royal Institute of Philosophy, Feb. 1994.
THOMSON, JUDITH (1996). See Harman, Gilbert.
TOULMIN, STEPHAN E. (1970). *An Examination of the Place of Reason in Ethics*, Cambridge.
TRIGG, ROGER (1980). Review of Alan Gewirth, *Reason and Morality*, *Mind*, 89: 149–51.
UNGER, P. (1975). *Ignorance: A Case for Skepticism*, Oxford.
URMSON, J. O. (1958). 'Saints and Heroes', in A. I. Melden (ed.), *Essays in Moral Philosophy*, Seattle, Wash.
VAN INWAGEN, PETER (1983). *An Essay on Free Will*, Oxford.
WALKER, RALPH C. S. (1982). *Kant*, London.
—— (1989a). 'Transcendental Arguments and Skepticism', in E. Schaper and W. Vossenkuhl (eds.), 55–76.
—— (1989b). '"Achtung" in the Grundlegung', in O. Höffe (ed.), *Grundlegung zur Metaphysik der Sitten. Ein kooperativer Kommentar*, Frankfurt (M.), 97–116.
—— (1993). Lectures on the *Grundlegung der Metaphysik der Sitten*, Oxford University, Michaelmas 1993 (unpublished).
—— (1999). 'Induction and Transcendental Arguments', in R. Stern (ed.), 13–29.
WALZER, MICHAEL (1987). *Interpretation and Social Criticism*, Cambridge, Mass.
WANDSCHNEIDER, DIETER (1982). *Raum, Zeit, Relativität. Grundbestimmungen der Physik in der Perspektive der Hegelschen Naturphilosophie*, Frankfurt (M.).

WARNOCK, MARY (1978). *Ethics Since 1900* (3rd edn.), Oxford.
WHITE, S. K. (1982). 'On the Normative Structure of Action: Gewirth and Habermas', *Review of Politics*, 44: 282–301.
WIGGINS, DAVID (1988). 'Truth, Invention and the Meaning of Life', in G. Sayre-McCord (ed.), 127–65.
WILKERSON, T. E. (1975). 'Transcendental Arguments Revisited', *Kant-Studien*, 66: 102–15.
—— (1976). *Kant's Critique of Pure Reason*, Oxford.
WILLIAMS, BERNARD A. O. (1966). 'Consistency and Realism', *Proceedings of the Aristotelian Society*, suppl. vol. 40: 1–22.
—— (1979). 'Internal and External Reasons', in R. Harrison (ed.), *Rational Action: Studies in Philosophy and Social Science*, Cambridge, 17–28.
—— (1985). *Ethics and the Limits of Philosophy*, London.
WILLIAMS, MICHAEL (1977). *Groundless Belief*, Oxford.
WIMMER, REINER (1980). *Universalisierung in der Ethik*, Frankfurt (M.).
WITTGENSTEIN, LUDWIG (1963). *Tractatus logico-philosophicus*, Frankfurt (M.).
—— (1970). *Über Gewißheit*, Frankfurt (M.).
—— (1982). *Philosophische Untersuchungen*, Frankfurt (M.).
WONG, D. B. (1984). *Moral Relativity*, London.

Index

Adorno, Theodor W. 27 n.19, 28
agency/action 94 f., 98–100, 118–121; what it implies 69, 71, 93, 97–106
Agrippa 26
Albert, Hans 26 n.17, 172 n.4
Altham, J. E. J. 189 n.15
Ameriks, Karl 43 n.14, 43 n.15
Annas, Julia 7 n.7
Anscombe, G. E. M. 99, 188
apagogic argument, *see* indirect argument
Apel, Karl-Otto vi f., 47 n.21, 52 n.25, 53, 64–92, 114, 114 n.15, 128, 130, 132 f., 146 n.12, 156, 159 n.18, 166 f., 172 n.4, 179–181
argument from agency vi, 93–128, 166; and moral realism 111 f.; objections against 116–128; starting point 94–97, 116–118; structure 113–116; transcendental conditional 97–106, 113, 115
argument from discourse vi, 64–92; and moral realism 74 f.; starting point 65–67, 75–79; transcendental conditional 67–69; objections 86–89
argument from normative consistency vii, 129–167, 171, 171 n.3, 189; objections 153–156, 166 f.; starting point 129–133, 156; structure 156–158; transcendental conditional 133–140, 146 f., 189
Aristotle 7, 18, 27, 45, 45 n.18, 46 n.19, 54, 59, 66, 101, 127 n.26, 142 f., 156, 169 n.2, 170, 177 n.7, 181, 187, 195
Aschenberg, Reinhold 56, 57 n.28, 91 n.19
Augustine 156
Austin, J. L. 65
Ayer, A. J. 3 n.2, 19 n.14

Bacon, Francis 141
Baier, Kurt 19 n.14
Barnes, Jonathan 7 n.7
Baum, Manfred 37 n.8
Beck, L. W. 39 n.12, 43 n.14
Benhabib, Seyla 76 n.9
Benn, S. I. 19 n.14

Bennett, Jonathan 30, 35 n.5, 57 n.27
Ben-Zeev, Aaron 112 n.14
Berlich, Alfred 53, 132
Beyleveld, Deryck 93 n.1, 95 f., 96 n.3, 101 n.8, 112 f., 112 n.14, 126 n.24
Blackburn, Simon 8, 12
Bond, E. J. 97 n.4, 100, 191 n.17
Boyd, Richard 8
Brink, David O. 8, 57 n.28, 186 n.13
Brooks, Richard 105
Brouwer, L. E. J. 58 n.29
Burnyeat, M. F. 7 n.7

Carnap, Rudolf 12, 15, 19 n.14, 76
Chisholm, Roderick 19 n.13
Chomsky, N. 131 n.1
conceptual scheme 55 f., 175
Conrad, Joseph 176
consensus theory of truth, *see* truth
contractual thories 23 ff., 73

Darwall, Stephen 3 n.2
Davidson, Donald 30, 55, 55 n.26
Davis, Felmon John 5 n.4
deduction in ethics 25 ff.
Dewey, John 139
Dialectically Necessary Method 93–116
dignity 162–166, 182
Diderot, Denis 169, 169 n.2
Diogenes Laertius 26
Descartes, Rene v, 7 n.6, 12, 132 n.5, 181
Dostoevsky, Fjodor 4 n.3

F! 161
fallibilism 132, 132 n.5, 172 n.4
Fichte, Johann Gottlieb 30, 44, 53, 60, 61 n.31
Finnis, John 45 n.18, 46 n.19, 47 n.20, 52, 52 n.25, 53, 58, 127 n.26, 135, 137, 153
Foot, Philippa 2 n.2, 19 n.14, 20 n.15, 187
freedom 94–96, 105; as positive value 102–106, 109, 117–120, 159–162

Frege, Gottlob 39
Freud, Sigmund 23, 57, 185
FUG 161

Galileo, G. 57
Galvin, Richard 10, 185
Geuss, Raymond 55 n.26
Gethmann, C. F. 54
Gewirth, Alan vi f., 2 n.2, 20, 20 n.15, 24, 79, 92, 93–128, 130, 133, 137, 142, 153, 154 n.15, 156 f., 159, 166 f., 174, 179, 191 n.17
Gibbard, Allain 8, 16
Goethe, J. W. v, 126
Goodman, Nelson 19 n.13
Gram, Moltke S. 31, 32 n.2, 37 n.8, 76 n.9
Grant, C. K. 51
Grundmann, Thomas 36 n.7, 38 n.11, 39 n.12, 39 n.13

Habermas, Jürgen 3 n.2, 5 n.4, 24, 73 n.7, 168, 180
Hare, Richard M. 8, 19 n.14
Harman, Gilbert 3 n.2, 9, 11, 19 n.14
Harrison, Jonathan 19 n.12, 26 n.18
Harrison, Ross 29, 132 n.4
Hegel, Georg Wilhelm Friedrich 30 f., 51, 171 n.3
Hegselmann, R. 54
Henrich, Dieter 32 n.2
Herodotus 9
Heslep, Robert D. 100 n.6
Hintikka, Jaakko 61 n.31
Hitchcock, Alfred 139
Hobbes, Thomas 24
Höffe, Ottfried 78 n.10
Hösle, Vittorio 26, 44 n.16, 47 n.21, 52 n.24, 52 n.25, 55, 60 n.30, 64 n.1, 74 n.8, 84, 132 n.3, 171 n.3, 172 n.4
Hogrebe, Wolfram 91 n.19
Horkheimer, Max 28, 72 n.6
Hossenfelder, Malte 33 n.3, 36 n.7
Hudson, W. D. 22 f., 96 n.2, 119 n.19
human dignity 130
human rights 165 n.26
Hume, David 2 n.1, 10, 18, 28, 101, 120, 169, 182, 184–188, 190 f.
Husserl, Edmund 30, 36
Hutcheson, Francis 20

Illies, Christian 81 n.12

Ilting, Karl-Heinz 43 n.14, 78, 78 n.10, 157 n.16
implications of acting, *see* agency
implications, of scepticism, *see* scepticism
indirect argument 37 n.8, 46, 46 n. 19, 95, 106, 113 f., 117 f., 146 f., 151, 158–160; not decisive? 56 ff.; versus lack of counter-arguments 49
induction in ethics 17 ff.
intuition/intuitionism 20 ff., 43 n.14, 51, 80 f., 82 n.13, 84, 156, 172, 177 n.8, 182
Isaye, Gaston 51, 58, 60 n.30, 174
Jonas, Hans 57 n.28
justification of moral realism 14 ff., 157 f.

Kafka, Franz 4 n.3, 145
Kant, Immanuel 3, 10 ff., 14, 18, 24, 27 n.19, 28, 30–32, 34–40, 42 f., 45 n.18, 50 n.23, 57, 57 n.27, 60 n.31, 78 n.10, 80, 81 n.12, 87, 91 n.19, 94, 101, 102 n.9, 103, 112 f., 120, 157 n.16, 158 n.17, 161 n.20, 162 f., 162 n.21, 165, 165 n. 25, 169 f., 171 n.3, 178, 184, 186, 194, 197
Keuth, H. 67
Kierkegaard, Søren 5, 12, 149, 169 n.1, 191 n.17
Koch, Dietrich 197 n.18
Körner, Stephan 35, 55 f.
Korsgaard, Christine 5, 8 n.8, 16 f., 23, 49, 103 n.10, 175, 184
Kuhlmann, Wolfang vi f., 52 n.25, 64 n.1, 65–67, 69, 70 n.5, 72, 74–76, 78 f., 84–91, 114 n.15, 146 n.12, 166, 180, 192
Kutschera, Franz von 6 n.5, 9

Lane, Melissa 49 n.22
Lange, H. 33 n.3, 39 n.12
laws of logic 58 ff., 141
Leibniz, Gottfried Wilhelm 48, 96 n.3, 101, 127 n.26
Lorenz, Konrad 36 n.6
Lucifer 149
Lukasiewicz, Jan 58
Luther, Martin 156
Lycan, Gregory 101 n.8

McDowell, John 61, 184, 189 n.15, 193
MacIntyre, Alasdair 109 n.13, 126, 127 n.25, 168–171, 171 n.3, 194
Mackie, J. L. 3 n.2, 6, 8 ff., 52 n.25
Mahowald, Mary B. 105

Malcolm, N. 30
Marlowe, Christopher 149–151
Marx, Karl 23
metaethics 2 ff., 11–14, 155 f.
Mill, John Stuart 97
Mitchell, D. 46 n. 18
Montaigne, Michel de 162
Montefiore, Alan 2 n.2, 20 n.15
Moore, G. E. 2 n.2, 3, 5, 16, 19 n.14, 20, 22, 76, 99, 111, 126 n.23, 158, 179
moral anti-realism vi, 1 f., 6–11
moral facts 3 ff.
moral judgements, justification 14–17, 23
moral realism vi, 1 ff., 90–99; in need of justification 14 ff; its 'truth thesis' 3 ff., 74, 112, 171–182; its 'moral-fact thesis' 4 f., 74, 112, 171, 192–197; its 'motivational thesis' 5 f., 74, 112, 171, 183–191
MP 165
Münchhausen trilemma 25 f., 33, 61

Nagel, Thomas 3 n.2, 5, 10, 17, 60, 114, 136, 141, 173, 184
Napoleon 41
Narveson, J. 124 n.21
naturalistic fallacy 18 ff., 21, 27 ff., 41, 63, 75–79, 90, 97, 99, 101, 106, 111, 157
NF 159
Nielsen, Kai v
Nietzsche, Friedrich 8, 12, 23, 28, 169 n.2, 170
Niquet, Marcel 36 n.7, 38 n.11
normative judgement 79–82; defined 79; truth of 143–146
normative inconsistency 130, 146 f., 151, 153 f., 154 n.14
normative need, see normative inconsistency
Nozick, Robert 15, 142, 191 n.16
NTJ 134

objectivation principle 125 f., 135 f., 148–151, 166
O'Neill, Onora 39, 44 n.16, 64 n.1, 68, 90, 91 n.19
original assumption of retorsive arguments, see transcendental arguments (retorsive argument, starting point)
OP, see objectivation principle
Orwell, George 122

Passmore, John A. 52 n.24
Peirce, Charles Sanders 30, 64 n.1, 68–70, 75, 82 n.13
performative condition, see transcendental conditional
Peters, R. S. 19 n.14, 64 n.1, 92
Phillips-Griffiths, A. 15, 26 n.18, 41 f., 64 n.1, 76, 88, 88 n.18, 162
Plato 4 f., 100, 127, 181, 194
Platts, Mark de Bretton 184, 188
Popper, Karl 18, 26 n.17, 49, 66, 77, 168, 185, 190
Pothast, Ulrich 96 n.2
Prichard, H. A. 4, 19 n.14
pragmatic implications, see transcendental conditional
Priest, G. 46 n.18, 58 n.29
principle of excluded middle 58
principle of non-contradiction 45, 58–60
Puolimatka, Tapio 100

Quine, W. V. O. 39 n.12, 192

Railton, Peter 8
Rawls, John 2 n.2, 16, 17 n.10, 19 n.13, 24, 73
reason, alternative forms 55 f., 67; as discourse 65, 67–73; its normativity 76–79, 90; its implications 117 ff.
reflexive transcendental argument, see transcendental argument (retorsive type)
Regis, Edward Jr. 93 n.1, 109 n.13, 127 n.27, retorsive argument, see transcendental argument
Ricoeur, Paul 23
Riedel, Manfred 78 n.10
rights 107–111
Röd, Wolfgang 38 n.10
Rorty, Richard 55, 169 n.2
Rosenberg, Jay F. 32 n.2, 36, 55
Ross, W. D. 4, 19 n.14
Royce, J. 64 n.1

de Sade, D. A. F. 28
sceptic/scepticism 6 f.; its implications 31 f., 45, 131; must be rational 6–8, 67 f., 76–8, 145 n.11
Schaper, Eva 55
Schlick, Moritz 7
Schneewind, J. B. 177 n.8
Schönrich, Gerhard 78 n.10
Schopenhauer, Arthur 185

Searle, John R. 65, 99
self-evidence 34 f., 40, 41, 46 n. 19, 95 f., 101, 113, 116, 135
Sextus Empiricus 18, 26
Shaftesbury, A. A. C. 20
Shakespeare, William 22, 177
Shoemaker, Sydney 30, 60
Sidgwick, Henry 19 f., 124, 172
Smith, Adam 169
Smith, Michael 10, 154 n.15, 183, 186 n.13, 188–190
Spector, Horacio 3 n.2
speech-act 45 n.17, 47, 51 f., 65 f., 133, 138 f.
Spinoza, Baruch de 121 n.20, 132
Stegmüller, Wolfgang 7 n.6
Steigleder, Klaus 93 n.1, 96 n.2, 106 n.11, 108, 110, 122
Stern, Robert 36
Stevenson, C. L. 19 n.14, 33 n.3
Stevenson, Leslie 38 n.10
Stine, William D. 62, 192
Stohs, Mark D. 126, 126 n.24
Strawson, Peter 30 f., 35 n.5, 38 n.9, 60
Stroud, Barry 53, 60–62, 60 n.31, 61 n.31, 110, 123, 126 f., 126 n.24, 145, 192, 197 n.18
Sturgeon, Nicholas 8
Sullivan, Roger J. 33

T! 140
Taylor, Charles 49 n.22
Taylor, Gabriele 99, 163
Thomas Aquinas 45 n.18, 54, 65, 65 n.2, 195
Thomson, Judith 9
Trigg, Roger 96 n.2
Toulmin, Stephan E. 19 n.14
transcendental arguments v f., 30–32, 169 f.; and deduction 54 f., 66 f., —explorational type 31, 32–44; its starting point 32–35, 41–44, 50 f.; its second premiss 35–40; its limitations 41–44, —retorsive type 44–63; definition 46; starting point 49–51, 54 f.; objections against 54–63
transcendental conditional 30 f., 33, 35–40, 45 ff., 47 ff., 51, 55, 65, 67–69, 115; and performative condition 51 ff., 58
transcendental deduction 32, 32 n. 2
truth 1 f., 65–67, 74, 127 n.26, 146, 175–179; as consensus vi, 65, 67–73, 82–86; and certainty 172 f.; its positive evaluation 65–67, 133–140, 155 f., 162, 164 n.23, 180; in practical matters 130, 131–133, 143–146, 173–181; tyranny of 168 f., 181 f.
truth-judging 129
TUG 155
Tugendhat, Ernst 24

Unger, P. 7
universality in ethics 15, 64, 79, 86–89, 108, 110 f., 114, 161 n.20
Urmson, J. O. 23

value 16 f., 79–81, 144
value judgement, see normative judgement

Walker, Ralph C. S. 7 n.6, 32 n.1, 33 n.3, 35, 35 n.5, 38, 38 n.10, 46 n.18, 57 n.27, 154 n.15
Walzer, Michael 9
Wandschneider, Dieter 197 n.18
Warnock, Mary 3 n.2
White, St. K. 107 n.12
Wiggins, David 195
Wilkerson, T. E. 32 n.2, 36 n.6, 174
Williams, Bernhard 6, 15, 98, 109 n.13, 121 n.20, 127 n.25, 178, 184
Williams, Michael 60, 62
Wimmer, Reiner 24, 73 n.7, 76 n.9
Wittgenstein, Ludwig 7 n.6, 12, 21, 30, 39, 67, 69, 84–86
Wong, D. B. 9, 112 n.14